Half-breed Traders
(Provincial Archives of Manitoba)

CANADA and the MÉTIS, 1869-1885

D. N. Sprague
with a foreword by Thomas R. Berger

Wilfrid Laurier University Press

This book has been published with the help of a grant from the Social Science Federation of Canada, using funds provided by the Social Sciences and Humanities Research Council of Canada.

Canadian Cataloguing in Publication Data

Sprague, D. N. (Douglas Neil), 1944-
　Canada and the Métis, 1869-1885

Bibliography: p.
Includes index.
ISBN 0-88920-958-8 (bound)　ISBN 0-88920-964-2 (pbk.)

1. Métis − Manitoba − History.*　2. Métis − Manitoba − Government relations.*　3. Red River Settlement − History.　I. Title.

FC3372.9.M4S69 1988　　　971.27′02　　　C88-093344-5
F1063.S69 1988

WILFRID LAURIER UNIVERSITY PRESS
Waterloo, Ontario, Canada　N2L 3C5

88 89 90 91 4 3 2 1

Cover design by *Vijen Vijendren*

Map 2 drawn by Victor Lytwyn

Printed in Canada

Canada and the Métis, 1869-1885 has been produced from a manuscript supplied in electronic form by the author.

Table of Contents

List of Illustrations

Foreword

The story of the Métis is one of the epics of Canadian history: the rise on the Prairies of a new nation of mixed blood ancestry, the emergence of a distinct culture, the formation in 1869-70 of the provisional government to defend their homeland, their dispersal. Yet in our own time the Métis have re-entered Canada's history, seeking to discover their own past, and to find a place for themselves in Canadian life.

The crucial year for the Métis was 1870. In that year Canada acquired the Red River Settlement, the provisional government of Louis Riel fled, and the dispersal of the Métis began. But it was in that same year that the Manitoba Act was passed by Canada's Parliament, and confirmed the following year by the Parliament of the United Kingdom, to ensure that the Métis would receive title to the river lots they occupied on the Red and Assiniboine and land for future generations. These were solemn promises made to the Métis by the Government of Canada—promises which were not kept.

In this book, Professor D.N. Sprague tells why the Métis did not receive the land that was supposed to be theirs under the Manitoba Act. John A. Macdonald and his Conservatives and Alexander Mackenzie and the Liberals did not honour the promises in the Manitoba Act. The Canadian Parliament passed a series of laws designed to undermine the rights the Métis had under the Manitoba Act. These laws prepared the way for settlers who moved westward to Manitoba from Ontario to acquire control of the provincial legislature. They, in turn, enacted a series of measures to ensure that the land allotted to the Métis would soon find its way into the hands of settlers entering the province from the East. Professor Sprague offers many examples of the methods used, such as legislation justifying the sale of land allotted to Métis children without any of the safeguards ordinarily required in connection with transactions with infants. Then there were powers of attorney, tax sales—any number of stratagems could be used, and were—to see that the land intended for the Métis and their families went to others. All branches of the government participated. It is a shameful tale, but one that must be told. It offers the explanation for the fact that today the Métis, once dominant at Red River, indeed the guardians of the community there, should now find themselves strangers in their own land.

In 1982, the Canadian Parliament belatedly recognized the Métis as one of the aboriginal peoples of Canada. It remains, to us, now that we know how they lost their land, to see that they get the land-base they were promised.

Thomas R. Berger
April 1987

Preface

The author's central purpose is to explain how the Red River Settlement, one of the most persistent[1] populations of North America from 1820 to 1869, dispersed almost entirely in the 1870s and failed to secure a new homeland by migration to the Canadian North West in the early 1880s. While students of other migrations are certain that push factors are as important as pulls in any mass exodus, in the case of the Red River Métis, the dispersal is usually attributed to some fatal flaw in the Métis character rather than to external pressures arising after 1870. The present study is an inquiry into the discouragements, formal and informal, that forced most of the Red River Métis from Manitoba to Saskatchewan and culminated in the rebellion of 1885.

Informal discouragements included intimidation of the original population by hundreds, then thousands of ultra-Protestants from Ontario who intended to establish new homes for themselves and to become a new majority transforming the Quebec of the West into a new Ontario. Newcomers appropriated Métis land and made the old settlers feel like strangers in a new land.

The Métis might have mounted an effective defence against such informal pressure had they not faced overwhelming formal discouragement from the acts of a colonial establishment created by the Government of Canada. Ottawa witheld self-government from Manitoba until a preferred

---

1. The evidence for the remarkable persistence of the Red River Settlement is census data compiled by the Hudson's Bay Company before 1849 in comparison with the figures reported in the first Canadian enumeration of the district renamed Manitoba in 1870. See D.N. Sprague and R.P. Frye, *The Genealogy of the First Métis Nation* (Winnipeg, 1983). Most of the families included in the earlier enumeration were included in the first census by Canada twenty years later. (The typical rate of persistence elsewhere in North America in the mid-nineteenth century was around thirty per cent for ten-year intervals). See David Gagan, *Hopeful Travellers: Families, Land, and Social Change in Mid-Victorian Peel County, Canada West* (Toronto, 1981), pp. 6, 95.

ix

majority was established. Facilitating the process were numerous Orders in Council and Statutes of Canada, which shifted the administration of insecure land titles from a legislature of the old settlers to a federal department whose primary mission was guaranteeing the security of the newcomers.

Since the formal process of discouragement was the more irresistable one, the operations of the Canadian bureaucreacy are the main focus of the study. The important evidence is communication between officials in the field and policy-makers in Ottawa. The highest level of consideration was frequently the office of the Prime Minister, occasionally operating independently of Cabinet or Parliament. And since Sir John A. Macdonald was the individual who occupied the prime ministerial position for eleven of the years between 1869 and 1885, his decisions are central to the story of formal discouragement. Yet Macdonald was only one of many unsympathetic actors in the drama. Given the pressure from the informal side, opportunities for accommodation of the Métis were easily missed by all operators of the apparatus of formal control. Whether such moments passed by mere carelessness or by deliberate inaction cannot be known with certainty in every instance, but one overall conclusion is inescapably obvious: the Government of Canada conceded a legal framework for the permanence of the Red River Settlement as a province in response to force in 1870, and subsequently presided over the dissolution of the terms of the Manitoba Act with approximately the same regret as would be exhibited by an unwilling victim escaping from a sales contract negotiated under duress.

Acknowledgements

Research support was provided by the Manitoba Métis Federation, the Canadian Department of Secretary of State (Canadian Studies Directorate), and the University of Manitoba Research Board. In the preparation of the manuscript, helpful criticism came from sceptical colleagues: Professor Thomas Flanagan at the University of Calgary, Dr. Philippe Mailhot at the Saint-Boniface Museum, Professor J.E. Rea at the University of Manitoba, and Professor Irene Spry of the University of Ottawa.

Sir John A. Macdonald, Nov. 1883
(Public Archives of Canada [C5332])

" . . . forgery of medical evidence . . . uncontrolled terror in early Manitoba . . . mock diplomacy in 1869-70. Certain nasty bits had been uncovered by establishment historians since 1936."

Chapter 1

Historiographical Introduction

"Rebellions" of native peoples disturbed Canadian history in 1869 and again in 1885. Neither encounter involved a massive number of "rebels," and both tended to be identified with a single person. In the first "Riel rebellion," Louis Riel probably had no more than 700 active adherents. In the second, the number of Métis taking up arms was less than 400. Not surprisingly, neither event was significant by the number of casualties. Only a few people died in the first instance; about fifty were killed on each side in the second conflict with Canada. Still, few historians would quarrel with the assertion that the Red River Resistance of 1869-70 and the North West Rebellion of 1885 had profound significance for the country as a whole because Canadians have debated heatedly and persistently the rights and wrongs of the roles played by the various participants for more than a century.

In the first frankly polemical accounts,[1] the most salient theme was the struggle of "civilization" against "barbarism" because the rebels in each case were the "natives" of a newly acquired country. An aggressive but compassionate New Dominion had defeated "semi-savage" obstacles to progress. And since the defeat of the Métis represented a conquest of persons whose language was French and religion was Roman Catholicism, the victory was a triumph for English-Protestant ascendancy at the same time. But so long as the French-Catholic minority in the rest of the country was not similarly vanquished, it would be impossible to achieve a "Canadian" consensus on the larger significance of the two "Riel Rebellions." Several traditions of hagiography and demonology posed conflicting claims to the larger truth.

In addition to the government-vindication tradition suggested above (the story with the New Dominion of Canada in the role of hero, the part of arch-villain played by "Dictator" Riel, and the Roman Catholic missionaries to the Métis falling somewhere in between), there was a French-

---

1. See George Bryce, *A Short History of the Canadian People* (London, 1887) or R.G. MacBeth, *Making the Canadian West* (Toronto, 1905).

1

Canadian version articulated by spokesmen for Canada's largest minority.[2] Here the tendency was to glorify saintly bishops and missionaries for their heroic struggle to "civilize" the Métis and to resist the tide of Orange-Protestant fanaticism emanating from Ontario. In the pro-French polemical tradition, Riel was a demented leader of a flawed but pitiable people. Louis Riel and the "semi-civilized" Métis ranked between the heroic clergy, on the one hand, and the anti-Catholic fanatics in and out of government, on the other hand.

Clearly, the government-vindication and the clerical-beatification polemics did not serve the national pride of the Métis who believed that they had followed neither dictator nor madman. Their version of events — largely a matter of oral tradition — passed from generation to generation in a number of different stories, occasionally surfacing in written petitions, then finally appearing as a comprehensive history published in 1935.[3] The official "history of the Métis Nation" depicted Riel as visionary and martyr. Neither insane nor dictatorial, he operated with foresight and consensus. The clergy were well meaning but cowardly; ultimately their cowardice turned them into betrayers of the cause and prime speculators in Métis land. Still, the clerical sin of cowardice paled beside the treachery of strangers who plotted the destruction of Riel and his people through the power of the state.

Sifting a more comprehensive truth from the competing polemical traditions became the challenge to academic historians in the twentieth century. To George Stanley, what was needed was to establish the good faith of each set of principal actors. His *Birth of Western Canada* (first published in 1936)[4] adopted a tragic stance. While praising the New Dominion for its zealous expansionism (a sign of "nationalism" and "aggressive civilization," both worthy attributes for Stanley), he still expressed sympathy for the frustrations of the clergy and the tragic losses of the Indians and the Métis. The tragedy was their "doom" as a people.

The natives had to fail. They were "primitive peoples" standing against the march of "civilization" (p. 88). At the minimum, they had to be pushed aside to make way for newcomers. The Métis plan to resist Canada in 1869 was absurd. Still, they did not deserve hatred for the attempt. Their one contemptible action in 1869-70 was the "cruel act of bloodshed" in

---

2. See D.P. Benoit, *Vie de Monseigneur Taché, archevêque de Saint-Boniface*, 2 vols. (Montreal, 1904); and A.G. Morice, *History of the Catholic Church in Western Canada*, 2 vols. (Toronto, 1910).

3. A.H. de Trémaudan, *Histoire de la Nation Métisse dans l'Ouest canadien* (Montreal, 1935). In English translation (by Elizabeth Maguet), the work is *Hold High Your Heads* (Winnipeg, 1982).

4. The place of publication was London, England. A generation later a Canadian firm acquired the copyright and reprinted the work in a resurrected but unrevised edition (Toronto, 1961).

the matter of Thomas Scott's execution for counter-insurgency. "The charges brought against Scott . . . were hardly offences that demanded the death penalty" (pp. 105-106). And even if Scott did deserve "a form of punishment used only as a last resort in civilized communities," his execution was politically inexpedient. The Métis invited terrible reprisals. Up to March 4, 1870 their resistance had been peaceful, "almost bloodless, but this regrettable event aroused those latent racial and religious passions which have been so deplorable a feature of Canadian history, and left bitter memories that were not soon forgotten" (p. 106).

Stanley's evidence that Canada might have forgiven the Métis for non-violent rebellion was that the Government of Canada continued to follow a process of conciliation through the passage of the Manitoba Act in May; the fatal error of the Scott matter meant that the government had to turn a blind eye to the violence of newcomers entering the new province thirsting for the blood of Scott's murderers. And since the key people of the provisional government had to be denied amnesty for the same reason, no Métis person could lead the government of Manitoba in the first critical years of the province's history.

"Sullen, suspicious and estranged from their [new] white neighbours and by the actions of the Canadians and the non-promulgation of the amnesty, almost immediately many métis began to look for new homes" (p. 179). Ineffectively led in their homeland, they sought a land of second chance west and north on the Saskatchewan River. Unfortunately, they soon discovered that their status as "first settlers in the North West Territories" did not exempt them from the provisions of the Dominion Lands Act (p. 251). Stanley believed Canada was wrong to have disregarded their new claims. "The attempt to impose an unfamiliar, and to the métis, unsatisfactory system of survey, and thus deprive them of their river-frontages and destroy their village community life, invited armed resistance" (p. 255).

No one could be surprised by the displaced Manitobans' retrieval of Louis Riel from exile in 1884. Nor surprised that he, in his turn, decided to follow the "tactics which he had employed in 1869 and 1870" (p. 314). He formed a second provisional government even though the clergy advised against such a move and condemned him for it. Their reaction was too strong, in Stanley's view. "Riel had no intention of fighting the Dominion with arms; it had not been necessary in 1869; it would not be necessary in 1885." Canada would be shocked into a negotiated settlement as before. "But instead of commissioners came troops" (p. 314).

Stanley did not hesitate to proclaim the "justice of the métis case" (p. 251). Canada's disregard of the Saskatchewan land question was clear. "The case against the Government is conclusive" (p. 261). Canada was guilty of "ministerial incompetence, parliamentary indifference, and administrative delay" (p. 244). Officials had committed "serious blunders'' (pp. 260-61) even though Canadian native policy in general was well intentioned, exhibiting "honesty, justice, and good faith"; Canada caused "no wars of extermination or compulsory migrations" (p. 214). In suppressing the rebellion of 1885, Canada's troops did little burning, looting, property damage, or killing. And "reason and conciliation ultimately prevailed" (p. 407).

Such was the first attempt at balanced interpretation. Stanley's curious mix of shallow praise and weak condemnation suggested that his *Birth of Western Canada* was merely the beginning of the larger task of mediation. The work attracted little attention in Canada at the time of publication in 1936. Reviewers tended to pass his conclusions with little criticism and less praise.[5] No one challenged his tortuous sequence: the Métis were determined to win a secure land base and political control over their homeland in 1869-70, showed no interest in land or politics in Manitoba in the 1870s, then became remarkably interested and determined again in Saskatchewan in 1884-85. Stanley attributed the erratic course of events to a certain petulance likely to be encountered in all primitive peoples who "felt that the country was theirs" (pp. 48-49).

The concept of primitivism disturbed a young W.L. Morton, as evidenced in an article (published in 1937) on the development of Red River institutional structures.[6] Without citing Stanley by name, Morton still presented a sharply contrasting analysis. He agreed that the Red River Settlement had become more and more "Indian" by intermarriage from 1820 to 1870, just as he readily conceded that most people in the Red River Settlement were more involved in freighting and the production of plains provisions than with full-time field agriculture. The contrast emerged in Morton's insistence that the settlement's striking backwardness was in government institutions because the Hudson's Bay Company had imposed a "seigniorial despotism" on the colony. The HBC-appointed council was "mild, often benevolent" but in no sense accountable to the residents of the parishes, not until 1869 (pp. 95-96). Then parish representatives united, perhaps not as a single unit (as one English-speaking member of the provisional government asserted) but "the degree of unity was sufficient to give good ground for Riel's attempt to form a united front and present terms to Canada" (p. 98).

What the rebels had done was not entirely well done. The Scott matter

---

5. In Stanley's view, *The Birth of Western Canada* (London, 1936) was "largely ignored" at the time of first publication. See his remarkably personal account of the development of the historiography before and since 1936 in his "Last Word on Louis Riel — the Man of Several Faces," in F. Laurie Barron and James B. Waldram, eds., *1885 and After: Native Society in Transition*, (Regina, 1986), pp. 3-22.

6. "The Red River Parish," in R.C. Lodge, ed., *Manitoba Essays*, (Toronto, 1937), pp. 92-105.

in particular was a "fatal blunder" but overall they had acted with "dignity" and true to the "old, proud claim of the Métis to be a 'new nation' [they had] mustered a militia and created representative institutions" (pp. 99, 102). When Canada admitted the Red River Settlement to Confederation as Manitoba, "the Dominion recognized rather than created" (p. 105). The question remained: if Manitobans were a well-rooted national people determined to defend their homeland from invasion by what Stanley had called an "almost foreign country" (pp. 48-49), why then was the dispersal of population so sudden and complete after winning a charter for national survival in the Manitoba Act?

Morton kept working on the problem and eventually found all that he cared to know in a two-volume monograph on "the Canadian half-breed" written in Paris by a French ethnographer during the Nazi occupation.[7] According to Marcel Giraud, the Métis were a "mixed-blood" people incapable of responding to their own best interests. Well-intentioned agents of civilization had tried to educate and mould them to greater competence but had failed. The Métis rejection of proper educational and moral instruction resulted in their decline, ruin, and extinction as a people.

Giraud saw nothing dignified or reasonable in their "nation" claim; he saw only vanity and violence. Defiance of Canada invited reprisal; the murder of Scott invited murders in revenge. The proof of Métis inferiority was their inability to fight an effective defence. "The attacks, the violent acts of every kind that were now directed against the Métis . . . aggravated the inherent weaknesses of their nature, of their upbringing and their antecedents, and precipitated the disintegration of their group" (p. 374). The reign of terror that began, paradoxically, with the arrival of troops sent to guarantee an orderly beginning for the new province continued with the arrival of new settlers because Ontarians, "grouped around their Orange Lodge, could commit the worst excesses with impunity" (p. 377). Yet Giraud refused to connect such violence to a larger pattern of denial of rights. Any injustices by the Government of Canada were "unintended" (pp. 381-382). The root cause of the dispersal was the fatal inferiority of the Métis themselves.

According to Giraud, the principal activities of freighting and the production of plains provisions for the Hudson's Bay Company were "distractions" rather than "occupations"; they were reflections of origin rather than rational adaptations likely to give way to new responses in subsequent historical development. Métis reluctance to take up full-time farming was proof that they were "incapable of understanding any plan of life other

---

7. Marcel Giraud, *Le Métis canadien: son rôle dans l'histoire des provinces de l'Ouest*, 2 vols. (Paris, 1945). The work is now available in English: *The Métis in the Canadian West*, translated by George Woodcock, 2 vols. (Edmonton, 1986). Page citations follow the Woodcock translation, vol. 2.

than nomadism.'' The few Métis who pretended to be farmers showed they were ''incapable of caring for them in a sensible manner'' (p. 388). They rapidly ran into debt and many sold their land to clergy hoping to ''substitute for these unambitious individuals a race whose qualities were in no way inferior to those of the immigrants of English or Germanic language'' (p. 390). It was no surprise to Giraud that the same cycle of agitation and violence followed the exodus to Saskatchewan and ''aggravated the causes of the decay from which this people was suffering'' (p. 452).

For the Manitoba historian learning to react against the word ''primitive'' as an interpretive category, the discovery of Marcel Giraud must have been disturbing. What W.L. Morton should have pointed out in his review of ''the Canadian half-breed''[8] in 1950 was that Giraud appeared to have done pioneering research in vast arrays of new material without learning to see beyond the literal to the functional meaning of written testimony, a weakness that was particularly evident in Giraud's use of missionary chronicles and clerical correspondence. Here, for example, was Giraud using Bishop Grandin of Saskatchewan to paint a gloomy prediction of Métis failure for Archbishop Taché of Manitoba: ''It will be just the same here — neither worse nor better as at St Boniface. Our poor Métis will leave their lands to strangers and withdraw as far as they can withdraw. They are a people without energy on whom one cannot count'' (p. 430). Instead of interpreting the letter as an indication of pedagogical frustration, Giraud cited Grandin's words for their literal meaning. He did not read the missionary bias. The same point missed Morton's notice.

''Giraud presents the Métis four square, in all his vivacity, colour and historical significance, depicts the first beginnings of the mixed race, its swift rise to 'national' consciousness, its half century of coherent life, and demonstrates the inevitability and pathos of its doom'' (pp. 61-62). Thus Morton abandoned his previous celebration of the ''autocthonous'' people settled in their neat little ''white washed houses clustered on the points and bays of the Red and Assiniboine Rivers.''[9] Following Giraud, Morton began to think of the Métis as the misfits of the West, distracted from true civilization by hunting and voyaging, activities that ''bound them ineluctably to nomadism and to barbarism.'' Their riverfront habitations were just ''rude log cabins,'' places for keeping their ''few possessions, carts, horses, perhaps a few cattle. There they cultivated rudely their potato patches, and tiny fields of grain. But the hunt, the trapline, the 'free' fur trade, drew them seasonally away'' (p. 65). They clung stubbornly to their ''primitive barbarism'' and followed the ''easier course'' away from field agriculture

---

8. In *The Beaver* (September 1950), pp. 3-7; reprinted in A.B. McKillop, ed., *Contexts of Canada's Past: Selected Essays of W.L. Morton* (Toronto, 1980), pp. 61-68. Page citations follow the McKillop edition.

9. Morton, ''Red River Parish,'' p. 89.

to the end of the wandering life, defeat, and the scaffold at Regina (pp. 62-63). If the Métis were victimized, they were willing victims, defeated finally by their own defects of character. "It was their tragedy that the instability and violence of Riel, reflecting the inherent instability and ready violence of his own uncertain people, ruined his achievement and destroyed his nation" (p. 67).

Six years later Morton was still endorsing Giraud's "magnificent study" but managed to cling to a fragment of his earlier denial of Red River primitivism. His history of the Red River "resistance,"[10] published in 1956 (and his general history of Manitoba[11] which appeared one year later), suggested that the nomadic Métis rebelled in 1869 not because they resisted learning the ways of a settled agricultural existence — not from an irrational defence of their alleged primitivism — but because they preferred instruction by French-speaking, Roman Catholic newcomers. "What the Métis chiefly feared in 1869 was not the entrance of the agricultural frontier of Ontario into Red River — and they would have welcomed that of Quebec — but the sudden influx of immigrants of English speech and Protestant faith" (p. 2). Riel recognized that "their evolution away from nomadism was incomplete" and feared that his people would be overwhelmed by the "inrush of British Canadian land-seekers from Ontario before the *métis* had finally abandoned the wandering life of hunters and tripmen and settled down as farmers in the parishes of the Red and Assiniboine" (p. 5). They strove to protect the stake of each individual to his rude private plot by protecting the French-Catholic character of the group as a whole.

It was the second more ambitious goal that brought them into conflict with Canada. Morton believed that "the Canadian government was entirely ready to grant the normal rights of British subjects to all civilized individuals in the North-West, without respect to race. But it had no idea that it was dealing with a corporate entity, a 'nation' by sentiment and by their own claim" (p. 3). And since the demand for "*corporate* rights" was considerably more than Canada was prepared to concede, the government naturally resisted. Included in the description of Canada's counter-resistance was Morton's disclosure that Donald A. Smith (the ranking Canadian officer of the Hudson's Bay Company recruited by the government in Montreal to travel to Red River in December 1869) accepted a mission of subversion more than conciliation: "the general purpose of his activities was clearly to create an anti-Riel party amongst the English and *métis* by the use of the influence of the Hudson's Bay Company, and by bribes" (p. 89). Morton

---

10. The term "resistance" appeared as Morton's own new label in his book-length editor's introduction to *Alexander Begg's Red River Journal and Other Papers Relative to the Red River Resistance of 1869-70* (Toronto, 1956).

11. *Manitoba: A History* (Toronto, 1957).

did not suggest that such a step disqualified the good faith expressed in the documents that Smith carried to conceal the covert mission. Morton's criticism was that the "game" was "tortuous and difficult," too much for one person to "play against the wary and entrenched Riel" (p. 84).

The "design" failed in its principal objective, and that failure led to the abortive counter-insurgency that culminated in Thomas Scott's death in March 1870. Morton suggested that the killing of Scott was "difficult to explain" because another counter-insurgent had been similarly tried and condemned but set free. William Gaddy had been captured, imprisoned, court-martialled, and ordered executed, then he disappeared. "The rumour was subsequently put about that he had been shot; but actually he had been led by a firing party away from the fort, and at the last moment released and told to leave the country" (p. 103). Morton was puzzled by the different conclusion of the Scott case. In Morton's speculation, Thomas Scott was the object of exceptional treatment because of the extraordinary hatred he and his guards shared for one another. He had to be executed or they would have killed him without the sanction of the provisional government. "The execution of Scott was preferable to his murder" (p. 115). The ceremonious shooting saved the illusion of orderly process, but the alternate form of killing Scott was still a fatal error. Before March 4, 1870 "all might have ended peacefully." After the execution, revenge became a necessary feature of any settlement acceptable to Ontario.

Morton's new version of the story raised a question concerning the Manitoba Act: if the Scott matter determined a vengeful outcome, why did Canada go on with the impression of conciliation, including the concession of the Manitoba Act in May? Here Morton explained that Prime Minister Macdonald was desperate for British participation in a military expedition to impose order, but the Colonial Office was "emphatic" that the Canadians first had to negotiate a settlement acceptable to the "Roman Catholic settlers." Without elaborating the point in detail, Morton asserted that the delegates from Red River "bargained hard" and if they had known "the pressure the Canadian representatives were under from the Colonial office to effect a settlement, would have bargained harder" (p. 135).

Morton's finding that Canada made large concessions to win British military aid and the disclosure that the Smith mission was an exercise in subversion as much as in diplomacy might have led some investigators to search for other signs of duplicity in the pacification of the Métis, especially in accounting for the massive exodus after 1870. But Giraud had given Morton all the reason he needed: the Métis were incurable nomads incapable of accepting agriculture. It was not necessary to ask if the land-promise provisions of the Manitoba Act had been broken along with the assurance of an amnesty. Curiously, though, Morton did present evidence that the government made no effort to control even its own "expedition of peace.'' To the officers and other ranks, "it was an expedition to avenge the murder of Scott."[12] The violence that followed (the general disorder Giraud had called a "reign of terror") Morton might have labeled the bleeding Kansas phase of Manitoba history. He recognized that the early expansion of Ontarians was more than a quest for individual plots by land-hungry pioneers. Homesteaders demanded neighbours like themselves. ''Whoever possessed the soil would give the new province their language, faith and laws.''[13] So they deliberately took up land that was already occupied, as well as apparently vacant tracts, and were sustained in such trespasses by the Government of Canada. Morton did not inquire if the support of interlopers had been promised in advance, if the Ontario bias was part of a deliberate strategy to assure Ontario's advantage in the race to determine whether Manitoba would remain a second Quebec. Morton asserted that Canada had done its best to move "with all possible speed to quiet fears and to ensure that the land rush would be peaceful and orderly."[14] In Morton's view, there were no serious blunders or intentional injustices in the administration of the Manitoba Act.

Morton's uncritical stance was taken one step further by Donald Creighton. His award-winning two-volume biography of Sir John A. Macdonald, which amounted to a general history of Canada, was published almost simultaneously with Morton's work on Manitoba. The nominal focus of the second volume[15] was Macdonald's prime ministerial career from 1867 to 1891, but the author's larger purpose was telling the story of the national government as personified in the country's founder and prototype leader. With such heroic scope, a few thousand Métis might have escaped the notice of another historian, but Creighton devoted several chapters to Macdonald's interaction with Riel and offered a thorough reinterpretation in the process.

In Creighton's rendition of the first episode, the story was of a rebellion by "half-breed rioters." Another country might have responded with force and asked questions later. Canada had to "behave in as patient and conciliatory a fashion as possible." Smith's was a straightforward diplomatic mission; and, when diplomacy failed, Riel gave "one final proof of the fact that military power was the one solid and constant basis of his provisional government" (p. 59). He murdered Thomas Scott. Still Canada persisted in the quest for a negotiated settlement because, from one side, Macdonald had to respond to pressure from the British, and, from another more immediate source, powerful pressure for a negotiated settlement came

---

12. Morton, *Manitoba,* p. 143.

13. Ibid., p. 154.

14. Ibid.

15. *John A. Macdonald;* vol. 2, *The Old Chieftain* (Toronto, 1955).

from the important French-Canadian wing of Macdonald's own party. The normally "docile troop" of French-Canadian Conservative supporters were bound to reject any settlement that did not satisfy the "fanatical" priest Riel had sent to Ottawa as his principal negotiator (pp. 62-63). Consequently, when Father Ritchot insisted upon "absurdly premature" provincial status for the Red River Settlement and held out for similarly unreasonable promises with respect to land, language, and schools, his will was done — but as a matter of expediency, for the sake of peace, rather than to strike a blueprint for the future.

Creighton's hostile rendition of the Métis and his unusually sympathetic depiction of Canada's duplicitous response to their demands became even more pronounced in his version of the second rebellion. But since Creighton worked from the perspective of Macdonald's full range of problems, the discussion of Canada's reaction to Métis demands acquired a reality absent from previous accounts. Creighton showed that the nuisance of Riel was tied to the leading preoccupation of the government in 1884-85. "The prime purpose of Canada was to achieve a separate political existence on the North American Continent." That was to be realized by the construction of the Canadian Pacific Railway (CPR), whose "prime function" was "to help in the building of the national economy and the national society which alone would make this ambition possible of achievement" (pp. 301-302).

A first effort to launch the railway had failed in 1873. A new beginning came in 1881 with Canada linking its fortunes to George Stephen, "perhaps the greatest creative genius in the whole history of Canadian finance" (p. 305). But Stephen could not work miracles. Canada had to subsidize the project enormously. Initial grants were "simply the first and most impressive pledges of a partnership which grew tighter and more inextricable with the passage of time" (p. 303). In 1883 and again in 1884 additional aid was demanded and provided. The later rescue "very nearly doubled the subsidy" (p. 376) and taxed Macdonald's powers of persuasion to his limit. Since the second subsidy was "out of all reason and all precedent" (p. 366), Macdonald called on his old friend and cofounder of Canada, Charles Tupper, then on diplomatic service in England. With Tupper temporarily seconded to Ottawa, Macdonald accomplished the great work of saving the railway in February 1884. Then, at the end of the stormy session, Macdonald sought a well-deserved rest at his summer home by the sea. Unfortunately, Macdonald's "summer holidays were no longer real holidays." He sought escape in June, but in July and August the "visitors and mails kept continually arriving. Besides, he wanted them to arrive" (pp. 383-384).

Thus Macdonald learned the disturbing news that "the evil genius of the Red River Rebellion" had returned to the North West in July of 1884 (p. 383). Trouble was brewing. The claims of the Manitoba "half breeds and the other squatters'' had been settled years before in Manitoba (p. 246), but having thrown away their opportunities to speculators, they enjoyed a brief ''spree,'' drifted west, and renewed the demand for land and cash. As before, they were calling themselves the Métis nation and claiming recognition on that account. ''In the settlement process they were a nation of squatters. Macdonald knew, as any lawyer knew, that squatters were notoriously suspicious, impatient, and stubborn people, and that the settlement of their ill-defined claims was probably the most exasperating and difficult problem that could confront a land-granting department'' (p. 369). Their complaints were without much substance, of course. ''Yet this did not mean that Macdonald considered the matter closed. The half-breed claims could be settled. . . .'' Even Riel might be transformed into a loyal client. ''The whole issue was a proper subject for compromise'' (p. 387).

Then, while still on holiday in August, Macdonald learned the more dreadful truth that Stephen was ''far from through his difficulties'' (p. 383). The president of the railway began to make ''disquieting hints'' in August and September that the ''enormous aid'' voted in February ''would not be enough to secure the completion of the Canadian Pacific Railway'' (p. 389). In the new crisis, Stephen sought British private assistance and persuaded Macdonald to accompany him on the mission to Baring Brothers in Britain. The leisurely crossing gave Stephen ample opportunity to reveal ''the deepest urgency of the Canadian Pacific's necessities'' (p. 394). Once in London, Macdonald ''began another set of equally lengthy discussions on the same subject with Tupper. Tupper emphatically agreed with him that a final effort to save the railway must be made'' (pp. 396-397). The question was one of strategy: ''How was he to convince his followers — his own Cabinet — that government aid to the Canadian Pacific was necessary once again?'' (p. 396). Creighton found nothing to indicate that either veteran foresaw a suitable combination of enabling circumstances. Not even Macdonald saw a way out of the problem of making additional subsidy politically palatable. He ''literally had not the faintest idea. But he had given his word to Stephen'' (p. 397).

In the meantime the western crisis had reached new, more dangerous proportions. On the eve of Macdonald's departure with Stephen, ''just before he left Ottawa,'' the Prime Minister had received what Creighton called a ''most disquieting'' report from Saskatchewan (p. 394). The Métis wanted more than their little plots, more even than some token cash in recognition of their imaginary share of Indian title. They were demanding both and two million acres of additional land and a royalty for themselves and the Indians to be paid in perpetuity on all future western development. For himself, Riel claimed a special personal indemnity in compensation for alleged past injuries. Later, with Macdonald and Stephen back in Canada, and the Métis demands still unmet, a more moderately worded petition arrived in December and came before Cabinet as one of the first items of business in the new year. "It was at this point, when the government expected negotiations and was prepared to make real concessions, that a most disquieting piece of news arrived from the north-west" (p. 413). Government agents had just learned that Riel would bring the entire protest to an abrupt and peaceful conclusion if a certain price were met. "My name is Riel and I want material," were his actual words, they said. "To Macdonald, it was a shattering revelation. It made the whole agitation seem a malevolent sham" (p. 414).

Of course Canada could not give in to blackmail. Nor was Macdonald frightened by the risk of standing on principle in the matter. "Deep in the final privacy of his being, he refused to believe that a single half-breed megalomaniac could destroy the west as a homeland for British Americans or that the track which was to bind Canada together would be permitted to fail for a few million dollars" (p. 415). Then the unexpected happened.

Before informing Riel that the government would never stoop to bribery, Canada took the precaution of informing the Métis that they might take their claims to a special commission which would hear "half-breed claims" in the spring. Wounded by his private disappointment, Riel sought revenge. He persuaded his deluded followers that no one's claim was safe and led everyone who called him leader into rebellion. At that point, according to Creighton, Macdonald stopped wondering what was going to happen, and started acting to make the best of a worsening situation which now included the financial collapse of the CPR. The two emergencies had developed separately yet coincidentally, and "together they might destroy him and his Canada." They had to be resolved separately, but they could be "played off against each other. And in that possibility did not there still lie a real hope? He could use the railway to defend the west. He could use the west to justify the railway" (p. 417).

And so he did. But in the discovery of the dramatic linkage of the railway to the rebellion, a scholar more critical than Creighton might have sought an earlier date for the connection. If the evidence established that Macdonald had linked the one with the other (perhaps as early as his first learning of the new difficulties facing the CPR late in August of 1884), such an investigator would necessarily have sought some intentional provocation in the superficial conciliation of January 1885. And if the evidence suggested that the government was playing a duplicitous game in 1884-85, as well as in 1869-70, the issue of Canadian good faith overall would come into a new perspective. In one form or another, the presumption of benevolence that was such a conspicuous anomaly of the historiography since Stanley's first attempt to balance the three polemical traditions in 1936 would finally have faced a direct challenge.

First one needed to question the fullness of Creighton's answer. Morton did not. He repeated Creighton's version in a history of Canada published in 1963.[16] Nor did Stanley challenge Creighton in a new biography of Riel which appeared in the same year.[17] The author of *The Birth of Western Canada* continued to sympathize with the tragic fate of the Métis leader and his people, but still did not question the presumption of government good faith. In the next decade, another historian sympathetic to the Métis, Lewis H. Thomas, published an eccentric study of Riel's treason trial and called Riel's execution a "judicial murder."[18] Otherwise the story of Métis-government relations as told by Canadian academics remained as Morton and Creighton had left the subject in the 1950s.

Feeling poorly served by establishment scholars, Métis people began to address the issues for themselves and refined their earlier polemical tradition for current consumption.[19] Only Quebec's new found anti-clericalism and heightened indifference to anything beyond the borders of the *québécois* homeland prevented a revival of the intermediate polemic glorifying the clergy. Since academic historians tend to think they are above "advocacy history," the government-vindication tradition embellished by Morton and Creighton reigned as the objective truth of the early

---

16. The full title was *The Kingdom of Canada: A General History from Earliest Times* (Toronto, 1963).

17. The title was simply *Louis Riel* (Toronto, 1963).

18. "A Judicial Murder — The Trial of Louis Riel," in Howard Palmer, ed., *The Settlement of the West* (Calgary, 1977).

19. Howard Adams, *Prison of Grass* (Toronto, 1975) is perhaps the best example of the genre. Other similar works followed from the patronage of the Gabriel Dumont Institute, an educational arm of the Association of Métis and Non-status Indians of Saskatchewan. They supported Martin Schulman's and Don McLean's development of Creighton's link of the railway to the North West Rebellion into a full-blown provocation thesis. See McLean and Schulman, appearing first as "Lawrence Clarke: Architect of Revolt," *Canadian Journal of Native Studies* 3 (1983), pp. 57-68. Mclean later published the same argument in more elaborate form as *1885: Métis Rebellion or Government Conspiracy?* (Winnipeg, 1985). Peripheral to the same trend dating from the late 1970s was the work of D.N. Sprague, which was supported by the Manitoba Métis Federation, examining the administration of the land promises of the Manitoba Act. His "The Manitoba Land Question, 1878-1882" *(Journal of Canadian Studies* 15 [1980], pp. 74-84) and "Government Lawlessness in the Administration of Manitoba Land Claims, 1876-1887" *(Manitoba Law Journal* 10 [1980], pp. 415-441) received more favourable consideration by academic historians. Adams and McLean were called "tendentious" (Stanley, "Last Word," p. 13; and Thomas Flanagan, "Louis Riel: A Review Essay," *Journal of Canadian Studies* 21 [1986], pp. 157-164), while Sprague's argument was considered scholarly if not fully proven (Thomas Flanagan, *Riel and the Rebellion 1885 Reconsidered* [Saskatoon, 1983], p. 26; and Gerald Friesen, *The Canadian Prairies* [Toronto, 1984], pp. 197-199). Several historians departing from (yet consistent with) Sprague in their own original research are Gerhard Ens, "Métis Lands in Manitoba, 1870-1887," *Manitoba History* 5 (1983), pp. 2-11; Diane Payment, *Batoche, 1870-1910* (Saint-Boniface, 1983); and Nicole St-Onge, "The Dissolution of a Métis Community: Pointe à Grouette, 1860-1885," *Studies in Political Economy* 18 (1985), pp. 149-172.

1980s. Then a scholarly reconsideration of the issues attracted attention in 1984.

The author of an intellectual biography of Riel and Deputy Editor of the Riel Papers, Thomas Flanagan, announced that there were serious flaws in the "conventional-account" of Canada-Métis relations.[20] Ironically, the "reigning orthodoxy" Flanagan attacked was "Stanley's version": the one work of an academic historian writing in English that concluded there were "serious unresolved grievances" driving the Métis to rebellion "after legal means of action had failed" in 1885 (p. viii). Flanagan asserted that "all subsequent historians" had drawn on Stanley's work. Flanagan appeared to ignore the progression of scholarship away from Stanley, and how his own contribution was completely conventional in that regard.

Flanagan took the story one step beyond Creighton. His "reconsideration" focused exclusively on the Métis in 1885. The crisis in the West did not appear in relation to the crisis with the railway. Nor did the rebellion of 1884-85 relate to the resistance of 1869-70. Flanagan denied that there were any direct links between the first action and the second except in the mind of Louis Riel, who considered the Manitoba Act and the promised amnesty a kind of treaty that left the Métis free to "remove themselves" from Confederation if the bargain were "broken in either of its branches" (p. 83). To Flanagan, no such provision existed in law. Consequently, there could be no legal basis for framing a provisional government a second time even if the promises of 1870 had been disregarded in the 1870s.

Dismissing Riel's rationale as a legal argument, Flanagan did not pursue its basis in fact. A sketch of the "government's performance in Manitoba" convinced him that the administration of the Manitoba Act had "left much to be desired." But, following Morton after Giraud, Thomas Flanagan thought that "the great migration had more to do with social pressure exerted by the white immigrants and the retreat of the buffalo . . ." (p. 26).

As migrants to Saskatchewan, the Métis did come into conflict with government officials. They had to, because they took up land as they pleased in "outright defiance of regulations" (p. 27). No wonder the government was reluctant to consider their claims. Officials were powerless to bend rules for Métis "squatters." They had to treat them "exactly the same as all other settlers according to legislation and settled policy" (p. 51). And officials treated them well. Flanagan reported that the Department of the Interior had conducted a case-by-case survey in 1884 to determine the precise nature of each claim, what part of the land could be granted as homestead (after the performance of adequate settlement duties), and what

---

20. Flanagan, *Riel and the Rebellion 1885 Reconsidered.* Flanagan's earlier work on Riel was *Louis "David" Riel: "Prophet of the New World"* (Toronto, 1979).

part was open for purchase because of its position in the rectangular survey. Then in 1885 the Métis received written notification of the results — before the rebellion. "Between 26 February and 7 March, a letter was sent to each of the claimants stating the terms on which he could make entry" (p. 47). Flanagan admitted that he was unable to find copies of the letters or other evidence to confirm his assertion that a "reasonable compromise" had settled the river-lot question before the rebellion began (p. 15). But he was positive that "no Métis were forced off their chosen lands" (p. 49).

Another argument developed by assumption and poorly supported assertion accompanied Flanagan's version of government reaction to the other principal Métis demand: cash compensation for extinguishing their share of Indian title. Flanagan believed that the formation of a "half breed claims commission" announced by telegram on 4 February should have ended agitation on the aboriginal title demand. His explanation for the continuation of protest echoed Creighton's assertion that Riel made conciliation look like provocation (p. 76). "The cryptic telegram, of which he made himself the interpreter, became evidence of the government's refusal to deal with the Métis — the exact opposite of its intended meaning" (p. 71). According to Flanagan, Riel had been plotting rebellion "almost from the beginning":

> Riel saw in the grievances of the Métis an opportunity to implement his theory that the Manitoba 'treaty' had been broken; that the Métis were the real owners of the North-West; that they could renegotiate entry into Confederation; that they must receive a seventh of the value of the land of the North-West as compensation for letting others live there; and they could seek an independent political destiny if these terms were not met. Collaborating with white agitators like Jackson who were chiefly interested in provincial status and responsible government, he embarked upon a complex and deliberately deceptive strategy of making successively more radical demands. A Bill of Rights amounting to a Declaration of Independence was envisioned almost from the beginning. Finally, when Riel realized there was an unbridgeable gap between himself and Jackson, he determined to go it alone, as he had in 1869. The Métis would take the lead, rise in arms, and carry the English half-breeds and white settlers with them. (pp. 99-100)

Canada had no choice but to deal firmly with the rebel leader after restoring order, but the government did overstep the limits of propriety in resorting to "forgery" of certain medical evidence to hasten Riel's hanging. According to Flanagan, "This is the one episode in the North West Rebellion in which the government may be accused, not of delays or mistaken judgment, but of bad faith" (p. 145). The rest was excusable. Any other errors were honest mistakes, "not part of a calculated campaign to destroy the Métis or deprive them of their rights" (p. 146).

No academic historian had echoed the official history more faithfully. No one had come closer to providing a complete echo of the "statement of leading facts'' prepared for the Governor General by the Department of the Interior in April 1885. The key elements of the interpretation were government fairness, on the one hand, and Métis intransigence (misled by Riel), on the other. In the official history, Canada was a helpless victim:

> The real causes of the agitation have . . . been beyond the control of the Government. As already pointed out, the half-breeds have asked for nothing reasonable at the hands of the Government which has not been granted to them; and there is indeed no instance in history where the standard of revolt has been raised, and blood been shed, so entirely without justification or provocation.[21]

The development of the historiography from Stanley, through Morton, Giraud, Creighton, and Flanagan would seem to indicate that each fresh version of history is not necessarily closer to full comprehension. On the other hand, if Flanagan's account (so similar to the official government version) were ultimately verified, the more important lesson could be that there is no vision more clear than the sight of the eye-witness. And yet the official history Flanagan embraced did not include his evidence of government forgery of medical evidence for the sake of expediting Riel's execution; nor did it draw Creighton's link of the crisis in the West to that of the East for the sake of the railway, or present either Giraud's documentation of uncontrolled terror in early Manitoba or Morton's story of mock diplomacy in 1869-70. Certain nasty bits had been uncovered by establishment historians since 1936. Are there other indications of duplicity? The question is still open. The question is important because it pertains to the logic of using minimal assumptions in explanation.

The central issue concerns the adoption of government good faith as a working assumption. Reformulators of the conventional account have found suggestions of bad faith, and still assumed that the latest discovery is an exceptional deviation from an overall pattern of benevolent accommodation. For developers of the government-vindication tradition the central problem has been Métis abandonment of opportunities in Manitoba and their blundering into a more perilous confrontation a second time in Saskatchewan. The presumption of government benevolence always calls for supporting assumptions about the Métis: ''primitivism'' with Stanley, or the assumption of incurable Métis ''nomadism'' by Giraud and Morton.

---

21. Public Archives of Canada (PAC), Sir John A. Macdonald Papers, MG 26 A, Incoming Correspondence, pp. 42338-42348, A.M. Burgess, Deputy Minister of the Interior, to Sir David L. Macpherson, Minister of the Interior. Flanagan came close to admitting that the intent of his book was to turn the historiographical clock back to the government's version of events. A review of his own and other recent work asserted that an ''attentive reader will see behind Stanley's analysis the oratory of Edward Blake,'' the leader of the Liberal Opposition in 1885. Flanagan considered his own book ''something of a return to the views of the Conservative government of 1885'' (''Louis Riel: Review Essay,'' p. 158.)

For Creighton and Flanagan, a tertiary presumption has been the political immorality of Riel and the incredible gullibility of his followers. Surely, the more reasonable starting point is suspending both sets of assumptions and asking what is logically the first question: Were the opportunities the Métis allegedly ignored in Manitoba genuine? Or did dispossession precede migration? If the evidence suggests that migration was a rational response to an intolerable situation, the migration would be explicable without resorting to assumptions of Métis non-adaptability. Then, with resettlement in Saskatchewan, the question that would require fewer assumptions than Flanagan's or Creighton's is whether the gestures of alleged conciliation in January and February of 1885 were objectively provocative. Is there evidence of deliberate provocation? If the provocations are not explicable accidents, what could Canada hope to gain by provoking Riel into forming a second provisional government? All such questions suggest that a path of fewer assumptions is possible — and appropriate — for a genuine reconsideration of the evidence.

H.Y. Hind, ca. 1869
(Provincial Archives of Manitoba)

"By depicting the Red River Settlement as a parody of proper colonization, Hind was telling his Canadian readers that the real development of the North West was yet to begin."

18

Chapter 2

Acquiring Canada's First Colony

Until the mid-1850s there was little talk of the land west of Lake Superior in Upper Canada. Canadians already had an agricultural frontier in the south-central region of present-day Ontario. Then, abruptly in 1854, the last "wild land" suitable for farming went up for auction in Bruce County. The leading newspaper of Toronto, George Brown's *Globe,* reported that an important milestone had just been passed. An era had ended. Canada needed "new worlds to conquer."[1]

The Canadian desire for a new agricultural frontier in the 1850s was stimulated by prosperity as much as by fear of confinement. Excellent wheat crops and record prices for grain in Britain (because of the Crimean War of 1854-56) encouraged farmers to sell every surplus bushel and to put every available acre into production.[2] Another incentive for land acquisition was to meet the demands of the next generation. In the nineteenth century, the "motive power of the family farm was the farm family" — especially sons. Young men legitimately hoped for "future compensation commensurate with their contribution to the economy of the family. . . ."[3]

Recognizing that there were foreseeable limits to farm consolidation within the old boundaries of Canada, self-appointed promoters of expansion joined the *Globe* in the late 1850s to advertise an unfamiliar West, far away and considerably to the north of the agricultural heartland then in production. What made the new *North* West all the more attractive to Canadians in the 1850s was the apparent ease of its acquisition because the Americans had conceded for the moment that the Indian territory west of Lake Superior, north of the forty-ninth parallel, was a protectorate of Britain and the British had delegated all ruling authority in the region to the Hudson's Bay Company (HBC). Periodically, however, the company's trade rights came up for renewal. One such occasion was in 1859. In anticipation of the

---

1. Doug Owram, *Promise of Eden: The Canadian Expansionist Movement and the Idea of the West, 1856-1900* (Toronto, 1980), p. 44.

2. John McCallum, *Unequal Beginnings: Agriculture and Economic Development in Quebec and Ontario until 1870* (Toronto, 1980), p. 20.

3. Gagan, *Hopeful Travellers,* p. 44.

event, the British government decided to strike a parliamentary committee to review the expediency of continuing the status quo or revoking HBC jurisdiction as a first step towards a more vigorous promotion of agricultural settlement on the prairies. Hearings began in 1857.[4]

One settlement did already have a well-established foothold in the southeast corner of HBC territory in the District of Assiniboia. According to a company census (taken in the spring of 1856), more than 1,000 families were situated on riverfront homesteads along the Red and Assiniboine rivers at the location of present-day Winnipeg.[5] The Red River Settlement was agricultural and settled in the sense that people had built houses and stables, kept gardens and livestock, raised a little grain, fished and cut wood, and put up hay for their horses and cattle in winter. But almost no one in the colony attempted to make a living solely from cash-crop agriculture. Nor did many people cover their occupancy of the land with the paper mysteries of "location tickets," "patents," or "transfers" which were such a marked feature of the settlement of Upper Canada from its earliest beginnings. The one "owner" of land in the Red River Settlement was the Hudson's Bay Company.[6] In that, and in many other respects, the colony was a kind of fur-trade company town more than a community of independent land owners determined to make money in the usual ways of land speculation and agricultural production. Indeed, almost every adult male at Red River in 1850 had some kind of tie to the HBC—selling the company his labour or selling some semi-finished commodity generated from local resources. Moreover, what a person sold to the company in the 1850s depended in large part on his father's relationship to the firm. That social distinction reflected a crucial ethnic division that was rooted deeply in the history of the fur trade, and explains settlement at Red River from the outset.

Before 1820, two companies competed for the fur resources of the region. In addition to the London-based HBC there was the Montreal-based North West Company. The Canadian challenger was able to compete with the older firm through its attachment to a population of *canadiens* who had ventured west, intermarried with native people, and remained in the territories as "freemen" after the expiration of their contracts.[7] Their *métis*

---

4. W.L. Morton gives a good general discussion in "The Northwest and Canada, 1857-1859," in his *The Critical Years: The Union of British North America, 1857-1873* (Toronto, 1964), pp. 21-40.

5. An abstract of the 1856 census is printed in the appendix of H.Y. Hind, *Narrative of the Canadian Red River Exploring Expedition of 1857 and of the Assiniboine and Saskatchewan Exploring Expeditions of 1858* (London, 1860), II, pp. 403-404.

6. For a qualification of the generalization, see Archer Martin, *The Hudson's Bay Company's Land Tenures and the Occupation of Assiniboia by Lord Selkirk's Settlers with a List of Grantees Under the Earl and the Company* (London, 1898).

7. The standard history of the HBC's Canadian rivals is M.W. Campbell, *The North West Company* (Toronto, 1957).

(mixed blood) progeny were scattered all through the Great Lakes region. But as the pressure of advancing settlement in Wisconsin and Minnesota forced them ever further west and north, large numbers of Métis migrated towards present-day Pembina, North Dakota, in the early 1800s.[8] The Nor'westers encouraged them to produce plains provisions, mainly pemmican (a preparation of dried buffalo meat, fat, and berries) on which voyageurs could subsist for months while en route to the fur-trade posts. Thus, an important key to the North West Company's challenge to the HBC was its ability to provision its trade from the hinterland itself. The Nor'westers thirty-six-foot canoes carried trade goods, not food, from Montreal. Since the Métis were an integral part of the Nor'westers success, employees were not discouraged from remaining in the North West after the expiration of their own terms of service.

No such encouragement was given to Hudson's Bay Company employees even if they had taken native women as spousal companions.[9] But in 1821, after a decade of ferocious competition, the North West Company merged with the HBC and the older organization reversed its policy of insisting on the repatriation of employees after retirement. At the same time, the restoration of monopoly conditions enabled the company to streamline its operations and eliminate almost one-third of the old labour force. Of the 700 employees let go in 1821,[10] many — perhaps most — had developed attachments to native women. They and their children (the "native English"[11]) were encouraged to retire to a small experimental colony promoted earlier by a Scottish peer with HBC sanction at the forks of the Red and Assiniboine rivers. From 1811 to 1816, Thomas Douglas, the Fifth Earl of Selkirk, had persuaded hundreds of poor Scot and Scot-Irish farmers to start afresh in his northern Garden of Eden. All but a handful had given up the attempt by 1821. After that date, those who remained were joined by the unemployed fur traders who decided not to abandon their native families and took up the company's offer of free rent at Red River.[12] A few years later, the Métis pemmican producers just over the

---

8. See Jacqueline Peterson, "Prelude to Red River: A Social Portrait of the Great lakes Métis," *Ethnohistory* 25 (1978), pp. 41-67.

9. See Jennifer Brown, *Strangers in Blood: Fur Trade Company Families in Indian Country* (Vancouver, 1980).

10. Philip Goldring, "Papers on the Labour System of the Hudson's Bay Company," in Parks Canada, *Manuscript Report Series,* no. 362, pp. 32-33.

11. "Native" is the term that was normally used to describe the part-Indian population of Red River in the census reports of the 1830s and 1840s. "Native English" is a term that Canadians used in polite correspondence to distinguish the "English half breeds" from the French Métis. See, for example, G.T. Denison, *Reminiscences of the Red River Rebellion of 1869* (Toronto, 1873), or PAC, Macdonald Papers, Incoming Correspondence, pp. 78093-78103, A.G. Archibald to John A. Macdonald, 20 December 1871.

12. About fifteen per cent of the unemployed fur traders took up the company's offer. See Sprague and Frye, *The Genealogy of the First Métis Nation,* p. 15.

international boundary at Pembina received a similar invitation (to keep them from trading with Americans and to secure their labour since the company that took shape by the late 1820s consumed more than sixty tons of pemmican per year).[13]

Generally, the pemmican producers of Red River in the 1850s were the children of the people who provisioned the HBC in the 1830s. Their population had more than doubled. They had more houses, stables, livestock, and acres under cultivation. Some had begun to work as freighters by cart or by boat, but the basic employment of the Métis in the 1850s was still as semi-independent producers of plains provisions. The other part-Indian population, the native English, had grown at a similar rate in demographic terms. They too had enlarged their number of river-front homesteads, and by the 1850s some were almost self-sufficient farmers who worked but little for the company. But most were still quite dependent on the HBC for their main income and tended to work at higher status jobs than the Métis, jobs best symbolized by the clerical-managerial position of "Apprentice Postmaster," created for native sons of former HBC officers.[14]

The question that preoccupied Canadians and the British in the mid-1850s was whether the limited agricultural development at Red River was to be explained by some inherent flaw in the people or by the climate and soil of the region. To that end, both governments sponsored expeditions of exploration in 1857 and both came to substantially the same conclusion — that the Red and Saskatchewan drainage basins had vast agricultural potential. The British group under Captain John Palliser focused its report on the "capabilities" of the country — the flora and fauna supported at present and in the foreseeable future. Palliser had little to say about previous ventures in settlement.[15] The Canadian group, led by H.Y. Hind, showed keener awareness of past and present human habitation of the North West because the Canadians were concerned as much about the question of ownership of the soil as about the discovery of a "fertile belt" capable of sustaining farms. Consequently, in the Hind report there was a lengthy examination of land use in the Red River Settlement.

Hind recited the colony's historical beginnings, observed that Lord Selkirk's venture had not prospered, and said that since there were "few accessions" of other newcomers from "distant countries" the settlement

---

13. Arthur Ray, *Indians in the Fur Trade: Their Role as Hunters, Trappers, and Middlemen in the Lands Southwest of Hudson Bay, 1660-1870* (Toronto, 1974), pp. 208-209.

14. Carol M. Judd, "Native Labour and Social Stratification in the Hudson's Bay Northern Department, 1770-1870," *Canadian Review of Sociology and Anthropology* 17 (1980), p. 312.

15. Irene Spry, ed., *An Account of John Palliser's British North American Exploring Expedition, 1857-1860* (Toronto, 1963).

had fallen into the hands of "half breeds," a fatal flaw for the proper development of the colony, according to Hind. He thought the "diminution of European settlers" brought the colony ever "nearer to the savage wild ness of Indian life." To be sure, the "neat whitewashed houses" along the river did give the appearance of an island of European civility in a sea of prairie wilderness — but only from a distance. On closer inspection, Hind said all was in disarray, "slovenly" and "careless."[16]

On the farm of Pierre Gladieux, for example, Hind found a cattle yard with horses and poultry roaming among swine and cows. In the stable, where Hind expected to see more signs of livestock, he found only a "neat, light, four wheeled carriage." But worst of all, from Hind's perspective, Gladieux was about to go off on a buffalo hunt in September before looking after his harvest of peas, wheat, and hay and an immense tree that lay in front of his house ready for cutting into firewood. Gladieux was a "half breed." Like others of his race, the man was "naturally improvident, and perhaps indolent," Hind said, "they prefer the wild life of the prairies to the tamer duties of a settled home."[17]

By depicting the Red River Settlement as a parody of proper colonization, Hind was telling his Canadian readers that the real development of the North West was yet to begin. The whole land was virgin country; the whole region was a new world to conquer. The Métis had no prior claim, "no paper or document of any kind to show that they held possession" of the river lots they occupied.[18] Those places were only their resting grounds between hunting excursions. Every "15th of June they start for their summer hunt of the buffalo" which was taking them ever greater distances away from Red River. Hind seemed to think that in time they might abandon the colony altogether. If not, should they have to be "thrust on one side" by a tide of incoming settlers, he recommended great care in the enterprise since "their full appreciation and enjoyment of a home in the prairie wilds during the winter and summer, would render them a very formidable enemy...."[19]

One thing was certain: it was the "destiny" of the North West to become a wealthy and prosperous region once it passed to "an energetic and civilized race, able to improve its vast capabilities and appreciate its marvellous beauties."[20] The same theme was echoed almost immediately by Hind's readers and admirers. A young Canadian lawyer named Alexander Morris quoted Hind at every turn, and warned that the region could

---

16. Hind, *Narrative of the Red River Expedition*, I, pp. 148, 222-223.

17. Ibid., pp. 164-165, 179.

18. Ibid., p. 190.

19. Ibid., pp. 180-181.

20. Ibid., p. 134.

not remain "unoccupied" for long: "if we do not proceed to settle it the Americans will. . . ." To launch "Nova Britannia" on the prairies, Morris urged immediate annexation to the "jurisdiction of Canada with power . . . to colonize the territory."[21]

The British and even the Hudson's Bay Company were not opposed to such a proposition. Edward Ellice of the HBC said glibly that "nothing is as easy as to acquire it. For a million sterling, they may buy . . . the whole territory north of forty-nine between Canada and the Rocky Mountains."[22] Nor did the British government see any difficulty in Canada's acquiring the North West. The problem for the Colonial Office was learning what Canada wanted. On the one hand, Canada claimed to be the true proprietors of the territory already (by virtue of inheritance from Quebec). On the other hand, one of the leading politicians of the United Province of Canada, John A. Macdonald, claimed that responsibilities of ownership were too burdensome in 1858 because "we would have no proper means of supervision over it—people would rush into it who from want of restraint would grow up into anything but a creditable population."[23] The result was that when the parliamentary committee reported its hearings there was no recommendation for annexation to Canada. An opportunity for expansion was missed in the late 1850s.

Macdonald and other leaders of the Government of Canada resisted expansion in the 1850s for reasons that were political and constitutional, as much as administrative or financial. The terms of union of Upper and Lower Canada in 1840 gave each section equal representation in Parliament. The 450,000 people in Upper Canada did not object until the 1850s when their population began to outnumber Lower Canada's—by more than 60,000 people, according to the census of 1851.[24] That disclosure gave rise to a cry for legislative redistribution or "rep by pop." The political problem for John A. Macdonald and his colleagues in the Government of Canada was that the concession of representation proportional to population was certain to upset the balance that kept Macdonald's group in power. By 1858, a recipe of appealing to the loyalism of Conservatives in Upper Canada and the conservatism of *canadiens* in Lower Canada usually enabled his coalition of "Liberal-Conservatives" to return as the dominant group in Parliament.

Macdonald's frustration at the end of the 1850s stemmed from

---

21. Alexander Morris, *Nova Britannia; or, Our New Canadian Dominion Foreshadowed, Being a Series of Lectures, Speeches, and Addresses* (Toronto, 1884), p. 25.

22. D.G. Creighton, *Sir John A. Macdonald;* vol. 1, *The Young Politician* (Toronto, 1956), p. 244.

23. Ibid., p. 286.

24. J.M.S. Careless, ed., *Colonists and Canadiens, 1760-1867* (Toronto, 1971), pp. 205, 240.

flagging support in Upper Canada as he seemed incapable of promoting the expansionist agenda promoted by Brown's *Globe*. If Canada annexed the North West and a horde of Protestant humanity rushed into the region from the adjacent English-speaking section of Canada, the cry for "rep by pop" would become even more irresistible in the fragile union. Another possibility was that open access to the North West would take thousands of young people from Canada West, "draining away our youth and strength," perhaps putting the predominantly Protestant part of the province back in a minority position and making Upper Canada vulnerable to a demand for "rep by pop" from Lower Canada. For both political reasons, Macdonald was "quite willing, personally, to leave that whole country a wilderness for the next half century." He did realize, however, that "if Englishmen did not go there, Yankees will." To prevent American annexation in the interim, Macdonald hoped that the British would administer the North West as a crown colony beginning in the 1860s.[25]

By 1865, however, a new incentive for expansion was arousing the interest of Upper Canada even more irresistably. The boom that had made people land hungry earlier had collapsed, and agricultural hard times prodded farmers to seek escape as a matter of survival.[26] Intensive production of one crop had led to soil exhaustion, and that made cereals vulnerable to disease and parasites such as rust and the wheat fly. Production plummeted. At the end of the 1850s an average Upper Canadian farm had produced 135 bushels of wheat for market every year; a decade later, the number fell to a mere 60 bushels per farm.[27] Consequently, the farmers faced a real crisis. "The problem was one of too many people competing for too few resources at a time when the wellsprings of the farm economy . . . were beginning to dry up."[28] Some farmers shifted from wheat to barley production to serve the rapidly growing market for beer-making in the State of Wisconsin. Many more redoubled their demand for opening the North West.

Since Upper Canada's new expansionist urge could not be resisted, and since it could not find an outlet within the existing constitutional arrangement, momentum developed in the early 1860s for an enlargement of the union which was moving ever closer to political deadlock. The separation of Upper and Lower Canada into the two provinces of Ontario and Quebec to look after "local" concerns and their recombination with the rest of British North America to pursue great "national" objects was

---

25. PAC, Macdonald Papers, Letter Books, vol. 8, pp. 8-11, Macdonald to Edward Watkin, 27 March 1865.

26. McCallum, *Unequal Beginnings*, p. 22.

27. Ibid.

28. Gagan, *Hopeful Travellers*, p. 71.

the panacea for the economic doldrums that one Ontario Member of Parliament described as a "general gloom" hanging "like a pall on the land."[29] Since Macdonald was committed to continuing his political career, he appeared at the forefront of the drive to create the new union and never lost control of his majority in the process. When the Parliament of the new Dominion met for the first time on November 8, 1867, John A. Macdonald was still Premier and newly eager to pursue expansionist goals. Before a month had passed, the government had resolutions before the House to annex the North West.

William McDougall, a long-time proponent of western annexation and the new Minister of Public Works, introduced the government's expansionist policy on December 4, 1867, saying that the time was long overdue for adding the great new land to Canada so that "the whole expanse from the Atlantic to the Pacific would be peopled with a race the same as ourselves."[30] The only objections to the declaration of intent by Ontario Members of Parliament concerned the justice of the Hudson's Bay Company's demand for compensation as a precondition for annexation. But George Cartier, Macdonald's Quebec lieutenant, hinted that the whole territory might be acquired for the "paltry sum of five or six million dollars."[31] That prompted a Maritimer to shift the debate to a different principle. He wondered if the people who already lived in the North West had been consulted. Since Nova Scotians had been more or less conscripted into the Canadians' federation, he wanted to know if the new targets for merger were "willing to come into the Union, or were they to be dragged in against their will also."[32]

When *Sir* John A. Macdonald (he received a knighthood for his success with the confederation scheme) finally spoke on the North West acquisition resolutions two days after the debate began, he ignored both criticisms. Macdonald took for granted that the HBC had to be consulted, but the wishes of the natives could be ignored because they were "incapable of the management of their own affairs." The necessary consultation was to talk to the HBC and "arrange with the Imperial Government . . . for powers enabling the Parliament of the Dominion to provide a constitution which might be amended as necessary hereafter, to adapt it to the growing requirements of the new country."[33] Two old opponents in the Province of

---

29. David Gagan, "Land, Population, and Social Change: The 'Critical Years' in Rural Canada West," *Canadian Historical Review* 59 (1978), p. 293.

30. Library of Parliament Scrapbook, Parliamentary Debates Reported by the *Ottawa Times* and the *Toronto Globe and Mail,* 4 December 1867, p. 64. Hereafter cited as Scrapbook Debates. The Official Parliamentary Debates did not become available until 1875 (Olga B. Bishop, *Canadian Official Publications* [Toronto, 1981], pp. 87-88).

31. Ibid., p. 65.

32. Ibid.

33. Ibid., 6 December 1867, p. 73.

Canada, Edward Blake and David Mills, suggested that it would be preferable for the Colonial Office to transform the HBC territory into a crown colony under British rule, with the North West coming into Confederation later with "the same rights of local self-government, free from federal control, as is already enjoyed by the provinces of this Dominion."[34] Mills thought that it would be inappropriate for Canada, in some respects still a colony itself, to have colonies of its own. Maritimers and some Quebeckers agreed.

In the end, however, it was the imperialism of Ontario—the power that had done so much to prompt Confederation in the first place—that carried the debate. Thus, Alexander Mackenzie, Member of Parliament for a depressed Ontario riding, stated that he was "prepared to do all in his power to assist in the acquisition and opening up of the North Western territory," even though he was the leader of Macdonald's opposition in all other respects.[35] Other Ontario expansionists reminded the House again and again that "we have no longer those vast tracts of fertile land" that gave rise to earlier prosperity. And William McDougall closed the debate by reminding Ontario Members of Parliament to "stand fast by the views which they had so constantly expressed, and which the people of Upper Canada endorsed."[36] They needed little prodding. Resolutions to acquire Canada's first colony passed on December 6, 1867, without division. Since Confederation was just five months old (and anything but well cemented), Joseph Howe, another disgruntled Maritimer, found the vote for "colonization and conquest and other grand ideas" mildly ridiculous.[37]

Given the overall enthusiasm and the haste with which the new Macdonald government pressed for parliamentary authorization to annex the North West, it might have been expected that he and his colleagues would have moved immediately on the project in 1868. But other matters, particularly a robust separatist movement led by Joseph Howe in Nova Scotia, precluded action anywhere but on the domestic front. The "Repealers" (so-called because they sought repeal of the British North America Act) were eventually neutralized by promises of "better terms" in the union and better offices for leading separatists (Joseph Howe, for example, became Superintendent General of Indian Affairs and Secretary of State for the Provinces, the two ministries that were likely to be the most involved in the North West as well as in dominion-provincial relations).[38] Only after Macdonald's personal diplomacy settled a pacification scheme on Nova

---

34. Ibid.
35. Ibid., 4 December 1867, p. 70.
36. Ibid., 6 December 1867, p. 74.
37. Ibid., p. 76
38. See Kenneth G. Pryke, *Nova Scotia and Confederation* (Toronto, 1979).

Scotia in the autumn of 1868 did a delegation consisting of the outspoken William McDougall and the more business-minded George Cartier go off to London to seek a bargain with the HBC.

Negotiating through British intermediaries, the Canadian delegates succeeded at the end of the first week of March 1869 in bringing the company to an arrangement that was likely to be acceptable to Canada. They promised to deposit 300,000 pounds sterling in guaranteed bonds in a London bank, to recognize a number of tax and territorial concessions (including the company's retention of one-twentieth of all the land suitable for agriculture). Then, for its part, the HBC would surrender all proprietary claims to the Crown, and the British sovereign would proclaim the Government of Canada the new colonial power in the North West.[39] But before the actual transfer, it was necessary for the Canadian Parliament to ratify the terms and conditions of the sale and to establish a policy for administering the colonization of the soon-to-be acquired territory.

When William McDougall introduced the transfer arrangement on May 28, boasting that Canada was "on the eve of securing the grand object for which our government was formed in 1864,"[40] no one disputed his claim. There was general consensus that annexation of the West was the principal goal of the Confederation movement that developed in Upper Canada in the three years before 1867. Even the chief spokesman for the opposition, Alexander Mackenzie, "gave credit to the delegates for their efforts in London." He quibbled that the reserve of one-twentieth was overly generous and asked why the government "had not brought down the measure they intended to introduce for the future government of the territory." But Mackenzie expressed "hearty support" for the arrangement "as a whole."[41] Consequently, on May 31, Parliament adopted an address "praying for the annexation of the North West," again, without division or debate.

Four days later, Sir John A. Macdonald introduced the bill to provide for the territory's colonization. The matter was complicated, however, by Canada's own colonial status. Constitutionally, Canada had no power to acquire and administer a colonial empire of its own. Section 146 of the British North America Act[42] did convey "power to admit Newfoundland, etc. into the Union," but the implication of the clause was as Mills had stated earlier—additions to Confederation were to enter as provinces. Macdonald's way around the constitutional problem was to frame the

---

39. See Canadian Sessional Papers (1869), no. 25.

40. Scrapbook Debates, 28 May 1869, p. 80.

41. Ibid.

42. The name of Canada's constitution was changed in 1982 to the Constitution Act (1867).

legislation with the implication that Canada was only taking a short interim step towards admitting another partner into Confederation. The bill provided that the region was to be *temporarily* run by a governor and council appointed in Ottawa. To be sure, the territorial viceroy was to make whatever "Laws, Institutions, and Ordinances" he saw fit, without any accountability to the inhabitants. But Macdonald assured the House of Commons that the "act would only remain in force until the end of the next session." He insisted that within one year the authoritarian "provisional" regime would be remodeled into "a more permanent government." Still, he did not promise that the arrangement to be created in a year or so would be a province or even elective in its institutions.[43]

Some members of the House were uneasy about the lack of detail concerning the "mature plan" that was contemplated. No public revelation was forthcoming from Sir John A. Macdonald on June 4 or at any time later. On June 18, during consideration of supplementary budget estimates, Luther Holton noticed that $1.5 million — a sum equivalent to about one-twentieth of the entire national revenue of the day — appeared rather cryptically under the "North West" account. What for? he asked. McDougall muttered that the need to improve communication with the territory called for expenditure, but Holton was dissatisfied with the answer. The next day he pressed more firmly and Macdonald attempted an explanation. He indicated that the government's intention was to establish immigration agents in Ireland and Scotland for recruiting newcomers for the North West. Anticipating a flood of immigrants, Canada needed a wagon-water route from the head of navigation on Lake Superior to the Red River Settlement. McDougall added that the money would also support a detailed survey of the land the settlers were likely to find most suitable for agriculture on their arrival. But neither he nor Macdonald said a word to reveal the shape of the "mature plan" for realizing the provincial status of the North West — not then, or the next day when the bill came up for second and final readings.[44]

One reason the measure passed with so little discussion is that Macdonald had waited until nearly the last day of a hectic session before revealing the barest hint of his government's colonial policy. Only as the House was anxiously expecting a recess did he bring his territorial government bill up for consideration. The assurance that nothing permanent was being enacted made it plain that Parliament would have occasion to go over the matter with more deliberate consideration in the near future. It remained to be seen what Macdonald envisioned for the long term.

Macdonald's private correspondence suggests that he intended to "keep it a crown colony" of Canada for considerably longer than the

---

43. Scrapbook Debates, 4 June 1869, p. 107.
44. Ibid., 18-19 June 1869, pp. 144-146.

temporary government scheme implied. Only after significant portions of the "fertile belt" in the Red and Saskatchewan drainage basins were well colonized would he consider taking all or part of the region into Confederation on a footing that would be more or less the same as that of the four original provinces.[45] In the meantime, the policy was to "grope quietly along," he said to one correspondent.[46] He was even more blunt with another. To J.Y. Bown, an Ontario Member of Parliament (and brother of a Canadian already at Red River), the Prime Minister said the game was to establish calm with the "wild people" of Red River by unspecified yet "considerable management" until enough newcomers like Bown's brother had moved west.[47] He predicted rather optimistically that the first wave of new settlers could accomplish the informal work of establishing Canadian sovereignty. "In another year," he wrote, "the present residents will be altogether swamped by the influx of strangers who will go in with the idea of becoming industrious & peaceable settlers." Macdonald added, "I am more apprehensive about the Indian difficulty than anything else."[48] Ironically, just as he was writing that Métis resistance to the transformation of the West would be relatively insignificant, the "present residents" of the Red River Settlement had already taken effective action to derail Macdonald's hope for an easy transition from HBC to Canadian rule.

---

45. PAC, Macdonald Papers, Letter Books, vol. 15, pp. 289-291, Macdonald to J.Y. Bown, 9 February 1871. Bown had written Macdonald on February 4 complaining about certain actions of Governor Archibald. Macdonald replied that Canada had no power to control Archibald's every move, and added: "If the original intention of keeping it a Crown Colony, to be governed by instructions from Ottawa, had been carried out, we would of course have been responsible for his actions. . . ."

46. Ibid., vol. 12, pp. 955-956, Macdonald to R.G. Haliburton, 9 July 1869.

47. Ibid., vol. 13, p. 237, Macdonald to J.Y. Bown, 14 October 1869.

48. Ibid.

William McDougall, 1867
(Public Archives of Canada [C8362])

"McDougall acted in accordance with his understanding of the instructions he had in hand, rather than in accordance with the changed plans in the mail from Ottawa."

32

Chapter 3

Asserting Canadian Authority Over Assiniboia

When the Canadian Prime Minister assured his private correspondents that the Red River Métis were likely to be "swamped" by newcomers, he probably envisioned settlers taking over land that the Métis occupied without title from the Hudson's Bay Company as well as homesteading on virgin soil. That was implied in the "Draft Order in Council for Uniting . . . the North-Western Territory to the Dominion of Canada." Only one clause addressed the land tenure of old settlers. Article 10 assured those who could document their tenure by reference to the company's Land Register that they had nothing to fear from the transfer: "All titles to land up to the 8th March 1869 conferred by the company are to be confirmed."[1] There was no provision for the cases that H.Y. Hind had reported were the most typical. There was no security for persons whose only proof of possession was their occupancy of the land.

In Canadian tradition, settlers without title were "squatters." To be sure, the practice was to treat such persons liberally if their "squatting" was on unsold Crown land and if the trespassers' occupancy was followed by significant improvements — development that met or exceeded the settlement duties expected of the official recipients of "free" land.[2] Apparently, Macdonald saw no reason to make different allowances for the Métis "squatters" in the North West.

The government's first concern was to know the location and extent of "titles conferred by the Company" so that suitable land from the rest of the territory might be set aside for the first wave of newcomers expected to

---

1. PAC, Macdonald Papers, Incoming Correspondence, p. 40208, "Draft Order in Council for Uniting Rupert's Land and the North-Western Territory to the Dominion of Canada."

2. Recipients of free land in Upper Canadian experience were military veterans expected to perform settlement duties before receiving Crown patents. The settlers receiving free grants that were not conditional on settlement and improvement were the pre-1789 Loyalists. See George C. Patterson, *Land Settlement in Upper Canada* (Toronto, 1920), pp. 21-32, 78-80, and 171.

emigrate from Ontario perhaps as early as the autumn of 1869. To that end, a team of land surveyors was sent to Red River in July. The leader of the group, John Stoughton Dennis (a lieutenant-colonel of militia), arrived in mid-August; the rest of his crew followed in time to begin work early in September.[3]

Before the surveys began, Dennis called on the HBC official who presided over the territory within a fifty-mile radius of Fort Garry, the Governor of the District of Assiniboia, William Mactavish. He told Dennis that Red River was not the same community Hind had visited ten years earlier. Dennis did know that the colony faced hard times because of drought and grasshoppers. The company had been collecting charitable donations in Canada and England for relief of the third of the population who faced starvation because of the failure of their crops, the hunt, and even the fishery. Indeed, the Government of Canada had contributed aid in the form of a public works project when forty (mainly local) men were put to work improving the cart road between Fort Garry and Lake of the Woods in the summer of 1868.[4] What was news to Dennis was the Governor's assertion that the natives were a hunting people rooted in the soil. Mactavish said that "as soon as the survey commences, the half breeds and Indians will come forward and assert their right to the land, and possibly stop work till their claim is satisfied."[5]

On August 21, Dennis reported the disturbing news to the Minister of Public Works, William McDougall, saying, "a considerable degree of irritation exists among the native population in view of surveys and settlements being made without the Indian title having been first extinguished. . . ." He warned that the "question must be regarded as the very greatest importance" and added that the "French half breeds . . . have gone so far as to threaten violence should surveys be attempted to be made."[6]

McDougall's repetition of the story that the Métis might become violent prompted Macdonald to provide armed support for his own nominee to replace Mactavish and to send his governor-designate to the North West almost immediately. Macdonald's man, none other than McDougall himself, left Ottawa in the last week of September—even before a new appointee could succeed him in the Public Works portfolio. Moreover, he departed in the company of a "large party" with several cases of rifles for equipping a police force to be recruited from the local population.[7]

---

3. A.C. Roberts, "The Surveys in the Red River Settlement in 1869," *The Canadian Surveyor* (1970), pp. 238-239.

4. George Stanley, *Louis Riel* (Toronto, 1963), p. 50.

5. Ibid., p. 57.

6. Roberts, "Surveys," p. 240.

7. PAC, Macdonald Papers, Letter Books, vol. 13, p. 237, Macdonald to J.Y. Bown, 14 October 1869. Macdonald later claimed that he knew nothing about the trouble over the surveys, "for it was only after McDougall had left Ottawa that he learned that

The plan was for McDougall and his entourage to travel by train as far as possible; then, upon reaching the end of steel at St Cloud, Minnesota, the Canadians were to follow the Crow Wing trail by ox cart and arrive at the border well before the transfer was to occur on December 1. In the meantime, Dennis and his surveyors were to confirm the boundaries of the Old Settlement Belt and to launch new surveys only on the periphery of the old.

What Macdonald did not realize is that the Métis were prepared to resist the slightest new incursion of strangers from Canada. Since the 1850s they had been witnessing the arrival of some of Canada's most acquisitive adventurers, exemplified best by John Christian Schultz, who arrived in 1861 to practise medicine.[8] However, it soon became apparent that the self-made Dr. Schultz was a speculator whose major ambition was cornering the land market in anticipation of the migration of pioneers from his native Ontario. In 1864, Schultz took over the *Nor'wester,* Red River's first newspaper, and used its pages to trumpet the need for the colony's liberation from the tyranny of the HBC. Preferring the adversary they already knew, the Métis emerged as the company's staunchest supporters. The Council of Assiniboia was not an authority they revered, but the existing government could be tolerated because in most respects it was powerless, and therefore irrelevant to their real concerns.[9] In an opposite yet similar twist, as soon as Schultz learned that the transfer was imminent, he sloughed off his earlier liberalism and declared that authoritarian government under Canada was entirely proper until the colony was better prepared for elective institutions.

In 1868 other Canadians as offensive to the Métis as Schultz came in to supervise the Dawson Road work. Charles Mair, for one, was a youthful poet who knew nothing about roadbuilding or its administration, but he did crave adventure and persuaded his friend, the Minister of Public Works, to give him the position of paymaster on the road project. Inevitably, Mair made the acquaintance of Schultz and just as predictably Dr. Schultz became the supplier of the provisions with which Mair paid the Métis crew. At the same time, Mair was writing letters to Ontario newspapers extolling the quality of the land that was free for the taking and not concealing his belief in the innate inferiority of persons of part-Indian ancestry. When he

---

Colonel Dennis had observed this discontent on the part of the half breeds in the preceding summer, and had reported it to his chief, who apparently thought so little of the circumstance that he did not mention it to his colleagues.'' See Joseph Pope, *Memoirs of the Right Honourable Sir John A. Macdonald,* 2 vols. (Ottawa, 1894), II, p. 51.

8. G.F. Reynolds, ''The Man Who Created the Corner of Portage and Main,'' Historical and Scientific Society of Manitoba, *Transactions* (1970), p. 8.

9. See Lionel Dorge, ''The Métis and *Canadien* Councillors of Assiniboia,'' *Beaver* 305 (1974), 1:12-19, 2:39-45, 3:51-58.

insulted the native wife of one of the settlement's most prominent persons, she struck back with an "overhauling" that included a slap in the face and several smacks with her riding whip.[10]

The rumour that people like Schultz and Mair were poised on Red River's doorstep by the thousands frightened as much as it angered all sectors of the native population. The Métis of one particular parish organized early in July to take direct and effective action to defend their land from interlopers. With the help — indeed, the prompting — of their priest, Father N.J. Ritchot, the people of St Norbert created patrols under two captains, Baptiste Tourond and Jean Baptiste Lépine.[11]

With Tourond and Lépine making certain throughout the summer of 1869 that "no stranger should establish himself on the lands" fronting on the Red and Assinibone rivers, it was evident to anyone who cared to notice that the Métis had in fact taken the first step towards creating a government. Since there were no other police already on the scene, it was equally evident that the Métis cavalry was likely to determine the shape of the order that was to succeed the HBC. If Tourond and Lépine were typical of the men who were going to emerge in the commanding roles, the leaders of the Métis shared a definite profile: they were in their forties, had *canadien* fathers, headed large families in their own generation, and had direct experience in the old economy of pemmican production as well as the newer livelihoods of freighting supplies for the HBC and subsistence farming. At the same time, Tourond and Lépine were both farmers without land grants. The land they "owned" they held by peaceable possession; their names did not appear in the HBC Land Register.[12]

Under the circumstances, it was predictable that older Métis with more lucrative ties to the company would attempt to head off the upstarts. In Ritchot's parish of St Norbert, the company's man was William Dease. He had an appointment on the Council of Assiniboia and was the registered owner of several large tracts of land.[13] As he moved to assert what he regarded as a more legitimate claim to leadership, Dease was joined by a group of similarly well-situated Métis from other parishes at the end of July.[14] They called a mass meeting to take place at Fort Garry on the 29th, and at the appointed hour, Dease told his compatriots that he and his

10. See J.E. Rea, "Bannatyne, A.G.B.," *Dictionary of Canadian Biography,* vol. 11, pp. 44-47.

11. Stanley, *Riel,* pp. 55-56.

12. See the data on the Lépine and Tourond families in Sprague and Frye, *Genealogy of the First Métis Nation,* household numbers 2923 and 4705.

13. Ibid., household number 1059.

14. According to Stanley, the associates of Dease were Pascal Breland, Joseph Genthon, and William Hallet *(Riel,* p. 56). See household numbers 508, 1927, and 2101 in Sprague and Frye, *Genealogy.*

associates were the authentic leaders and true defenders of Métis society. Dease asserted that the nub of the entire matter was the 300,000 pounds to be paid by Canada to the HBC. Since the actual owners of the soil were the natives, the Métis should demand money from the company, rather than resisting Canada and the surveys.[15]

A challenger to Dease who emerged as the leading spokesman for the Métis position, distinct from the company and the Canadian expansionists, was a young protegé of Ritchot willing to act on Ritchot's view that Dease and his friends were only posturing — were willing tools of Schultz, diverting attention from the real danger which was land loss. Ritchot's man was no hunter or farmer or even a resident of the colony for the last ten years, having only recently returned to his parents' home at Red River after a decade's absence for the pursuit of an education in Montreal.[16] But the young man had learned the art of speaking well. Indeed, he must have reminded those who heard him of his recently deceased father, who had mobilized the Métis twenty years earlier to resist the HBC in a trade matter that seemed of similar importance then. In 1849 they had followed one Louis Riel for freedom of trade; in the autumn of 1869 they would turn to Louis Riel the younger to get security for their land.[17]

Unfortunately for Colonel Dennis, Ritchot's parish was the one his crew had skirted even as they moved peripherally along the colony's western boundary. Their intention was to run an imaginary line perpendicular to the border with the United States about ten miles west of the Red River all the way from the boundary to the Assiniboine River (see Map 1). From the government's standpoint, the "Winnipeg meridian" could cause no offense, and at first no counter measures followed. But in the first week of October, a crew started to mark off sections in an easterly direction towards the Red River just south of the Assiniboine. On October 9 Dennis reported that all was still well; his men were "making good progress" and "nearly as far as the Red River." They were still outside the two-mile limit delineated by the Hudson's Bay Company in its survey of the mid-1830s. What he did not appreciate fully is that everyone in the colony observed a four-mile limit: an inner two miles of cleared and wooded land from which people took their fuel, crops, and building timber, and an outer two miles left in prairie sod as hay land. On October 11, the surveyors reached what they called the southern boundary of Section 6, Township 7, Range II, east of the Winnipeg meridian when the old settlers of the area ordered a halt

---

15. Stanley, *Riel*, pp. 56-57.

16. Ibid., pp. 18-34.

17. A standard account of the free-trade crisis appears in W.L. Morton, *Manitoba: History of a Province* (Toronto, 1957), p. 87. A work that shows that the company managed the matter to its own advantage is J.S. Galbraith, *The Little Emperor: Governor Simpson of the Hudson's Bay Company* (Toronto, 1976).

Map 1:
The Red River Settlement and the First Dominion Surveys

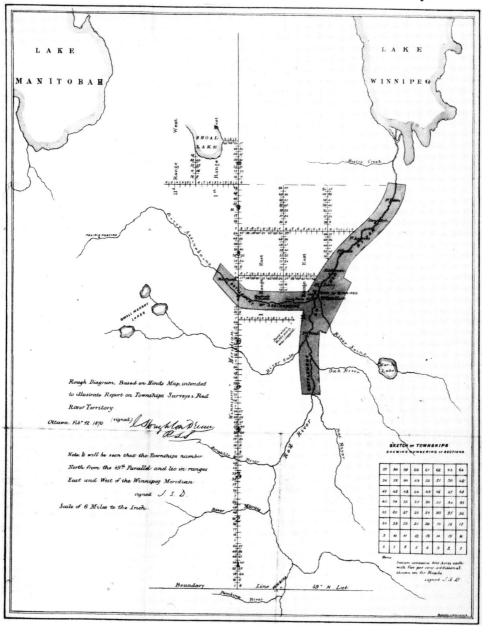

Source: PAC, National Map Collection, H12/740/Red River

because they said the crew was trespassing on the hay land of Edouard Marion.[18] Marion and sixteen of his neighbours ordered them off the land. Among the sixteen was Baptiste Tourond, the captain of the patrol in the area, but Louis Riel did the talking. He spoke English. A.C. Webb, the survey crew leader, asked Riel to give him each man's name, jotted the information into his field notes, and vacated the scene without further trouble.

The reaction of Colonel Dennis was less calm than that of Webb. Dennis went to the nominal authorities and demanded strong measures to punish those who interfered with his surveys.[19] Subsequently, they did ask for an explanation of events. Once again, Riel spoke for his neighbours. He asserted simply yet firmly that Canada "had no right to make surveys . . . without the express permission of the people of the Settlement."[20]

How, though, were the "people of the settlement" to express such permission? No representative assembly existed under company auspices. The nearest approximation to an elected government was the apparatus that came into existence each spring to govern the hundreds of families who still participated in the buffalo hunt, travelling as one or two expeditions southwest to the location of the herds. Within each were groups of families that formed particular teams. Each chose a captain. The captains chose their principal leader and he presided over the council of captains, the body that set regulations and met each day to handle offenders against the community's laws. The captains of the hunt were true representatives of the people; their council was a genuine though extra-legal government.[21] Even after the hunt declined in economic importance, its political organization had a social significance that continued.

The traditional organization of the hunt gave the Métis a political structure with which to resist the surveys. The new importance of farming[22] gave them their motive. As the protest broadened, each group of concerned families selected its captain. They met in St Norbert as the council of the whole people, declared on October 16 that they were the National Committee of the Métis, and chose a president, John Bruce. Since the expected struggle was to be a contest of speechmakers, the committee elected a secretary, Louis Riel.[23]

---

18. Not André Nault, as is usually reported, for example, in Stanley, *Riel*, p. 59. See Roberts, "Surveys," p. 244.

19. PAC, Macdonald Papers, Letter Books, vol. 13, p. 482, Macdonald to William McDougall, 20 November 1869.

20. Stanley, *Riel*, p. 59.

21. For a vivid description of the political organization of the hunt, see Joseph Kinsey Howard, *The Strange Empire of Louis Riel* (New York, 1952), pp. 257-262.

22. See Sprague and Frye, *Genealogy of the First Métis Nation*, pp. 16-24, for the changes in the relative importance of hunting, freighting, and farming to the Métis between 1830 and 1870.

23. Stanley, *Riel*, p. 61.

Soon disturbing news convinced the National Committee that the resistance to Canada might become an armed conflict as well as a war of words. On October 20, Métis witnesses to McDougall's arrival at St Cloud came home to report that they had seen several cases of the latest repeating rifles in the Canadians' baggage. Anticipating that McDougall's entourage would reach the border near the end of the month, the committee's next move was to take steps to prevent the governor from entering the territory with his load of carbines.[24]

Father Ritchot may have advised Riel that the best way to prevent trouble was to keep McDougall out of the settlement — away from Schultz and the other Canadians. The National Committee agreed. On October 21, they authorized barring the road to the United States, and drafted the famous dispatch to the governor-designate: ''The National Committee of the Métis of Red River orders William McDougall not to enter the Territory of the North West without special permission of the above-mentioned committee.''[25]

The note reached McDougall as he was about to enter Rupert's Land, after having reached the border on October 30. Three days later he continued as far as the Hudson's Bay Company post just to the north of the line, and was met by a company of Métis cavalry escorting McDougall's advance man, Captain D.R. Cameron, out of Assiniboia. Their commander, Ambroise Lépine,[26] then ordered McDougall off the land, and escorted the whole group back to the boundary on November 2. Pointing to the ground in front of his horse, Lépine said, ''You must not return beyond this line.''[27]

Confident that time was on his side — that he was soon to be joined by Canadians already in the settlement or with a force sent overland by Macdonald — McDougall embarked upon a period of waiting, expecting that all obstacles would vanish in time for his triumphal entry on the transfer date of December 1.[28]

In the meantime, the Métis National Committee took steps to consolidate its power. Its troops took Fort Garry in a bloodless coup on November 2, then devised means to recruit at least passive support from the rest of the population. The committee invited the native English of the Protestant parishes to elect twelve representatives to join an equal number of Métis deputies elected from the Catholic districts, and suggested November 16 was not

---

24. Ibid., p. 62.
25. Ibid.
26. The brother of Baptiste Lépine. See Sprague and Frye, *Genealogy,* household number 2920.
27. Stanley, *Riel,* p. 65.
28. PAC, Macdonald Papers, Incoming Correspondence, pp. 40751-40758, McDougall to Macdonald, 31 October 1869.

too soon for a first meeting to "consider the present political state of the country, and to adopt such measures as may be deemed best for the future welfare of the same." Elections followed and Protestants met Catholics on the appointed day.[29]

November 16 was also the approximate time of Macdonald's first learning of the interruption of the surveys and the subsequent barring of McDougall from the settlement.[30] His sources of information were American newspapers forwarded to Ottawa, not dispatches from the governor-designate. Then, about November 20, Macdonald received McDougall's first report. Evidently the Métis feared exclusion from the " 'law' (meaning the Council), that the half breeds would be all driven back from the River & their land given to others, etc., etc." In the long term, the solution was to "call for volunteers from Canada to *settle* the country with a good Rifle among the implements of husbandry in each case." That would prevent a recurrence of the annoyance of such crises. For the moment, though, McDougall said, "I am not frightened & don't believe the insurrection will last a week. . . ."[31]

Macdonald agreed in his reply of November 20 that McDougall's trouble was only "some little opposition" and that everything might proceed according to plan. Canada would not send a military force even though many of the Ontario volunteers were prepared to go to the North West through the United States disguised as settlers. For the moment, Macdonald thought that the most appropriate response was judicious use of patronage and sending influential French-Canadians to the scene.

> It occurs to me that you should ascertain from Governor McTavish to name the two leading half-breeds in the Territory, and inform them at once that you will take them into your council. This man Riel, who appears to be a moving spirit, is a clever fellow, and you should endeavour to retain him as an officer in your future police. If you do this promptly it will be a most convincing proof that you are not going to leave the half-breeds out of the Law.[32]

The good-will ambassadors to be sent from Quebec were a priest with missionary experience in the West, Father J.-B. Thibault, and a French-Canadian militia officer, Colonel Charles de Salaberry. Their assignment was to convince the Métis that all "stories as to the intentions of Canada to deprive them of their lands & to govern . . . without any reference to the residents" were totally untrue.[33]

---

29. Stanley, *Riel*, p. 68.

30. Creighton, *Old Chieftain*, p. 43.

31. PAC, Macdonald Papers, Incoming Correspondence, pp. 40752, 40754, McDougall to Macdonald, 31 October 1869.

32. Ibid., Letter Books, vol. 13, p. 481, Macdonald to McDougall, 20 November 1869.

33. Ibid., p. 515, Macdonald to Rose, 23 November 1869.

Macdonald concluded the letter with a warning that McDougall should avoid the temptation of blasting his way into the colony. "The point you must never forget," Macdonald stressed, "is that you are approaching a foreign country under the government of the Hudson's Bay Company. . . . You cannot force your way in. . . ."[34]

Evidently content that all would be resolved in the West, Macdonald sought confirmation that everything was still moving smoothly on the London end. The Prime Minister used the recently completed trans-Atlantic cable on November 22 to telegraph Canada's financial agent, John Rose, asking whether the money had been "paid over." At the same time, the telegram reported that McDougall had been stopped by an "armed Force of half breeds" and the insurgents had appointed a "provisional committee or Government."[35]

Although Macdonald may have intended nothing more by his question than literally to ask if the sale had been completed, the prompting sparked an idea in the clever imagination of Rose who subsequently launched a series of letters and telegrams urging delay of the transfer until peaceable possession could be assured. On November 25 he observed: "It is one thing to have to evict troublesome tenants" after a change of landlords. That Canada had anticipated from the beginning. Under the unexpected present circumstances, Rose observed, "we do not yet have the entry of the door." Why "pay for an estate if we can't get possession?"[36] The next day, a telegram from Rose to Macdonald was even more blunt: "Government and Company urging surrender [meaning payment]. Shall I claim delay? If so let Governor [General] cable . . . immediate."[37]

The advantage of delay was obvious — all responsibility for defeating the insurgents would fall to the HBC and the British. Canada could avoid the expense and humiliation that was certain if the suppression of the "half breeds" proved more complicated than McDougall or Macdonald imagined. Indeed, Sir John A. Macdonald himself should have appreciated as much as soon as he first learned of the disturbance from newspaper accounts in mid-November. He responded rather dimly, at first, because a crushing burden of personal financial troubles and family sorrow had pushed him into nearly continual drunkenness in the autumn of 1869. As the public crisis first broke he was not on top of developments. Later, as the trouble at Red River began to overshadow his own private tribulations, he became more clear-sighted. He saw that Rose was right. November 26 was

---

34. Ibid., p. 481, Macdonald to McDougall, 20 November 1869.

35. Ibid., Incoming Correspondence, p. 40224, Macdonald telegram to John Rose, 22 November 1869.

36. Ibid., p. 40241, Rose to Macdonald, 25 November 1869.

37. Ibid., p. 40249, Rose telegram to Macdonald, 26 November 1869.

not too late to stall the British.[38] However, the same cable that informed the Colonial Office of Canada's refusal to accept the transfer, "unless quiet possession can be given," asserted too confidently that "Macdougall will remain near frontier waiting favourable opportunity for peaceable ingress."[39]

McDougall was waiting at Pembina — still expecting to become Governor on December 1, and Macdonald's letter of November 20 authorized him to take control of the territory by any means short of force. With the refusal to accept the transfer communicated to the British on November 26, it was imperative that McDougall receive new instructions before December 1. Macdonald did not write on the 26th, but he did send a dispatch the next day telling the expectant governor to stay where he was and to forego proclaiming his authority: "You ought not to swear that you will perform duties that you are, by the action of the Insurgents, prevented from performing."[40]

If Macdonald wanted the message to reach McDougall in time, he would have had to send the information by telegram as far as Fort Abercrombie (south of Pembina on the Red River), and to have had it carried the rest of the way by riders on fast horses. (Macdonald had learned on November 25 that the best ordinary mail connections required at least twelve days by railway and ox cart.)[41] Consequently, when the Prime Minister chose to send his important dispatch of November 27 by ordinary mail, he had to know that the letter could not arrive at Pembina in time to make a difference on December 1 and he admitted as much the same day when he wrote another cabinet colleague that he feared the worst — not because his man on the spot had defective instructions, but because McDougall was too "high handed" to "do the right thing."[42]

On December 1 McDougall acted in accordance with his understanding of the instructions he had in hand, rather than in accordance with the

---

38. Creighton acknowledges that Macdonald's chronic drinking became acute in the autumn of 1869 *(Old Chieftain,* p. 41). Still, he asserts it was Macdonald's "quick lawyer's eye" (p. 47) which spotted the no-payment-without-peaceable-possession remedy. Creighton ignores the week-long pause before Macdonald's telegram of the 26th, and he ignores the telegram of Rose that finally prodded Macdonald into action. Creighton tells the story as follows: "John Rose . . . had written a little complacently [that everything was ready for the transfer]. . . . But he could be stopped. Canada could refuse to accept the transfer until peace was restored. . . . It was the one neat quick way out. And Macdonald determined to take it" (p. 48).

39. PAC, Macdonald Papers, Incoming Correspondence, pp. 40255-40256, draft telegram from Governor General to Lord Granville, 26 November 1869.

40. Ibid., Letter Books, vol. 13, p. 614, Macdonald to McDougall, 27 November 1869.

41. Ibid., Incoming Correspondence, p. 40830, H.P. Dwight telegram to Macdonald, 25 November 1869.

42. Ibid., Letter Books, vol. 13, p. 585, Macdonald to George Cartier, 27 November 1869.

changed plans that were in the mail from Ottawa. In the small hours of the morning, McDougall crossed the border and shouted the proclamation of his gubernatorial power into the frosty silence of the darkened prairie. For the benefit of the live audience, printed copies of the proclamation went up all over the Red River Settlement later in the day. Ironically, the proclamation of the transfer had a tonic effect on the council of delegates that had been lost in pointless wrangling since first meeting on November 16.[43]

McDougall's assertion that the transfer was an accomplished fact, like it or not, prompted a proposal from Riel: "If Mr. McDougall is really our Governor today, our chances are better than ever. He has no more to do than prove to us his desire to treat us well. If he guarantees our rights, I am one of those who will go to him in order to escort him as far as the seat of his government."[44] On that point all parties agreed—depending upon what was meant by "our rights." Riel then proposed a short recess to prepare a draft list. The others agreed to wait and see.

Two hours later Riel tabled a fifteen-point document which the principal spokesman for the native English, James Ross, accepted in substance. Riel proposed nothing more than an elected government (with exclusive power over all matters "local to the Territory"), equal status for the French and English languages, and secure land tenure for everyone (not just registered freeholders). According to the wording of the land-rights article, Canada had to guarantee "all privileges, customs and usages existing at the time of the transfer . . ." (which was broader than the confirmation of titles that Macdonald contemplated in the Draft Order in Council governing the transfer). On the land-rights issue it appeared that the native English and the Métis were united. The snag that developed was over the status of the extra-legal government then in existence. Riel's party demanded the power to deny McDougall entry until he recognized their rights. Ross objected that such a proviso had no meaning unless the council of delegates was the legal government of the colony; only the Queen of England could make them the government of Assiniboia. To declare otherwise would be an act of rebellion.[45]

Thus the council broke up on December 1. It infuriated Riel to have agreed on their rights and failed on a procedure for enforcing them. He held the native English entirely to blame and condemned them for cowardice. "Go, return peacefully to your farms! Stay in the arms of your wives," Riel shouted. "But watch us act. We are going ahead to work and obtain the guarantee of our rights and yours."[46]

43. Stanley, *Riel,* p. 68-72.

44. Ibid., p. 73.

45. Ibid., p. 74.

46. Ibid.

The immediate result of the apparent, irreparable division between the two native populations of Red River was an opportunity for the Canadian party to assert its own dominance despite its numbers. In 1869 there were about 6,000 Métis, 4,000 native English, and less than 1,000 Canadians in Assiniboia.[47] Of course, the Canadians were confident that they would achieve the dominant position in the North West eventually. The question that concerned them on December 1 was whether the defeat of Riel would occur immediately, with local resources, or later with outside help. One measure of the impatience of the Canadians is that they chose to make a bold move immediately, on their own. Schultz and Mair persuaded McDougall to commission Dennis as the "Lieutenant and Conservator of the Peace" to recruit an army of sympathizers from the native English.[48] But Mair and Schultz made two fatal miscalculations. They overestimated both the competence of Colonel Dennis as a general and the willingness of the English "half breeds" to fight the French in open war.[49]

As soon as Riel learned of the plot he moved against the most likely sources of trouble which were the stores and saloons in the little village of Winnipeg. When a group of about fifty Canadians and their sympathizers barricaded themselves in Schultz's store and prepared for a siege on December 7, the Métis broke the plot on the same day by rolling some artillery from the fort up to Schultz's door and daring them not to surrender. In a moment the Métis gained entry, then marched Schultz and his co-conspirators to jail in Fort Garry.[50] As soon as Dennis learned of his colleagues' capture, he too gave up the fight, in his case, by fleeing overland to Minnesota. As he trekked through the snow on foot, he must have burned with anger and ached with hope for some future opportunity to avenge his disgrace.[51]

McDougall, for his part, became another embittered actor once he learned of Macdonald's amended instructions too late to avoid the embarrassment of his premature proclamation of the transfer. After making one

---

47. According to the census of Manitoba taken one year later (after a considerable influx of newcomers), the balance of population was 1,611 "whites"; 5,696 "French Métis"; and 4,082 "English Métis." *Canadian Sessional Papers*, no. 20 (1871), p. 91.

48. Ibid, pp. 74-75.

49. A contrary view, one that argues that the two native populations were "implacable enemies," is expressed by Frits Pannekoek, "The Rev. Griffiths Owen Corbett and the Red River Civil War of 1869-70," *Canadian Historical Review* 57 (1976), pp. 133-149. But Pannekoek admits that the native English were still not willing to become the completely compliant tools of the Canadians and they were too divided among one another to define and fight for their own independent objectives.

50. Stanley, *Riel,* pp. 75-76.

51. See the accusations of Joseph Royal, PAC, Macdonald Papers, Incoming Correspondence, pp. 88884-88890, Royal to Macdonald, 2 November 1880; and the denial by Dennis, pp. 88880-88883, 10 November 1880.

final attempt to impress Riel with the futility of continuing the "insurrection," he left for Ottawa with Dennis in late December. Later, Macdonald complained that McDougall had made "the greatest possible mess of everything."[52]

The Prime Minister might have judged McDougall less harshly if the would-be governor had not launched a public campaign of personal vindication in the new year.[53] Macdonald would not admit that he shared any of the blame for mishandling the matter. At the same time, he feared that public agitation might spoil a second ambassadorial mission he had set in motion early in December.

The ambassador following Thibault and de Salaberry was Donald A. Smith, the highest ranking Hudson's Bay Company officer in North America. But the role the Prime Minister assigned to Smith was more daring than the assignment given to the others. The task Macdonald proposed (and Smith accepted) was for the official to go to Red River "as a sort of commissioner [but actually] . . . to make arrangements for the dispersion of the Insurgents, and the dissolution of their committee."[54]

On the same day Smith left for the West, Macdonald sent a letter to McDougall informing him of Smith's mission in unmistakable terms. "It is hoped here," he said, "that while Mssrs. Thibault & de Salaberry are acting upon the French half-breeds, Mr. Smith will be able to strengthen, encourage and organize the English & Scotch half breeds & the whites who are loyal to Canada, so pray sit down with the gentlemen & lay out a plan of operations."[55] Ignorant that the scheme had already failed with McDougall using Dennis, the Prime Minister cheerily instructed his man at Pembina to work with Smith in devising "a plan by which he might quietly & without observation, organize a body of Scotch & English to take possession of Fort Garry. . . ."[56]

First Thibault and de Salaberry (then Smith in his turn) discovered that McDougall had already acted and failed in their assigned mission. Worse, Thibault became a convert to the Métis cause soon after his arrival in the settlement in late December,[57] and Smith failed in the undercover aspect of his assignment. Later, Macdonald confided to Rose that he thought Smith was "incapacitated from usefulness by the most wretched physical

---

52. Ibid., Letter Books, vol. 13, p. 812, Macdonald to H.C. Langevin, 28 December 1869.

53. "McDougall is very sore about his fiasco . . . tries to put blame upon everybody else. . . . Without reading the documents you really could not understand the extremity of the folly he displayed in the west." Ibid., p. 966, Macdonald to Rose, 26 January 1870.

54. Ibid., p. 648, Macdonald to Rose, 5 December 1869.

55. Ibid., p. 713, Macdonald to McDougall, 12 December 1869.

56. Ibid.

57. Ibid., p. 85.

cowardice.'' It seemed he had chosen the wrong man: ''our selection of him was rather unfortunate.''[58]

Closer to the reality of the situation, Smith was afraid of provoking the Métis by seeming to be too friendly with the native English, and he did not get very far in bribing Riel. Instead, he persuaded the people in the settlement that Canada recognized they were a distinct political community and intended to respect their rights as a condition for their joining Confederation. In other words, the cover assignment became the whole mission. By fulfilling only the throw-away part of his task, Smith made a dramatic contribution to the increasingly complicated embarrassment of Macdonald's government.

Rather than defeating the insurgents by covert action,[59] Smith made promises that went beyond his instructions. Moreover, the whole community of Red River heard Donald A. Smith tell the people that they had absolutely nothing to fear from Canada. In a mass meeting that took place in the court yard of Fort Garry on January 19, 1870 (and continued the next day), they heard Canada's ambassador elaborate what he understood to be the government's intentions. By the time the performance was over, nothing remained but to set forth the conditions for the people's own terms of transfer. Riel closed the meeting by playing with the Canadian sneer that the people were ''half breeds'': ''We claim no half rights . . . but all the rights we are entitled to. Those rights will be set forth by our representatives, and what is more, Gentlemen, we will get them.''[60]

The method was to elect a larger council, a convention of forty delegates to enumerate the people's concerns, and to send a deputation to Ottawa to obtain appropriate recognition of their bill of rights. The first step, the election, was completed at once, in time for an initial meeting of the convention on January 26. Then, rather than debating the list of rights the Riel party had prepared on December 1, the convention struck a subcommittee to prepare a new non-partisan list. Six people accepted the appointment. Since the group consisted of a divided trio of Métis, and three English-speaking ''half breeds'' who were sceptical about the wisdom of resisting the transfer too openly, there was a real danger that the six people involved would soon become lost in personal bickering and disagreement.

---

58. The disappointment in Smith was expressed by Charles Tupper writing to Macdonald from Pembina, 30 December (ibid., Incoming Correspondence, pp. 41003-41004), then elaborated in private conversation once Tupper returned to Ottawa, and finally repeated by Macdonald himself to Rose on 21 January (ibid., Letter Book, vol. 13, p. 931).

59. In mid-February Macdonald still hoped that Smith might ''cause to be removed quietly and without observation some material portions of the machinery of your steamer at Fort Garry, otherwise, it might be employed in bringing supplies in the spring to the Insurgent camp'' (ibid., pp. 1056-1057, Macdonald to Smith, 16 February 1870).

60. Stanley, *Riel,* p. 91.

Somewhat surprisingly, they reported within three days that they had agreed to a text that was remarkably similar to Riel's

After debating and approving the revised list, the members of the entire convention then demanded specific assurances from Smith that the government in Ottawa would be likely to concede the demands that were emerging as the consensus of the diverse groups of native people at Red River. They handed the ambassador the document at 11:00 a.m. on February 7 and told Smith that he was expected to appear before the convention at 1:00 p.m. with his reply. They wanted simple answers — yes or no to each article. Smith reported later that he could give the delegates most of the assurances they wanted, but he refused to reply with a simple yes to each demand. Articles 6 and 15, for example, called for autonomy that amounted to provincial status — elective territorial institutions and parliamentary representation. Both would be "fully and liberally considered," said Smith. Two other articles called for bilingual proceedings in the legislature and the courts. Bilingualism would be "unquestionably . . . provided for," Smith promised. Still other articles (8, 14, 16, and 17) reflected the universal anxiety that the existing population would lose proprietorial control of its homeland. Here Smith asserted that "property held by residents in peaceable possession will be secured." He saw no problem with article 16 either: "That all properties, rights and privileges, as hitherto enjoyed by us, be respected and the recognition and arrangement of local customs, usages and privileges, be made under the control of the Local Legislature." In fact, the only article that received an answer as indefinite as maybe was the demand for a broad franchise because Smith was uncertain that the lack of a property qualification and the inclusion of Indians would be acceptable to Canada.[61]

Encouraged that their principal concerns were certain to be accommodated, the convention concluded the next day that there was good reason for accepting Macdonald's invitation to send a deputation to Ottawa. To give such a negotiating team a more official standing (as well as to provide continuity in the transition of power), Riel urged the convention of forty to transform itself into the provisional government of the territory. "The Provisional Government is an actual fact," he said. "Why not recognize it? . . . It has accomplished some good. Help it do more." Since the logic of Riel's proposal was nearly irrefutable, the convention agreed that the same committee that drafted the list of rights should produce a draft constitution. When that work passed on February 10, Louis Riel emerged as President, James Ross accepted the office of Chief Justice, and other notables representing every faction but the Canadian party filled the remaining offices.[62]

---

61. PAC, Macdonald Papers, Incoming Correspondence, pp. 41335-41350, D.A. Smith to Joseph Howe, 12 April 1870.

62. Stanley, *Riel,* p. 98.

From Sir John A. Macdonald's standpoint, the worst set of circumstances imaginable had developed. The "wild people" of the settlement had created an extra-legal authority that went unchallenged by the HBC, and the population he had counted on to "seize Fort Garry and hold it against all comers" had not risen. Instead, they had joined the insurgents and pressured Smith into a role that Macdonald specifically repudiated in a private letter to his friend John Rose.[63] When Macdonald learned at the end of February that Smith had given firm promises and de facto recognition to the provisional government, he became convinced that nothing short of war was likely to get the "half breeds" out of Fort Garry.[64]

The difficulty with Smith's promises was that Macdonald was reluctant to venture beyond two concessions. The Prime Minister had written Smith that there was "no objection to *two-thirds* of the Council being selected from among the Residents." But the council he envisioned was still an advisory body in a territorial government. The other concession, elective institutions, would follow as "soon as the Territory is in a positon to bear the burden and assume the responsibilities."[65] Clearly, neither point represented a significant departure from his original plan for territorial administration. In that sense, both positions reflected a rather intransigent attitude towards the Métis and their demands. Similarly, Macdonald refused to move from his original position on the land question. He still held that the only residents with unqualified security were persons whose "titles" were conferred by the HBC. The rest were to be accommodated by "a very liberal land policy as to the future settlement of the country."[66] Settlers without titles would have to prove compliance with yet-to-be-specified settlement duties. The Prime Minister refused to consider pre-emptive land rights for persons whose only claim was occupancy by itself. Macdonald did express confidence that the "propositions adopted at the Red River conference are, most of them, reasonable enough, and can easily be disposed of with the delegates," but he harboured grave misgivings about what would happen when the delegates returned home with their

63. Macdonald was certain that "conciliatory propositions would be rejected by our Parliament." PAC, Macdonald Papers, Letter Books, vol 13, p. 933, Macdonald to Rose, 21 January 1870; see also ibid., vol. 13, pp. 24-28, Macdonald to Rose, 23 February 1870.

64. The same displeasure would appear to explain the government's reluctance to thank Smith for his services; "it was not until February 22, 1872, nearly two years after his services were rendered, that Mr. Smith received any official recognition of what he had done. He was then thanked in a lengthy letter by the Governor-General in Council." Beckles Willson, *Lord Strathcona: The Story of His Life* (London, 1902), p. 90.

65. Ibid., vol. 13, p. 848, Macdonald to Smith, 3 January 1870.

66. Ibid., p. 850.

"inadmissible" demands not granted. Macdonald had "no great confidence in his [Riel's] ratifying any arrangement made here with the delegates."[67] Consequently, the Prime Minister made new efforts to prepare a military expedition for departure in the spring.

In making his military preparations, Macdonald recognized that a force of British regular troops would be more effective than the Canadian militia. In the first place, the "half breeds" were more likely to be intimidated by the imperial power of Britain. And secondly, the presence of an imperial force would discourage Americans from thinking that Canada was alone and powerless to assert sovereignty over the North West.[68] The problem was getting them into Assiniboia: "once there they can easily . . . be replaced by a Canadian Force."[69]

Macdonald's Cabinet colleagues approved the scheme. The difficulty was with the British. They feared that intimidating the natives would anger the Americans.[70] Consequently, the colonial office held back, even after events at Red River took a new — and bloody — turn following the failure of a second plot by the Canadian party to seize Fort Garry in mid-February. The most troublesome character in the second episode was, of course, Thomas Scott,[71] back in jail on February 18 and engaged in nearly endless taunting of his guards, a kind of harrassment that reached a critical point on February 28. To Scott's surprise, they entered his cell, dragged him outside, and started to beat the man senseless. Others intervened in time and saved his life.

Instead of changing the guard or muzzling the prisoner to prevent his murder, President Riel struck a special tribunal to try Scott for his most recent "treason" against the provisional government. On March 3 a majority of the members of the military-style court martial voted for the death penalty and informed Scott that he should prepare himself for death by firing squad the next day. The condemned man called them a "pack of cowards" and boasted they would not dare to kill him. He was correct to a point, but new evidence suggests that the tribunal did intend to give him the scare of a lifetime.[72]

The next day, Thomas Scott was taken from his cell and placed in front of a squad of marksmen looking like executioners, but the captain of the guard is said to have loaded their guns in preparation for the event with "powder and wad" only. Unfortunately for Scott (and Riel), an

---

67. Ibid., vol. 14, p. 49, Macdonald to Rose, 11 March 1870.

68. Ibid., Incoming Correspondence, pp. 40423-40433, Minute of Council, 4 February 1870.

69. Ibid., Letter Books, vol. 14, p. 48, Macdonald to Rose, 11 March 1870.

70. Ibid., Incoming Correspondence, p. 40458, Rose to Macdonald, 22 February 1870.

71. Stanley, *Riel,* p. 111.

72. Irene Spry, ed., "The Memories of George William Sanderson," *Canadian Ethnic Studies* 17 (1985), pp. 115-134.

uncontrollable Irish nationalist adventurer in the crowd of onlookers refused to be satisfied with a mock execution. William O'Donoghue wanted the Orangeman dead. Consequently, according to George Sanderson, on the command to fire, O'Donoghue's revolver discharged at the same time the firing squad shot its harmless blanks, and Scott fell dying in the snow. Then Francois Guillemette stepped forward and delivered the coup de grace.[73]

The possibility that the killing of Thomas Scott was a kind of accident (or at least a murder for which William O'Donoghue was more directly responsible than the provisional government) did not appear in American newspapers when the story reached St Paul, Minnesota, several days later.[74] Nor did Ontario newspapers reveal the fuller truth then or later. Their news was that a pure flower of Ontario youth had been savagely murdered by a "half breed papist rabble," and the issue changed from a matter of frustrated expansion into a question of the status of Protestants and Catholics in Canada.[75] After March of 1870, any accommodation of the Métis had to be denounced in Ontario as the appeasement of Catholic murderers and any failure to accommodate the French-Catholic Métis would be interpreted as "Protestant fanaticism" in Quebec. From March of 1870, all Canadians — Quebeckers as well as the others — would agree with Macdonald that some kind of armed force was needed, if only to protect the Métis from vengeful Orangemen.

As Macdonald continued his effort to bring the British into the Canadian consensus, his problem was their continuing anxiety about offending the Americans. The Colonial Secretary, Lord Granville, stipulated that Britain would not participate in an expedition unless and until "reasonable terms" were granted to the "Roman Catholic settlers."[76] Macdonald held out for his own terms. As late as April 9 he was still insisting that he would only receive the delegates.[77] Just as firm in his position, Granville wanted to know the "result of negotiations" before he would commit his country to military assistance.[78] Fearing that the results of the negotiations were

---

73. Stanley, *Riel*, p. 161.

74. Nor did this version of events come through in any account of the execution written by Riel. His position was that the provisional government had a duty to punish Scott for his "treachery." Thus, Riel freely admitted a role played by himself in the "tribunal," and he never denied that the court had committed the "culprit" to death. At no time did Riel suggest that the event of March 4 was intended as a mock execution. He never attempted to shift responsibility to O'Donoghue. But just before Riel's own execution, the last time anyone asked him about the matter, Riel did say that Scott's execution had been "mismanaged," unfortunately without explaining how. See George Stanley, ed., *The Collected Writings of Louis Riel*, 5 vols. (Edmonton, 1985), I, p. 310, 421; and V, p. 110, 583.

75. A.I. Silver, *The French Canadian Idea of Confederation, 1864-1900* (Toronto, 1982), pp. 75-82.

76. PAC, Macdonald Papers, Incoming Correspondence, p. 40471, Lord Granville telegram to Governor General, Sir John Young, 5 March 1870.

77. Ibid., p. 40584, Macdonald to Governor General, 9 April 1870.

78. Ibid., p. 40583, Granville telegram to Governor General, 9 April 1870.

likely to be rejected by Riel, Macdonald despaired. He feared that there had to be some kind of "conquest," while the British wanted an assurance that there would be no war. That was the bind. "Lord Granville says . . . that if we accept the country, England will send troops, but . . . he says the troops are not to be used to force the people to unite with Canada, in other words to be of no use."[79]

The nub of the problem was Macdonald's unwillingness to grant the necessary concessions and his recognition that it was politically impossible for him to do so after Scott's "barbarous murder."[80] His assurance to the British that he wanted troops only as a "friendly garrison" (not as a "hostile force") was transparent to the Colonial Office whose own experience in such matters was broad enough to recognize that peaceful military occupation was impossible without substantial concessions in advance.

On April 23 the British made a final offer. They would contribute a force and the troops could advance using all the firepower at their disposal, but only to enforce a mutually acceptable settlement. In the cryptic language of the telegram: "Canadian Gov't to accept decision of H.M's Gov't on disputed points of Settler's Bill of Rights."[81]

Thus the double-bind tightened: negotiations would have to be genuine or the armed force would be entirely Canadian; if the force were nothing but militia, the fighting was likely to be intense. In the event of a Canadian war against the "half breeds," the insurgents were certain to seek American aid, and there were numerous indications that the United States was not likely to turn its back on an opportunity to assert its own influence over the North West. Such an outcome could be avoided by seeming to comply with the insurgents' demands, in preparation for real subordination of the "half breeds" and reconciliation with Ontario in time for the next election (constitutionally as far distant as the autumn of 1872). Macdonald saw his best remaining chance, and he took it.

---

79. Ibid., p. 40585, Macdonald to Governor General, 10 April 1870.
80. Ibid., Letter Books, vol. 14, pp. 131-132, Macdonald to Carnarvon, 14 April 1870.
81. Ibid., Incoming Correspondence, pp. 40593-49594, Granville telegram to Governor General, 23 April 1870.

N.J. Ritchot, ca. 1870
(Provincial Archives of Manitoba)

"The appointment of Ritchot was the nearest that Riel could come to participating in the negotiations himself."

Chapter 4

Negotiating with Delegates from the North West

A three-person delegation from the North West arrived in Ottawa on April 11, 1870, ready to begin negotiations. To Macdonald's horror, two of the committee members were brought before an Ottawa magistrate on charges of complicity in the "premeditated murder" of Thomas Scott within forty-eight hours of their arrival. Nothing could have impugned his previous assurances of a kind reception more thoroughly and disrupted the settlement he envisioned more emphatically because negotiation in apparent good faith was a prerequisite for securing the military assistance the British were reluctant to concede in early April.

Macdonald had agreed that someone would give the delegates a kind reception in Ottawa. Telegraphic messages between the Governor General and the Colonial Office do not indicate who was to speak for Canada, or the scope of the possible concessions. The messages did imply that the Prime Minister did not contemplate meeting the representatives himself. Nor did he foresee the approval of extravagant concessions from anyone else. Macdonald believed that he already had an understanding with Bishop Taché, and he thought Taché was "satisfied with the terms accorded to himself and his church."[1]

The Prime Minister does not seem to have expected much more to develop from the meetings with the delegates. Still, he did not intend to treat them harshly. Macdonald's horror at the arrests on April 13 arose from his fear that the event would give the British new cause to question his previously asserted good faith. A week later, with criminal charges still pending and Canada apparently doing nothing to frustrate the proceedings, Granville cabled for an explanation. "Did Canadian gov't authorize arrests of delegates?" he asked. "Full information desired by telegraph," he demanded.[2] A few hours later, the official Canadian answer flashed back over the wire. "Canadian gov't did not authorize arrest of delegates. A

---

1. PAC, Records of the Governor General's Office, Records of the Governor General, RG 7 G 13, vol. 3, Sir John Young telegram to Lord Granville, 11 April 1870.

2. Ibid., Granville telegram to Young, 18 April 1870.

brother of deceased Scott laid information on oath against two of the three as accessories before the fact.'' To make the assertion all the more credible, the same message revealed the ''secret'' that Macdonald was assuming full responsibility for the cost of the delegates' legal defence.[3]

The British were reassured but a question remained about the flexibility of Canada in responding to the North West representatives once they laid their terms before the government. That particle of remaining doubt is probably what prompted Granville to send the telegram of April 23 in which he asserted that if Canada persisted in the request for British military aid, the Colonial Office would reserve the right to decide what was reasonable and unreasonable in the settlers' demands.

The threat of British intervention was followed by a termination of criminal proceedings and a decision of the Prime Minister to become involved in the negotiations directly. According to the journal[4] kept by the most important of Riel's negotiators, Father N.-J. Ritchot,[5] the first ''audience'' that Saturday ran from 11 a.m. until late afternoon and was ''pretty well confined to asking questions or requests for information.''[6] The tone of the questions, and the repeated assurances that Canada intended to accommodate all the delegates' suggestions, pleased Ritchot immensely. He and the others went away believing that a good settlement would result.

The following Monday morning the discussions resumed with the Prime Minister still playing a leading role on the Canadian side. Encouraged by the previous meeting, the delegates stated their demands boldly. They said that they expected ambassadorial status for themselves and a general welcome for the population, with Canada taking the territory as a new province in Confederation. Another facet of the demanded welcome was a general amnesty for all occurrences before the transfer. Ritchot stressed that such a pardon was the indispensable starting point, it was the ''*sine qua non* of any settlement.''[7] Subsequently, when Macdonald seemed only to resist the concession of provincial status, Ritchot thought that the Prime Minister was conceding the amnesty point and wished to move on.

Macdonald insisted that the North West territory could not become a

---

3. Ibid., Young cypher telegram to Granville, 18 April 1870.

4. Reproduced in W.L. Morton, ed., *Manitoba: The Birth of a Province* (Winnipeg, 1965), pp. 132-160.

5. The two other delegates were Alfred H. Scott (a Winnipeg bartender) and Judge John Black (''Recorder of Rupert's Land,'' the principal law officer of the Red River Settlement). The appointment of Ritchot was the nearest that Riel could come to participating in the negotiations himself. See Stanley, *Riel*, p. 123-124; and Philippe R. Mailhot, ''Ritchot's Resistance: Abbé Noel Joseph Ritchot and the Creation and Transformation of Manitoba,'' (Unpublished PhD Thesis: University of Manitoba, 1986).

6. Stanley, *Riel,* p. 136.

7. Ibid., p. 138.

province without a period of preparation, perhaps as brief as twelve months. For several hours they haggled—with Macdonald agreeing to shorter and shorter periods of preparation until he finally conceded that pro vincial status might be granted at once, at least to the District of Assiniboia.

Overnight Ritchot must have decided that the amnesty question demanded similarly explicit resolution because he brought the subject up again the next day, on April 26. Macdonald hesitated, saying, "the affair was not within their competence."[8] According to Ritchot, he did agree that a general amnesty was a prerequisite to a peaceful transfer, and assured Ritchot that Canada would "undertake to get the matter settled" by advising the Governor General to seek a guarantee of safety from prosecution from the Queen before, and as a condition of, her transfer of authority from the Hudson's Bay Company. Ritchot and the others were at first sceptical that such a procedure would serve, then felt reassured, and finally agreed that the amnesty could be treated separately so long as it was settled.

By the time of the fourth meeting on Wednesday, April 27, the Canadian negotiators were ready to respond with a draft of a settlement that covered the matters acknowledged to be within the power of Canada. The document was proposed as a series of legislative amendments to the temporary government act of the previous session of Parliament and was acceptable to the delegates in most respects. They approved what was provided for self-government and on cultural matters, but rejected the treatment of the land question because a clause vested control of all lands in the Dominion. Ritchot insisted that the new province should have the same power over natural resources as the others. When Macdonald and Cartier insisted that Canada had committed itself to considerable expenditure to buy out the interest of the HBC, and looked forward to even greater potential costs in the extinguishment of Indian title, they claimed full justification for controlling at least the vacant land as Dominion territory. Ritchot's reply was to resurrect the demand that William Dease had promoted at Red River the previous summer—the idea that persons of part-Indian ancestry should claim a share of the compensation paid to Indians in recognition of their inherited part of the aboriginal title.

At first Cartier and Macdonald resisted the idea that the Métis and native English might have aboriginal rights at the same time that they claimed rights as settlers. According to Ritchot, they replied that "the settlers of the North West . . . having obtained a form of government fitting for civilized men ought not to claim also the privileges granted to Indians."[9] But Ritchot insisted that dual status was the only equitable way to resolve the impasse on the land control issue.

Ultimately, Cartier and Macdonald both appeared to agree. They said that the native people at Red River could have self-government and

---

8. Ibid., p. 139.
9. Ibid., p. 141.

homesteads (the rights of "civilized men") and still claim a share of the aboriginal title ("the privileges granted to Indians"). The only sticking point after April 27 seemed to be the amount of land that was the appropriate compensation. Ritchot insisted that each person of part-Indian ancestry ought to have a right to select a tract equivalent to 200 acres for himself and each member of his family. Macdonald and Cartier held out for considerably less.

With apparently only the quantity of land still in dispute, the Canadian negotiators put their understanding of the agreement on general principles into a draft of a bill that Macdonald proposed to lay before Parliament within the week. When confronted with the text on Thursday, April 28, Ritchot observed that the Indian title clause was unsatisfactory not only for the amount of land to be granted, but also for the lack of a specific mode of distribution and form of tenure of the grants. Ritchot wanted to continue the discussions until both matters were resolved. Macdonald, however, had become "indisposed," and Cartier attempted to continue the negotiations by himself on Friday and Saturday. Finally, on Monday, May 2, Macdonald rejoined the group and the two sides came to an understanding. Ritchot was jubilant:

> We continued to claim 1,500,000 acres and we agreed on the mode of distribution as follows, that is to say: The land will be chosen throughout the province ... in several different lots in various places, if it is judged to be proper by the local legislature which ought itself to distribute these parcels to heads of families in proportion to the number of children existing at the time of the distribution; that these lands should then be distributed among the children by their parents or guardians, always under the supervision of the above mentioned local legislature which could pass laws to ensure the continuance of these lands in the half breed families.[10]

Macdonald's own notes corroborate what Ritchot recorded. In the Prime Minister's version, the text of the clause was:

> That in order to compensate the claims of the half breed population as partly inheriting the Indian rights, there shall be placed at the disposal of the local legislature one million and a half acres of land to be selected anywhere in the territory of the Province of Manitoba, by the said legislature, in separate or joint lots, having regard to the usages and customs of the country, out of all the lands not now possessed, to be distributed as soon as practicable amongst the different heads of half breed families according to the number of children of both sexes then existing in each family under such legislative enactments which may be found advisable to secure the transmission and holding of the said lands amongst the half breed families — To extinguish Indian claims.[11]

With an agreement apparently sealed, the next step was to get the

---

10. Ibid., p. 143.

11. PAC, Macdonald Papers, Incoming Correspondence, pp. 40641-40642.

matter through Parliament. Later in the day, Macdonald introduced the House to the general terms of the bill.[12] He indicated that the territorial government act of the previous session was to be amended, setting aside a small portion of the North West, giving it provincial status and a form of government "subject to alteration by the People" if at any time later they believed the mix of institutions no longer suited their circumstances.[13] Macdonald explained that a large influx of newcomers was expected within the year. For that reason, it was necessary to quiet the fears of the present population with certain guarantees that their land was assured. With regard to the newcomers, a police force was being dispatched with British assistance. Consequently, orderly immigration and future development was assured.

Initially the Opposition did not quarrel with the details of the proposal. On May 2, no one disputed, for example, the official bilingualism or public support to denominational schools that was provided. What the Opposition attacked was the more fundamental principle of negotiating with "rebels," granting them provincial status, and encumbering the territory with land promises that seemed to impede the rapid settlement that was anticipated. More particularly, the dual status accorded to the native people struck the leader of the Opposition, Alexander Mackenzie, as especially bizarre. He said that he could not understand how "half breeds" might receive land as settlers and also come forward claiming land as Indians. In Mackenzie's view, the "half breeds were either Indians or not."[14]

Cartier answered that they did not propose to give the "half breeds" an "Indian reserve." The land granted in recognition of their share of Indian title was to be given "to heads of families to settle their children." Macdonald indicated that the British had already set such a precedent with their policy of giving Loyalists land "for purposes of settlement of their children." In the present instance, the only difference was that there was vastly more land available in the expanse of the territory that was not affected by the settlement of "half breed" claims at Red River.[15]

Macdonald's problem was that the Opposition reacted to the jarring inconsistency between the Prime Minister's assertion that the terms of the settlement were temporary provisions, bound to be adjusted by the new

---

12. Most of the debate for that evening and on subsequent days appears in Morton's *The Birth of a Province* as "Extracts from the Debates on the Manitoba Bill, May 2-May 9, 1870," pp. 161-227.

13. The verbatim text of Macdonald's remarks concerning the temporary nature of the constitutional provisions of the settlement was as follows: "All these clauses and stipulations are, of course, subject to alteration by the people themselves, except so far as they relate to the appointment of the Lieut.-Governor, which of course, rests upon the same authority as in the other Provinces of the Dominion. In all other respects they may alter their Constitutions as they please" (ibid., p. 167). The "same authority" to which Macdonald referred was his understanding of section 92 (1) of the BNA Act.

14. Ibid., p. 172.

15. Ibid., p. 176, 199.

population about to pour into the territory in the summer, and the implication of the land clauses that the population already there was fixed for the present and the next generation in their own little province. Consequently, the land clauses had to be altered.

The revised text still promised land for the children but eliminated all reference to the timing and method of the distribution, as well as any suggestion of trusteeship to be observed by the provincial legislature. The new text promised 1.4 million acres "towards extinguishment of the Indian Title . . . of the half breed residents" on terms, and conditions, in a process and at a time that was largely unspecified except to say that a distribution was to be made by the Lieutenant Governor

> under regulations to be from time to time made by the Governor General in Council, . . . in such parts of the Province as he may deem expedient, . . . and divide the same among the children of the half breed heads of families residing in the province at the time of the said transfer to Canada and the same shall be granted to the said children respectively, in such mode and on such conditions as to settlement and otherwise, as the Governor General in Council may from time to time determine.[16]

Similarly, the security of the parents' claims became less definite. The words agreed to earlier were to "change peaceable occupancy to title," protecting persons on granted or ungranted land, both within and beyond the limits of the old HBC survey.[17] The new text was less sweeping, and the intent of "quieting . . . titles, and assuring to the settlers . . . the peaceable possession of the lands now held by them" was obscured in a tangle of sub-clauses emphasizing a hierarchy of uncertain tenures that may or may not have covered every case with the same security that was assured on May 2.[18]

When Ritchot discovered how completely and abruptly Macdonald had retreated from the terms that were agreed to on Monday morning — how the agreement had become "very much modified" by May 4 — he aroused his colleagues to demand reinstatement of what had been previously conceded. Ritchot's account of what followed appears in the journal entry of May 5:

> We saw Sir George and Sir John; we complained to them. They declared that in practice it amounted to the same thing. For us they promised that they would give us by Order in Council, before departure, assurance of the carrying out of our verbal understandings; but that for the present it would be impossible to get the Bill passed if one changed its form. . . .[19]

---

16. Statutes of Canada (1870), Chapter 33: An Act to amend and continue the Act 32 and 33 Victoria, chapter 3; and to establish and provide for the Government of the Province of Manitoba, section 31.

17. Ritchot's journal, in Morton, *Birth of a Province,* p. 140-141; and PAC, Macdonald Papers, Incoming Correspondence, pp. 40605-40610.

18. Statutes of Canada (1870), Chapter 3, section 32.

The broken agreement of May 2 was then covered by fresh assurances, an understanding that some of the settlement would appear in the statute, and the rest would be covered by Orders in Council consistent with the original terms. Since the delegates appreciated that the circumstances called for devious handling of the Opposition, they agreed to go along with what Macdonald proposed.

Then all matters moved swiftly towards a conclusion between May 5 and May 10. The Governor General reported to the Colonial Office that a settlement satisfactory to the delegates was in a form that was likely to pass Parliament, and requested permission to order the troops to Red River.[20] On May 6, Granville replied, "Yes, the troops may proceed." Then the House of Commons went through a final two days of debate, and passed the bill at midnight on May 10. The delegates did not receive the Orders in Council they were promised, but before leaving Ottawa, Ritchot did obtain a letter from Cartier promising that all the tenures outlined in section 32 would receive the same consideration: "so soon as the Government can grant the necessary titles, no payment shall be required from any persons . . . ." Equally encouraging was a postscript adding:

> I have, moreover, the high honour of assuring you, not so much on my part as on that of my colleagues, that regarding the subject of the 1,400,000 acres of land reserved by the 31st Section of the Manitoba Act for the benefit of half breed families, the regulations which ought to be established from time to time by the Governor General in council concerning this reserve, will be of a nature for recognizing the desires of the half breed residents, and for guaranteeing, in a manner that is at once efficient and just, the division of this expanse of land among the children of the heads of half breed families living in the province of Manitoba, at the time of the transfer to Canada.[21]

Only one legislative loose end remained. Two members of the Opposition, Alexander Mackenzie and David Mills, had challenged the constitutionality of the Manitoba Act because it granted representation in the Senate that did not appear to be contemplated by section 147 of the British North America Act.[22] They had suggested that a "state of tutelage" for the territory would give time to clarify the representation issue as well as a period to settle the country with persons who were already familiar with British-style government. Macdonald had replied that no one could know whether the bill was unconstitutional until its final provisions were set.

---

19. Ritchot's journal, p. 147.

20. PAC, RG 7 G 13, vol. 3, John Young to Lord Granville, 3 May 1870; ibid., 5 May 1870.

21. *Journals of the House of Commons of Canada,* VIII (1874), "Appendix 6: Report of the Select Committee on the Causes of the Difficulties in the North West Territory in 1869-70," p. 74, Cartier to Ritchot and Scott, 23 May 1870. The postscript of the same letter also appears in PAC, Records of the Department of the Interior, RG 15, vol. 230, file 167.

22. On May 4, see debates in Morton, *Birth of a Province,* pp. 207, 211.

Then, "Imperial Confirmation" could be obtained in due course if British sanction were needed.

Six months later Macdonald decided that confirming legislation was indeed desirable, first, to clarify Canada's power to provide parliamentary representation for new provinces and, secondly, in anticipation of the future of Manitoba, to establish a power for adjusting Manitoba's boundaries once it was certain that the province was not developing into a "new Quebec." Macdonald anticipated that newcomers to the little "postage stamp" province would soon outnumber the "half breed" population so completely it would be expedient to enlarge the boundaries of the minuscule province to a more respectable size.[23]

With both purposes in mind, Macdonald wrote a brief letter to the Governor General on December 29, including the text of the legislation he contemplated.[24] On January 3, the Queen's representative dutifully forwarded the letter to Britain.[25] A week after the Colonial Office received Young's dispatch, Lord Kimberley (the new Colonial Secretary) was ready to comply with the Canadian request, even to the point of adding a power that Macdonald had not mentioned. A similar recent appeal from the government of New Zealand had asked for authority to make new counties out of old. It may have seemed sensible to Kimberley that Canada would someday wish to merge some of Quebec into Ontario, or amalgamate the Maritimes into a wider union, just as the national legislature would certainly find it expedient to create or dissolve provincial entities in the North West territory from time to time. Consequently, he attached the New Zealand power to the Canadian proposal, giving Canada authority to "withdraw part of the territory of any province and legislate therefore."[26] Since the provisions of his draft legislation were "not in exact conformity" with Macdonald's draft, Kimberley decided to delay passage "until Sir J. Macdonald . . . shall have seen it."[27]

---

23. A curious letter from R.G. Haliburton of Nova Scotia warned Macdonald that even the Maritime provinces would react violently "If . . . the attempt is made to make Manitoba anything else than an English province having English laws and the English language. . . ." Making the Manitoba Act permanent would provoke "a storm that will sweep everything before it." Haliburton indicated that he "found the public generally give *you* credit for wishing to do what is right in this matter; & it may strengthen your hands to know that in carrying out your views, you will be borne out by the public sentiment of the country." PAC, Macdonald Papers, Incoming Correspondence, pp. 156724-156735, Haliburton to Macdonald, 7 October 1870.

24. Ibid, Transcripts, vol. 583, Macdonald to Sir John Young, 29 December 1870. The text of the amendment as originally proposed is printed in D.N. Sprague, "The Manitoba Land Question, 1870-1882," *Journal of Canadian Studies* 15 (1980), p. 84.

25. PAC, Colonial Office Papers, MG 11, C042/696, pp. 2-4, Young to Lord Kimberley, 3 January 1871 (received 19 January 1871).

26. Ibid., pp. 14-15, draft text of BNA Act of 1871, [January, 1871].

27. Ibid., pp. 6-7, marginal note on "Minute Paper" initialled by Kimberley, [January, 1871].

The text that left England on January 26 arrived in Macdonald's hands in mid-February. Evidently, the Prime Minister was somewhat startled by the broadened power, and feared the political repercussions of its passage — the criticism that was bound to arise from those who would claim that Canada wished to meddle with the political geography of the original provinces in Confederation. As a result, Macdonald jettisoned the Kimberley amendment, and, in his own redraft, he added a clause indicating his faith in the future population of the North West by making the federal power to create constitutions for new provinces a one-time only proposition.[28] Macdonald's new draft explicitly disowned all federal responsibility for Manitoba's constitution, and stipulated a similar immunity for any other new province receiving a constitution by Dominion statute. Then, as Macdonald was about to depart to Washington, D.C., on diplomatic business, he handed the matter to Cartier on February 26, instructing him that the latest draft should be the one ''sent home to England to be passed by the Parliament there.'' Macdonald stressed that the covering letter from the Governor General to Kimberley must ''point out that all the provinces of the Dominion should hold the same status that the four [sic] Provinces now composing the Dominion . . . hold.''[29]

Cartier did as he was told. The new draft giving Parliament a once-only power to enact constitutions for new provinces went to Sir John Young, and he dutifully forwarded the package to the Colonial Office on March 2.[30] Then the Canadian House of Commons entered the process as Cartier sought parliamentary approval for the *fait accompli*.

The House condemned the government on March 27 for its failure to consult the elected representatives of the people of Canada before proposing changes to the national constitution.[31] On April 8, a frustrated Governor General telegraphed the Colonial Office to halt the legislative process there until the Canadian legislators settled on their preferred text.[32]

In the course of the subsequent parliamentary debate, there were no dramatic changes suggested.[33] Still, the debate did shed light on the members' views of what they had done previously in ratifying Macdonald's settlement of the Red River crisis. David Mills stated that ''the Manitoba Act was passed . . . to meet the peculiar circumstances which prevailed in the province at the time, and to enable the Government to restore peace there.'' Mills suggested that Macdonald's assurance that it was a

---

28. Ibid., C042/697, pp. 28-31.
29. PAC, Macdonald Papers, Letter Books, vol. 15, pp. 378-379, Macdonald to Cartier, 26 February 1871.
30. PAC, Colonial Office Papers, MG 11, CO42/697, pp. 18-28.
31. Ibid., pp. 270-282, clippings from debates reported in *Ottawa Times*.
32. PAC, RG 7 G 13, vol. 4, telegram, Young to Kimberley, 8 April 1871.
33. PAC, MG 11, CO42/697, p. 533, text of Canadian draft adopted by Joint Resolution of Parliament.

"temporary measure to be replaced by a better matured Act at some subsequent time" was essential to the bill's passage.[34] Turning to the draft of the bill then before the House, Mills observed that the act for Manitoba would become "unalterable" unless the provincial legislature wanted it changed. Yet the majority of the Canadian Parliament thought, like Macdonald, that the future population of Manitoba could be trusted to secure what was needed.[35] As a result, the draft resolutions did pass on April 12, and the British responded as requested in June.[36] With that which was "temporary" under the authority of Canada then unalterable, except by the legislature of Manitoba,[37] it became more important than ever to make certain that the "Riel party" and its sympathizers were displaced from all positions of real political power in the fledgling "half breed" province of Manitoba.

---

34. Extract of Parliamentary debate in ibid., pp. 278-280.

35. Macdonald had recently calmed one of his more outspoken critics of the Manitoba Act thus: "The granting of responsible government was, in my opinion, premature, but it is the best form of government for the new settlers who will go there in schools this next season. They will ere long be able to exercise their influence as electors, and mould the Institutions according to their own ideas." PAC, Macdonald Papers, Letter Books, vol. 15, pp. 289-291, Macdonald to J.Y. Bown, 9 February 1871.

36. Statutes of Great Britain (1871), Chapter 28: An Act respecting the establishment of Provinces in the Dominion of Canada.

37. The impact of the BNA Act (1871) on the scope of provincial power became a matter of judicial interpretation much later. It is important to note that in the nineteenth century politicians seem to have interpreted section 92 (1) of the BNA Act much more broadly than the twentieth century Supreme Court of Canada. When the newcomers first began to act as Macdonald expected in the mid-1870s (and changed the "provincial parliament" from a bicameral to a single chamber legislature) there was little controversy. Indeed, one of the few opponents of the elimination of bicameralism argued that the innovation was objectionable mainly because the one change tended to divert attention from more "necessary" alterations: disposing of denominational schools and the official status of the French language. See J.H. O'Donnell, *Manitoba Matters: Being a Short Chapter Devoted and Dedicated to the Davis-Royal Administration, The Autonomy of Provinces no Longer respected, Ottawa Dictates, Manitoba Obeys* (Winnipeg, 1875).

Alexander Morris, 1875
(Public Archives of Canada [(C26837)])

"Morris began to wonder if the great effort that was needed to keep Riel out of politics was worth the trouble."

Chapter 5

Eliminating the Riel Factor from Manitoba Politics

News of the delegates' accomplishments in Ottawa preceded their homecoming, and since Father Ritchot was known to be the principal negotiator, he returned to a hero's welcome.[1] By the same token, the responsibility for explaining the settlement in all its aspects fell on Ritchot's shoulders at a special meeting of the Legislative Assembly of the provisional government called by President Riel for June 24.

On the appointed day, Ritchot addressed the Fort Garry assembly in French, pausing from time to time as Riel translated for the English-speaking minority. They indicated that the result of the negotiation was the Manitoba Act and other promises to follow by Order in Council and Royal Proclamation. A general amnesty, for example, was expected with the arrival of the Lieutenant Governor (a Nova Scotian named Adams G. Archibald). He was to arrive about July 15, the new date set for the transfer, and the first day in the history of the new province.

Provincial status had been considered earlier by the representatives of the parishes and rejected[2] in favour of a cheaper territorial administration but no one objected to the *fait accompli* on June 24. Nor did anyone complain that the whole settlement was not spelled out in every detail in the Manitoba Act.[3] The audience cheered their President and his principal

---

1. Stanley's *Riel*, pp. 147-213, is the standard account of the Manitoba reaction to the delegates' work in Ottawa and the subsequent difficulty on the amnesty question. His is the account followed here, except when evidence not cited by Stanley suggests a different emphasis or elaboration.

2. Most historians consider the revision of the Bill of Rights in this and other respects to be conclusive proof of a dictatorial style on Riel's part. See, for example, Creighton, *Old Chieftain,* pp. 61-63 and Morton, *Birth of a Province,* pp. xvi-xviii. It is important to note, however, that such changes appear to have been more significant to historians after the fact than to Riel's colleagues in the provisional government in 1870.

3. "General meeting held at Fort Garry. Manitoba Bill accepted unanimously" (PAC, Records of the Governor General, RG 7 G 13, vol. 3, Young telegram to Granville, 8 July 1870). See also the eyewitness account in Provincial Archives of Manitoba (hereafter cited as PAM), William Coldwell Papers, MG 2 14, item 528, "Rev. Mr. Ritchot Thanks the Legislature," 24 June 1870.

delegate when they had finished, and the same assembly voted unanimously to ratify what was before them.[4] The only issue the representatives discussed further was the kind of honour-guard they thought appropriate for Archibald, and how far they might travel east for escorting the gentleman safely to Red River.

Of course, the Government of Canada had no intention of exposing Archibald to unruly subjects.[5] That was the purpose of the "Red River Expeditionary Force" of about 1,200 troops.[6] They departed by fast steamship from Collingwood, Ontario, in May but one delay after another impeded their progress. First the Americans stopped them at the canal connecting Lake Huron and Lake Superior until the British ambassador in Washington repeated the assurance that the delegates had from Canada, to the effect that the army was on a "mission of peace" and carried a proclamation of general amnesty and no warrants for arrest. Then, once the troops completed the boat trip to Fort William and began the trek following the old fur-trade route to Red River, they encountered the first of more than seventy portages of supplies and artillery, which explained why they did not reach the last leg of their journey at the source of the Winnipeg River on Lake of the Woods until August.

By that time, the date of the transfer was long passed. Since Archibald had not arrived at the expected time, Riel began to doubt the good faith of Canada's promises. Finally, on August 23, he received word that the advance guard of the army, the British 60th rifles, had come up from Lake Winnipeg as far as Point Douglas, only one bend in the Red River from Fort Garry. Late that night, Riel went within sight of their camp fires, stood in the rain, and listened to the sound of the soldiers' excitement over the next day's expected activities.

In the morning, the first of the troops marched the last miles to the fort. Later, their commander falsely reported that the "inhabitants welcomed troops as deliverers from oppression and plunder." The truth was that no crowd stood along the muddy road to embrace the vanguard of their supposed liberators, and there were no "half breed banditti" to be routed from the fort.[7] The gates of Fort Garry stood open; inside, the place was

4. Stanley, *Riel*, pp. 148-149.

5. The Governor General informed the Colonial Office on 8 June 1870 that "the Ministers wish Mr. Archibald so to time his arrival as to reach Fort Garry immediately after HM troops shall have established themselves there" (PAC, Records of the Governor General, RG 7 G 10, vol. 4, Young to Granville). Later, he reported a slightly different arrangement: "the Lt Gov shall proceed via Lake Superior and join the troops. If, on his arrival at the Lake of the Woods, he finds everything quiet . . . he can at his own discretion precede the troops . . ." (ibid., Young to Kimberley, 27 July 1870).

6. The force consisted of 373 British troops and 2 battalions of Canadian militia (382 men from Ontario, 389 from Quebec). See Stanley, *Birth of Western Canada*, p. 131.

7. PAC, Records of the Governor General, RG 7 G 13, Young telegram to Lord Granville, 1 September 1870.

empty. Moments before, Riel had received a warning that his life was in danger. "For the love of God, clear out," the messenger shouted, "you are going to be lynched."[8]

Riel had fled in time. There was no hanging on August 24, only a flag-raising ceremony that Riel himself witnessed from the safety of the steps of Taché's cathedral on the other side of the river. He stood there with the Bishop watching the troops race into the empty fort, whooping for blood and finding no one to hang or to shoot. Feeling disappointment and anger of his own, Riel turned to Taché and said, "It appears that we have been deceived."

If Taché had known the intentions of the British colonel commanding the troops, he would have agreed with Riel. Colonel Wolseley wrote later that there was "sad disappointment in all ranks" when they found the fort empty. Forgetting the alleged purpose of his mission, Wolseley confessed in his memoirs that Riel had three choices on August 24: he could surrender and hang for murder; he could resist and hang for treason; or he could run and hope for escape. There was no amnesty that included the "murderers" of Scott.[9] The day before Wolseley's arrival, however, Taché had returned from an errand of his own to confirm in Ottawa the promise Ritchot had brought to Red River in mid-June. Taché obtained the assurance he sought from Cartier. Unfortunately, Sir George Cartier was mistaken in his expectations, as much as were the others.

To unravel the pattern of deception that came to a focus on August 24, it is necessary to return to the record of the negotiations in April and May. Early in the discussions (on April 26), the Prime Minister asserted that Canada could not include the amnesty in the settlement to be enacted by Parliament because the matter was not within the jurisdiction of the Dominion until the transfer was completed. When Ritchot insisted that a general amnesty was the *sine qua non* of a peaceful transition, Macdonald and Cartier conceded — according to Ritchot's account of April 26 — that "they would undertake to get the matter settled and that it was easy by such or such means that they indicated to us. . . ."[10]

A week later, the day after agreeing to the text of the Manitoba Act that was first introduced to Parliament, the delegates met the Governor General, Sir John Young (soon elevated to the peerage as Lord Lisgar). Five people attended the meeting on May 3. In addition to the three delegates and Young, the fifth participant was Sir Clinton Murdoch, personal representative of Lord Granville, who was monitoring Canada's handling of the negotiations. They chatted in general about the settlement; then, according to Ritchot, Young turned to the amnesty issue and said, "no one . . . who had taken part in those unfortunate violation of laws

---

8. Stanley, *Riel*, p. 155.

9. Ibid.

10. Ritchot's journal, in Morton's *Birth of a Province*, p. 139.

would be troubled. . . .'' Murdoch added that "Her Majesty's government desired only one thing, which was to re-establish peace and to pass the sponge over all the facts and illegal acts which had taken place in the North West and its territories.''[11] Ritchot replied that the delegates needed the promise in writing, but Murdoch expressed surprise that anyone could question the reliability of a vice-regal promise simply because it was verbal: "when one dealt with men such as those before whom we were, it was not necessary to dot all the *i*'s.[12] Still, the delegates insisted that "the people would not be satisfied" with anything less than a written promise. Young then repeated his assurance that "everything would go well, that the settlers of the North West could be reassured that no one would be troubled.''

The next day Cartier asked Ritchot if the meeting with the Governor General had proceeded satisfactorily. Ritchot answered that the delegates were "well satisfied" that Britain would provide what Canada could not, and returned to the part of the settlement that Cartier wished to reopen in view of the parliamentary debate that had begun on May 2. More than two weeks elapsed before Ritchot's attention could return to the amnesty question. Then there was a second meeting with the Governor General on May 19, a meeting attended by four people: Ritchot and Scott accompanied by Cartier, meeting Sir John Young (without Murdoch). According to Ritchot's journal entry of May 19, he repeated his insistence that he must have something in writing to confirm what Murdoch and Young had promised verbally on May 3. Finally Young gave in to Ritchot's pressure and agreed to furnish a document saying that "Her Majesty was going to proclaim a general amnesty immediately" and that the proclamation would arrive with the Lieutenant Governor.[13]

Ritchot expected to receive Young's letter the next day. When no communication arrived on May 20, or during the next several days, he returned to Cartier who explained on May 24 that Young and Murdoch had reconsidered the matter and had found a different procedure more appropriate. They had decided that the committal of the Queen to an amnesty before it was requested through the Colonial Office was a breach of form. It was more appropriate for the delegates to petition the Queen through the Governor General. When Ritchot resisted the petition proposal, Cartier responded with profuse assurances that the process was "only a matter of form.''[14]

Finally Ritchot agreed to pursue the amnesty as suggested and Cartier's secretary prepared the petition for Ritchot's signature on May 26. At the same time, Cartier reiterated his certainty that the outcome was "only a matter of form." What Cartier did not realize is that the Governor

---

11. Ibid., p. 146.
12. Ibid.
13. Ibid., 154.
14. Ibid., pp. 155-156.

General had no intention of supporting an amnesty on Cartier's authority alone.

As far as Cartier knew, he was the minister primarily responsible for the matter. When Young asked for a full "report on the petition," he made the request to Cartier; and it was Cartier who responded on June 8 with a full "narrative of facts . . . leaning towards safety for the conduct of the insurgents."[15] Normally such a document would have gone from its author for approval by Cabinet and then to the Governor General as a Minute of Council. But Parliament was not in session. Macdonald was gravely ill, and most of the other ministers were away from Ottawa on summer holidays. Only two other Cabinet ministers saw Cartier's report. Neither voiced any particular objection, not even to the passage in which Sir George advised against any exceptions to the amnesty because the exclusion of Riel, for example, would "tend to perpetuate a feeling of irritation. . . ."[16]

Notwithstanding approval by Cabinet (such as it was), Sir John Young sent the report on the amnesty to the Colonial Secretary on June 9 with a covering letter asserting that the document was "not to be regarded as a Minute of Council nor as the expression of cabinet."[17]

Clearly, Young did not think that Cartier had the authority to promote the position he and Macdonald's colleagues proposed. Simultaneously, however, Cartier was completing other delicate negotiations and made promises that were even more sweeping in their consequences. All were reported to Granville without any of the disqualification Young heaped onto the amnesty report. Apparently Cartier had the authority to promise a delegation from British Columbia a transcontinental railway, to be started within two years and completed in ten,[18] but he could not draft the rationale for the amnesty he and Macdonald promised the Red River delegates on April 26. The difference between the two matters was not a difference in Cartier's authority, but his consistency with the wishes of Sir John A. Macdonald as they were known to Sir John Young. Thus Cartier's role in the amnesty is only part of the story, the rest is the part played by Macdonald.

When Cartier and Macdonald learned that the amnesty issue was the sine qua non of negotiations on April 26 and both negotiators for Canada promised the delegates that they would have what they demanded — but

---

15. PAC, Macdonald Papers, Incoming Correspondence, pp. 41654-41657, Francis Hincks to Macdonald, 18 March 1874.

16. The reading of the report by the other ministers, Hincks and Campbell, is mentioned in the letter by Hincks to Maconald, 18 March 1874, cited above. The memorandum itself is printed in the "Report of the Select Committee on the Causes of the Difficulties in the North West Territory in 1869-70," in *Journals of the House of Commons of Canada*, 8 (1874), appendix 6, item 131, pp. 171-178; a manuscript copy appears in PAC, Macdonald Papers, Incoming Correspondence, pp. 41435-41454.

17. "Report of the Select Committee," item 126, p. 169, Young to Granville, 9 June 1870.

18. For Cartier's role in the negotiations for the admission of British Columbia to Confederation, June 6-9 and June 25, see W.L. Morton, *The Critical Years: The Union of British North America, 1857-1873* (Toronto, 1964), pp. 247-248.

from the Crown directly, not from Canada — Macdonald reported to Murdoch that two demands were impossible. Murdoch then informed Granville on April 28 that two "clearly inadmissible" demands had arisen. One involved vesting control of the territory in the local inhabitants. The other "would secure an indemnity to Riel and his abettors for the execution of Scott, and to all others for the plunder of the Hudson's Bay Company's stores, and for other damages committed during the disturbances, concessions which this Government could not venture even if it had the power to grant. . . ."[19]

Murdoch indicated that, under the circumstances of the negotiations, "there was no choice but to reject these terms and to endeavor to arrange others that would not be open to objection." No details of the arrangements appeared in Murdoch's report of April 28. He did not write, for example, that the land question was nearing a settlement by the appearance of a compromise, nor that the amnesty was being disposed of by a more complicated subterfuge. Murdoch did not suggest that the delegates were given a promise Macdonald had no intention of keeping, or that Macdonald's strategy called for Young and Murdoch to join him in deceiving the delegates (and Cartier as well). The conclusion seems inescapable, however, that the "arrangement" to which Murdoch referred was exactly such action.

In concocting the ruse, Macdonald must have dreaded the inevitable conflict it would cause with Cartier. By April 28, the stress had become so intolerable that Sir John began to drink — apparently with the intention of remaining "indisposed" for some considerable period because he was still drunk on Friday and took to his bed over the weekend with nothing but a large stock of newspapers and his favourite port wine.

No one close to Macdonald knew how much longer his "break out" would continue.[20] Finally, the lack of progress that Cartier was making in concluding the negotiations between April 29 and May 1 prompted the Prime Minister to drag himself over to Cartier's for one last meeting on Monday morning, May 2, where a final round of concessions completed the negotiation charade. Then, Macdonald drew upon his phenomenal stamina to go into the House of Commons later in the day to characterize the settlement in words that were coherent if not elegant. And so he continued for the next several days.

On May 6 Macdonald reached the limit of his endurance. Just after eating a quiet lunch in his office, he felt a sudden sharp pain that sent him writhing in agony to the floor. A physician came to the Prime Minister's aid

---

19. "Report of the Select Committee," item 135, pp. 193-194, Murdoch to F. Rogers, Undersecretary of the Colonial Office, 28 April 1870; a manuscript copy appears in the PAC, Macdonald Papers, Incoming Correspondence, pp. 41640-41642.

20. According to Creighton, Macdonald was "sick of Riel, and Red River, and these interminable negotiations. The piled papers lay on the desk in front of him. The gaze of the delegates was fixed upon him with implacable ferret-like intentness." That drove him to drink. See Creighton's *Old Chieftain*, pp. 66-67.

a few moments later and concluded that the aging politician suffered from "biliary calculus" (gall stones). The violent pain signalled the passing of one stone, doubtless there were others. Dr. Grant prescribed complete immobility, and turned the Prime Minister's office in the East Block into a sick room for the duration of the crisis.[21]

Since there were no more attacks like the one of May 6, Macdonald began to show enough recovery to be moved as far as the more comfortable main room of the Speaker's chambers on June 2. He continued to improve and the doctor ordered the completion of Macdonald's convalescence on Prince Edward Island. There, in July and August, the Prime Minister "received few letters and sent fewer replies."[22]

In Macdonald's absence, Cartier became Acting Prime Minister and handled all matters including the amnesty. But since the Governor General knew that Macdonald's views differed from Cartier's, he disqualified the amnesty report of June 8 and subsequently secured Macdonald's approval for his action. In July Macdonald confirmed that "neither the Governor General nor the Cabinet should be committed to the General Amnesty." Even the lesser proposal of clemency for all but the "murderers" of Scott was to "proceed from England without advice from Canada."[23]

Meanwhile, Cartier continued to believe that the general amnesty was forthcoming, even though he did recognize that public opinion in Ontario was too strong to proclaim it immediately. Canada would have to delay at least until the people of Red River welcomed their governor, and established their undoubted loyalty.[24] Taché feared that the delay running into July had a different, sinister meaning. That was why the Bishop had set off to Ottawa for reassurance.

According to Taché's account of his meeting with Cartier, the acting prime minister asserted that the "thing has not changed"[25] and encouraged Bishop Taché to see for himself in a meeting with the Governor General who was on holiday at Niagara. Indeed, Cartier suggested that they might travel there together. By the time they reached Kingston, however, they had become so fearful of public meetings protesting the Manitoba Act that the two decided to by-pass Toronto. They travelled separately, with the "rebel Bishop" completing the journey by himself through the United States. Then the Governor General refused Taché the expected assurance. Instead, Young sent him back to Cartier saying, "he knows my views upon the subject and he will tell you all."[26]

---

21. The account of the nearly fatal illness, complete with a description of the peculiar method of hospitalization is in ibid., pp. 68-72.

22. Ibid., p. 72.

23. PAC, Records of the Governor General, RG 7 G 12, vol. 73, pp. 242-245, quoted in Young to Granville, 21 July 1870.

24. "Report of the Select Committee," item 16, pp. 38-39, Cartier to Taché, 5 July 1870.

25. Quoted in Stanley, *Riel*, p. 150.

26. Ibid., p. 151.

Young knew Cartier could only repeat what Sir George already knew, but the Governor General preferred having Cartier spinning the old yarn to repeating the lie himself. Since Cartier still believed[27] that the matter was settled in principle — only the right moment was lacking for implementation — he dutifully repeated the "all" that the Governor General demanded and enabled Taché to return to Red River satisfied that a general amnesty was forthcoming. The Bishop arrived at his "palace" opposite Fort Garry on August 23, and told Riel that "there was not the slightest danger." The next day, Taché still hoped that he had not been "deceived" as he stood beside the former President watching the troops swarming into the fort.

Riel fled to safety at St Joseph's, a Métis community a few miles west of Pembina in the United States. Canadians hunting for him found alternate satisfaction in the stoning to death of Elzéar Goulet and the shooting of Franois Guillemette (Goulet, for sitting on the tribunal that condemned Scott and Guillemette for firing the second shot in the execution).[28] There was no civil administration to keep the peace. In fact, the Orange Order was the first social or political institution established after the transfer when Orangemen among the volunteers set up Loyal Orange Lodge 1307 at Fort Garry on September 18. In the next several months, the majority of the population of the little village of Winnipeg joined the Mother Lodge in initiations that occurred twice a week, every week over the winter.[29]

When Archibald finally arrived on September 2, he perceived immediately that the Canadians were the unruly element of the population. His first report to Ottawa asserted that there was little difficulty between the native English and the Métis, and he hoped Riel would continue his "voluntary" exile until the mood of the Canadians became less violent.[30] In the interim, Riel left the leadership of Manitoba in the hands of persons who, like himself, were educated in Montreal, but unlike Riel, were not implicated in the events of 1869-70. Both trustees were in Quebec until the summer of 1870. One was Joseph Dubuc, old friend and schoolmate of Riel. The other was Joseph Royal, sent to Riel's aid on Cartier's recommendation.[31]

As the "outrages" of the Canadians against the Métis continued even after Archibald's establishment of a civilian police force, many Métis began to wonder if they should not launch a second resistance or at least seek outside help in the enforcement of the settlement with Canada. Riel

---

27. PAC, Records of the Governor General, RG 7 G 12, vol. 73, pp. 242-245, Young to Granville, 21 July 1870.
28. Other "outrages" are itemized in Stanley, *Riel*, pp. 159-161.
29. Cecil J. Houston and William J. Smyth, *The Sash Canada Wore: A Historical Geography of the Orange Order in Canada* (Toronto, 1980), pp. 58-59.
30. "Report of the Select Committee," item 88, p. 137, Archibald to Cartier, 3 September 1870. On the same theme, see also PAC, Macdonald Papers, Incoming Correspondence, pp. 24960-24967, Archibald to Macdonald, 9 October 1871.
31. Stanley, *Riel*, p. 165.

recognized the potential for disaster in such discontent when William B. O'Donoghue reappeared in a fresh, even more troublesome role. When Scott's killer returned, it was to seek support for a movement to annex the territory to the United States. Hoping to prevent a drift of the Métis to O'Donoghue's cause, Riel left the security of St Joseph's for a public meeting at St Norbert on September 17, and argued that the "treaty" with Canada was far better than anything they could expect from the Americans. To O'Donoghue's chagrin, the rest of the group agreed. Instead of adopting a petition asking the United States to annex Manitoba to Dakota territory, they petitioned President Grant to ask Queen Victoria to demand enforcement of the Manitoba Act. Then Riel returned to St Joseph's.[32]

By the end of September it was clear that the leader of the Métis might come and go more or less as he pleased in the parishes south of the Assiniboine River. In that sense his exile was not only a voluntary one, but also little more than an inconvenience. As soon as Archibald inaugurated the "true constitution of Manitoba," Riel expected his people would control the legislature and set the stage for the former President to become Premier.[33]

Before elections could take place, boundaries for electoral districts had to be drawn; before drawing the electoral map, there had to be a census for an equitable apportionment of the twenty-four seats in the provincial legislature. With the additional purpose of locating and enrolling the persons entitled to land under the Manitoba Act, Archibald took steps to enumerate the population in October. Five teams of enumerators canvassed as many census districts. Each team consisted of a Métis and a native English settler working independently, comparing their results only when the task was completed. According to the "French Report," there were 5,757 "French Half Breeds" and 4,083 "English Half Breeds" in a total population of 11,963. The English enumerators reported 5,696 of the first group and 4,082 of the second in a total of 11,967.[34] Such double enumeration, and the similarity of the two tabulations, tended to support Archibald's later contention that the accuracy and impartiality of the enumeration were beyond reproach.

As soon as the results were known (early in December), the Lieutenant Governor drew electoral boundaries proportional to population, and true to Riel's prediction, the "Rielites" triumphed in the subsequent election, taking seventeen of the twenty-four seats. Schultz was defeated, as were all other Canadians except Royal and Dubuc.[35]

The Orange faction (also known as the Ontario party) was determined

32. Ibid., pp. 161-163.
33. George Stanley, general editor, *The Collected Writings of Louis Riel*, 5 vols. (Edmonton, 1985), I, pp. 120-121, Riel to Joseph Dubuc, 21 October 1870.
34. *Canadian Sessional Papers*, no. 20 (1871), p. 91.
35. Stanley, *Riel*, pp. 165-167.

that such a result would not be repeated in the voting to choose the four members for the House of Commons. Rioting, bribery, and more subtle intimidation ensured subsequently that three out of the four successful candidates were anti-Riel English. Two of the honourable members, Lynch and Schultz, were Orangemen.[36] That success, and the orgy of brawling at the polls, convinced Archibald that the lust for vengeance had run its course. Since the Ontario party was also about to receive a generous balm of cash compensation for alleged suffering during the late "insurrection," Archibald reasoned that all except the most violent Orangemen would tolerate a general amnesty if it were proclaimed in the summer of 1871. Remembering previous conversations with Cartier[37] and a letter from Macdonald in which the Prime Minister seemed concerned only about the proper timing,[38] Archibald wrote Cartier in May asking him about clemency. "Don't you think it quite time now to have that matter settled?" he suggested. In the same letter, Archibald enclosed a note from the native English politician, John Norquay, agreeing that "the spirit of Clear Gritism which was rampant... is gradually subsiding." Norquay agreed that a general amnesty would be tolerated in the summer of 1871.[39]

Cartier passed Archibald's letter on to the Prime Minister, but Macdonald did not reply. He might have thought that his earlier letter still applied. The earlier instruction was

> to discourage any pressure for a general amnesty on the one hand, and, at the same time, to convey the assurance verbally that those who have only been guilty of taking up arms to keep out McDougall to obtain a constitution for the country will not be molested. Time, the great curer of evils will soon calm down the apprehension of those engaged in the rising and all will go well with you especially if Riel and those directly implicated in Scott's death submit to voluntary exile.[40]

Clearly, Archibald had misinterpreted the Prime Minister's position. The second half of the quotation indicated an expression of concern about the supporters of Riel, not the Orange fanatics. Macdonald hoped and expected that by Riel's exile the Métis would eventually lose track of their leader and in that loss forget their former claims to national status. Then all would "go well" for Canada's colonization of Manitoba and the rest of the North West.

---

36. Houston and Smyth, *The Sash Canada Wore,* p 58.

37. Referring to his briefing with Cartier and Francis Hincks before his departure to Manitoba in a letter to Macdonald (2 December 1871), Archibald said, "I have taken care not to allude to anything which was confidentially communicated to me by Sir George or Sir Francis while you were ill, and have committed nobody but myself" (PAC, Macdonald Papers, Incoming Correspondence, pp. 78062-78065).

38. Ibid., Letter Books, vol. 14, p. 422, Macdonald to Archibald, 1 November 1870.

39. PAC, Macdonald Papers, Incoming Correspondence, pp. 41536-41541, Archibald to Cartier, 28 May 1871.

40. Ibid., Letter Books, vol. 14, p. 422, Macdonald to Archibald, 11 November 1870.

Macdonald should have clarified the misunderstanding as soon as the matter came to his notice in June 1871, but he did not, probably because he knew that he could not tell the whole truth to Archibald without the facts getting to Cartier. Consequently, one deception led to another and the entire matter became exceedingly more complicated in the autumn of 1871 with a second attempt by O'Donoghue to exploit the Métis for his own purposes.

By September 1871, with none of the promises fulfilled, O'Donoghue believed that, if he crossed the border with a small force of his followers at Pembina, he might attract hundreds of dissatisfied Métis before reaching Fort Garry. Together, they might take the fort, throw out the "Ontario bandits," and seek the protection of the United States to secure their independence.

As soon as Riel learned of O'Donoghue's new plan, he returned to Manitoba and called a meeting of the Métis captains from every parish to take place at St Vital on September 26. On the appointed day, Riel brought them to the same resolution they had adopted the year before. In the new crisis, however, Riel recognized that by withholding his support from Archibald until the last minute, he might force the amnesty so long delayed. Consequently, when Archibald finally learned that Manitoba was about to be invaded, and issued a proclamation on October 4 calling everyone to "rally round the flag of our common country," the native English responded at once, but the Métis waited for some indication that past promises would be fulfilled. They did not have long to wait. On October 5 Archibald gave them what they wanted when the Governor authorized Father Ritchot to tell Riel that "the co-operation of the Métis and their leaders in the support of the Crown . . . cannot be looked upon otherwise than as entitling them to most favourable consideration." Then several companies of Métis cavalry mustered at St Boniface and Riel promised Archibald in writing that "so long as our services continue to be required, you may rely on us."[41]

Before the Métis departed for the frontier to reinforce troops already on the scene, Joseph Royal (speaker of the provincial legislature), asked Archibald to cross the river and review the 200 men ready for war on Canada's behalf. The Lieutenant Governor accepted the invitation in an instant and met the men in their traditional dress (light blue capote, bright red sash, dark corduroy trousers, and knee-high moccasins). Then he shook hands with their leaders, one by one, taking in friendship even the right hand of Louis Riel.

The meeting of the former President and the Lieutenant Governor on October 8, 1871, might have marked the end of a lingering twenty-four-month crisis. Instead, the handshaking incident only brought Orangemen to new heights of vituperation in Ontario. Macdonald told Archibald later in the month that "Scott's murder by Riel, & the handshaking are the topics

---

41. Stanley, *Riel,* pp. 169-174.

that we have to fear on the stump & at the Hustings before the next General Elections and if no change takes place some of our best friends will be unseated as supporters of the present government."[42]

What made the episode particularly unforgivable to critics outside Manitoba was a total lack of apparent necessity. The facts reported in the eastern press were that Archibald learned that a Fenian raid was imminent on October 3; he issued a call to arms to the loyal population on October 4; O'Donoghue made his move on October 5; and, on the same day, the whole invading force of less than fifty men was taken by an American border patrol, thus ending the crisis even before it began. What Archibald found everyone ignoring was that, in the opinion of the Canadians commanding at the "front," the crisis was far from over with the arrest of O'Donoghue's first contingent. As late as the morning of October 8, Archibald was still receiving panicky dispatches for more reinforcements.[43]

Archibald's defence of his action to Macdonald focused on the other military reality that he "had either to go over to St Boniface, or risk giving offence to half, and that the most warlike half of the population at the moment when they were assuming an attitude that I had been urging on them ever since the invasion was threatened."[44] For his fellow Nova Scotian, Joseph Howe, Archibald added a constitutional dimension to the justification explaining that the majority of the French- and English-speaking Manitobans had approved his action. "It seems to me," he continued, "that the people here must be allowed to be judges of how to manage their own affairs...." Archibald reminded Howe that Manitoba was a province with as much right to autonomy as Nova Scotia or the others and suggested that "you can hardly hope to carry on responsible Government by inflicting death penalties on the leaders of the majority of the electors."[45]

The real issue was that the renewal of excited denunciations reflected a broad-based prejudice in Ontario that Manitoba was not a province to be trusted with the same powers as the others. Thus Riel became convinced that no matter how "loyal" he was, he would never be loyal enough for the "wicked" men in Ottawa. Consequently, after November 1871 he hinted to Taché that he was not going to continue standing outside affairs, waiting indefinitely. That led the Bishop to intercede once more on Riel's behalf and he did obtain a significant concession at the end of December when Macdonald agreed to pay the costs of maintaining Riel, his associate

42. PAC, Macdonald Papers, Letter Books, vol. 16, pp. 537-542, Macdonald to Archibald, 30 November 1871.

43. Stanley, *Riel,* p. 174.

44. PAC, Macdonald Papers, Incoming Correspondence, pp. 78093-78103, Archibald to Macdonald, 20 December 1871.

45. "Report of the Select Committee," item 107, p. 151, Archibald to Howe, 20 January 1872.

Lépine (and their families), if they would agree to "leave the country and be absent for at least a year."[46] The implication was clear enough. If they accepted one more year of voluntary exile, they could come home in 1873 expecting a resumption of their political careers — exactly as Sir George Cartier had gone into exile after his youthful participation on the rebel side in the "troubles" of 1837.[47]

There was a critical difference, however, between Cartier's experience and that of Lépine and Riel. No one hunted Cartier with a price on his head, whereas the legislature of Ontario had offered a $5,000 reward[48] in 1871 for the capture of the persons responsible for Scott's death. Since bounty hunters could take their quarry more easily from a St Paul hotel than various guarded places in Manitoba, Lépine and Riel might have felt both would be more secure at home (even without an amnesty). Consequently, Lépine returned to St Vital in May, and Riel followed in June.

If Riel's return assured his safety, coming home brought him peace of mind on other accounts as well. Riel was better able to look after his mother, younger brothers, and sisters,[49] and he could attend to speculative interests that included a claim to a potentially valuable parcel of real estate near the Lake Manitoba terminus of a prospective canal the government was considering as a link between the Red and Saskatchewan river systems.[50] Above all, however, Riel's return enabled him to play a leading role in the politics of his "small nation."[51]

By July, his political intentions were well known. He would seek election to the House of Commons and, after a seat had been vacated for him in the provincial legislature, Riel would force Macdonald to concede the amnesty or deny responsible government by refusing to recognize the wish of the elected majority in its choice for premier. Campaigning openly in the French-speaking parishes, Riel recognized that his continuing popularity was his greatest security, and Sir John A. Macdonald conceded as much after Riel's political intentions were reported to the Prime Minister by Manitoba informants.[52]

46. PAC, Macdonald Papers, Letter Books, vol. 16, p. 682, Macdonald to Taché, 27 December 1871; vol. 19, p. 544-545, Macdonald cypher letter to Alexander Morris, 6 January 1873.

47. PAM, Riel Papers, item 60, Royal to Riel, 17 December 1870.

48. Stanley, *Riel,* p. 178.

49. See Riel Papers, I, pp. 194, 201-202, 205 (letters to his mother and sister Marie) for indications of Riel's anxiety about the well-being of his family.

50. A concluding paragraph in a letter to his mother, 17 May 1872, suggests that Riel was worried about the security of his claim to the property and urged her to get one of Reil's cousins to plant some acres conspicuously in barley and to send him any news about the government's plans to proceed with the project (ibid., I, p. 212).

51. Ibid., I, pp. 206-208, 213-216, 220-221.

52. PAC, Macdonald Papers, Incoming Correspondence, pp. 110715, Gilbert McMicken cypher telegram to Macdonald, 13 July 1872.

Macdonald's concession was to grumble then, as he did later, that Riel had "cheated and deceived" him, but short of posting a guard in every Métis home in Manitoba, or having Louis Riel assassinated, there was nothing that could be done to check the embarrassment of Riel's return. In any case, Macdonald was more preoccupied at the time with getting his "friends" re-elected elsewhere, an exercise that was complicated by many different election days across the country. The absence of simultaneous elections dictated easy victories first to help bring the more reluctant ridings along later, or to rescue important candidates defeated in one place by running them in another. Thus, in 1872, after Cartier suffered defeat in Montreal, Macdonald instructed Archibald to "get Sir George elected in your province." Knowing that Riel was about to take the riding of Provencher in Manitoba, and fearing another episode like a handshaking if Riel yielded to Cartier, Macdonald added two more sentences to the same coded message: "Do not however let your late President resign in his favour. That would make mischief in Ontario."[53]

Archibald was happy to follow Macdonald's instructions but Riel was the only likely winner who was open to offers of rewards for temporary retirement from the federal scene. When the Governor notified the Prime Minister that Taché believed that the minimum price ought to be the amnesty, Macdonald responded with an assurance on September 12 that "Sir George will do all he can to meet wishes of the parties." Since that was almost what was demanded, Macdonald said, "This statement should be satisfactory."[54] When Taché passed the message on to Riel, the former President replied that the government had to reaffirm its commitment to the whole "treaty" of 1870. Once again, Macdonald responded in language that seemed to serve while still leaving room for evasion: "Cartier who is at Montreal agrees with me as to pledges. It will be his interest to secure the approbation of his constituents and he can be of more service to them than any other man."[55]

Refusing to be more specific, Macdonald still obtained the result he wanted. Riel declined the nomination on September 14; no other local candidate accepted in Riel's place; and Cartier won the seat by acclamation. Then Taché informed Macdonald that, since they had done their part, "I hope we will be rewarded by the grant of the amnesty which alone can secure peace to this country." At the same time, Taché made a pitch for keeping Archibald in the office of Lieutenant Governor: "he is really the right man in the right place and the Dominion is greatly indebted to him."[56]

By mid-September, however, Archibald was virtually out of office

---

53. Ibid., p. 85929, Macdonald cypher telegram to Archibald, 7 September 1872.
54. Ibid., p. 85944, Macdonald cypher telegram to Archibald, 12 September 1872.
55. Ibid., p. 85942, Macdonald cypher telegram to Archibald, 13 September 1872.
56. Ibid., pp. 41552-41553, Taché to Macdonald, 15 September 1872.

already. Angered and embittered by the outrage over the handshaking episode (and other matters, discussed in the next chapter), he had offered Macdonald his resignation on the eve of the new year and, four months later, the offer to go quietly became a request to be released at once.[57] Macdonald responded by urging Archibald to stay until an appropriate replacement could be found, a task that presented considerable difficulty because the Prime Minister was already discouraged in his quest for a suitable Chief Justice for the Manitoba Superior Court created the year before.[58] It was not until the summer of 1872 that Macdonald found his "Chief" in Alexander Morris — one of the original proponents of Canada's expansion westward, a lawyer of some talent, and a more tactful expansionist than McDougall. At the same time, while Morris was a conciliator, Macdonald had reason to believe that his recruit would be more firm in the cause of building "Nova Britannia" in the West than Archibald had been. When Macdonald sent him to Manitoba in August, he probably thought Morris would be a good successor to the gubernatorial office if he succeeded in the judicial appointment.

Morris arrived in Winnipeg on August 13, 1872.[59] By the end of the month, he was sending Macdonald valuable information indicating that he was likely to be one of the government's best sources of political intelligence as well. Indeed, Morris may have played a role in the Cartier election. At least he appeared to be receiving part of the thanks for the affair when Macdonald wrote him on September 26 saying how pleased he was with the way that the matter was "managed." In the same letter, Macdonald confirmed that Morris was becoming "Administrator" as well as Chief Justice.[60] After September 26, Sir John A. Macdonald addressed all the significant communications about Riel to Morris, not to Archibald.

There was plenty to communicate because the reality became plain in October that the Métis leader was still determined to force the amnesty on the local level. The strategy was for the sitting member for St Vital to

57. Ibid., pp. 78107-78109, Archibald to Macdonald, 31 December 1871; and pp. 78177, Archibald cypher telegram to Macdonald, 30 March 1872.

58. At Macdonald's insistence, the tribunal was renamed the "Court of Queen's Bench." Ontario and Nova Scotia lawyers were extremely worried that the judicial system might follow Quebec models because the majority of the province was French-speaking. In names and forms and the appointment of personnel, Macdonald made certain that the Manitoba judicial system resembled that of Ontario. See PAC Macdonald Papers, Letter Books, vol. 16, pp. 19, 537-542, Macdonald to Archibald, 12 July 1871 and 30 November 1871; and vol. 18, pp. 546-549, Macdonald to Morris, 24 September 1872. See also, ibid., Incoming Correspondence, pp. 77983-77992, Archibald to Macdonald, 8 November 1871 and pp. 113998-114001, Morris to Macdonald, 16 January 1873.

59. See Dale and Lee Gibson, *Substantial Justice: Law and Lawyers in Manitoba, 1670-1970* (Winnipeg, 1972), pp. 94-99.

60. PAC, Macdonald Papers, Letter Books, vol. 18, p. 571, Macdonald to Morris, 26 September 1872.

resign in Riel's favour, and force Macdonald's hand on the responsible government question. On October 11, Macdonald wrote that he preferred the risk of arresting and convicting Riel for murder to seeing the Métis leader become Premier of Manitoba. "The quarrel with Riel must come sooner or later," he confided to Morris. "We may as well have it now . . . if there are any warrants out they should be executed against Riel. He should be arrested for the murder of Scott & put upon his trial."[61]

Morris responded[62] that the situation was not as critical as Macdonald thought. Nothing would happen before a by-election confirmed Riel's election, and that could be frustrated, first, by delay (because Archibald was about to leave the province without a successor in the office of Lieutenant Governor). With executive functions only partially in the hands of Morris in his role of Administrator, the perfect delay was pleading incapacity to sign the writ for an election, "leaving it to be dealt with hereafter by the Governor." Such a situation would buy time to defeat the candidate either by bribery of the electorate ("with $1,000 Riel could be beaten in St Vital") or by intimidation ("Have warned Royal that if Riel persists, warrant will inevitably be issued").

Ultimately, the threat of legal proceedings was the effective discouragement to Riel's seeking the premiership in 1872. On December 3 a failed attempt to arrest him sent the Métis leader back into hiding.[63] Then delegations, deputations, petitioners, and Taché appealed for the amnesty in the old manner, with the same result as before.

By mid-December, Morris began to wonder if the great effort that was needed to keep Riel out of politics was worth the trouble. "It is a pity," he suggested, that "this amnesty could not be settled," particularly since Taché was so "warm" on the subject. "Could not Cartier get the English gov't to dispose of it on their own responsibility . . .?"[64]

Macdonald's response was to write his other confidant in Manitoba, Gilbert McMicken, asking him to see Morris and "revive his recollection of affairs." In Macdonald's version of the relevant history, the "circumstances connected with the Amnesty were these":

> When the disturbance first broke out, and McDougall was prevented from entering into the Province . . . Lord Lisgar, by express instructions from England, invited the malcontents by Proclamation to lay their grievances before him, and promised an Amnesty if they would lay down their arms and cease to obstruct the entry of the Canadian Authorities. . . . [Unfortunately] they continued in rebellion until the arrival of the Military

61. Ibid., pp. 681-682, Macdonald to Morris, 11 October 1872.

62. The advice from Morris is found in two messages; see ibid., Incoming Correspondence, pp. 113890-113892, Morris to Macdonald, 8 November 1872, and p. 113901, Morris cypher telegram to Macdonald, 16 November 1872.

63. Stanley, *Riel,* p. 188.

64. PAC, Macdonald Papers, Incoming Correspondence, pp. 113948-113951, Morris to Macdonald, 11 December 1872.

Expedition at Fort Garry in September.

The people therefore forfeited all claim to amnesty. However, I fancy there will be no difficulty in getting Her Majesty's Government to grant an amnesty except to the murderers of Scott.

The delegates sent down here by the people demanded a Constitution for Manitoba, with representative Institutions and responsible Government and insisted upon it. The Canadian gov't, for peace sake, yielded and the Manitoba Act was passed. But by the passage of that Act, at the request of the people there, the Dominion Government were deprived of all authority in the administration. This was not the voluntary wish of the Canadian Gov't, it was forced upon them by the Agents of the insurgents themselves.

As it is now the Gov. General's authority is limited altogether to the exercise of the pardoning power after conviction. His commission as Governor General gives him no power to prevent any criminal from being arrested and tried and sentenced.[65]

There were no more suggestions from Morris for clemency that would include Riel. Of course, Taché still pressed the demand. In January 1873, he threatened to publish all that he knew on the subject if the amnesty were not granted immediately.[66] Anticipating such action from Taché, Macdonald had already asked Morris to have a "straight up and down talk with the Archbishop" in order to "ascertain all that he can say on the subject."[67]

When Morris eventually reported on the matter, the news was unsettling to say the least. He suggested that "vague promises were made but there is little evidence of it," meaning almost nothing in writing.[68] Still, prudence called for denials from everyone who talked to Ritchot at the time of the negotiations on April 26, May 3, and May 19, 1870. Murdoch's subsequent letter was ideally suited to Macdonald's purpose. "I have no recollection," he wrote in March 1873, "of any promise or expectation of an amnesty to Riel and his associates having been held out by Lord Lisgar, when Mr. Ritchot had an interview with him in my presence or at any other time."[69]

Cartier was less sweeping in his denial. "I always took the same ground we both did," he wrote Macdonald on February 23, "namely that the question of an amnesty was not for our decision, but for the Queen and Imperial Government. In his interview of the nineteenth Lord Lisgar also gave assurance to Father Ritchot that the military expedition was going to Red River not to arrest anyone. . . ."[70] Clearly, for Cartier, the issue was

---

65. Ibid., Letter Books, vol. 19, pp. 528-531, Macdonald to McMicken, 4 January 1873.

66. Ibid., Incoming Correspondence, pp. 41580-41583, Tache to Macdonald, 25 January 1873; also printed in "Report of the Select Committee," item 20, pp. 49-50.

67. PAC, Macdonald Papers, Transcripts, vol. 583, Macdonald to Morris, 16 December 1872.

68. Ibid., Incoming Correspondence, pp. 114043-114050, Morris to Macdonald, 12 February 1873.

69. "Report of the Select Committee," item 53, p. 104, Murdoch to Herbert, 5 March 1873.

70. Ibid., item 125, p. 105, Cartier to Macdonald, 5 March 1873.

not whether the delegates were promised that the whole population was "safe from all harm" but who was to guarantee the immunity from prosecution. Recognizing that Cartier's position was a distinction without a difference, Macdonald wrote again hoping for a more useful denial,[71] but before his faithful Quebec lieutenant could respond, Sir George lapsed into the final phase of the illness that had taken him to Britain for treatment shortly after the 1872 elections.

The death Sir George Cartier in May of 1873 renewed the problem of the amnesty. Riel decided to run for the vacant seat, and Taché awaited the government's handling of his election before publishing the pamphlet he had written on the amnesty promise. Macdonald knew that he could not delay calling the by-election indefinitely, but by setting the date for November the Prime Minister thought he had enough time to eliminate Riel by political manoeuvring. Reports from his most trusted informants in Manitoba indicated that the Riel party had been disintegrating since January 1873.[72] Consequently, the opportune moment to grant an official "amnesty for all ... except to those who were concerned in the murder of Thomas Scott" seemed at hand. A general proclamation in the summer of 1873 would isolate Riel and "drive him out of the country, which is a consummation devoutly to be wished." The less preferable alternative was Riel's arrest and trial because of the potential for acquittal or a hung jury "and while he is there he will be a continual fire brand."[73] Unfortunately for Macdonald, the British insisted that Canada had to recommend the matter first.[74]

Thwarted from the preferred political strategy, but still determined to eliminate Riel by any means short of assassination, a second attempt to arrest Riel occurred on September 14. Constables could not find him, but they did seize Ambroise Lépine, and the court indicted the lesser villain one month later. Then, thirty days after Lépine's first court appearance, the voters of Provencher chose Louis Riel to fill Cartier's vacant seat in Parliament.[75]

In 1874, proceedings against Lépine and Riel worked as parallel developments to bring the amnesty issue to a crisis and resolution. Another variable in the story was the change of government in Ottawa in November 1873 following scandalous disclosures concerning the Conservatives' electioneering in 1872. The result was that Riel arrived in the capital almost the

71. PAC, Macdonald Papers, Incoming Correspondence, pp. 41572-41578, Macdonald to Cartier, 22 March 1873.

72. Ibid., pp. 114010-114015, Morris to Macdonald, 26 January 1873; pp. 110786-110791, McMicken to Macdonald, 29 January 1873; and pp. 114028-114033, Morris to Macdonald, 7 February 1873.

73. Ibid., Transcripts, vol. 583, Macdonald to Dufferin, 2 June 1873.

74. Ibid., Incoming Correspondence, pp. 41619-41629, Kimberley to Dufferin 24 July 1873.

75. Stanley, *Riel,* pp. 191-195.

same day that the new government led by Alexander Mackenzie decided to seek a more thorough condemnation of Macdonald's corruption in a general election, and Riel saw Parliament dissolved before he could take his seat. But Provencher re-elected him in February 1874. After his second return to Ottawa, the House of Commons demanded his expulsion in April. At the same time as that bizarre proceeding, Taché published the facts of the long-withheld amnesty and the House decided to form a committee to collect evidence of its own.[76]

Neither the new evidence collected by the parliamentary committee in April and May nor a third election of Riel in Provencher broke the impasse. The rush to resolution developed after the Court of Queen's Bench in Manitoba found Ambroise Lépine guilty of murder and worthy of hanging in the matter of Thomas Scott. At that point early in 1875, the Governor General intervened to proclaim that two years' of imprisonment and permanent deprivation of political rights were the appropriate punishments. By implication, Riel deserved a similar release from the threat of execution. Consequently, when Parliament disqualified the member for Provencher from taking his seat in the House of Commons the second time (in February 1875), he and Lépine were both excused from murder charges conditional on a deprivation of political rights and a five-year banishment from British territory.[77]

Mackenzie might have preferred to have hanged both, but he knew as well as Macdonald that the Canadian union was still a fragile entity demanding "prudence and moderation . . . to prevent the discordant elements from ending in a blowup."[78] Thus, Mackenzie followed the Governor General's lead in moderating the Orangemen's cry for blood against the Riel sympathizers' demand for unconditional amnesty. In any case, said Mackenzie, his hands were tied. The evidence presented to the select committee proved that Macdonald had promised clemency.

Of course, Macdonald denied[79] any such promise had ever been given by his government and denounced Mackenzie's proposal of the five-year banishment as an "absolute pardon." Elaborating his objections in a private letter he wanted burned, Macdonald explained that, since Riel and Lépine were likely to pass their exile in the United States, "the Haven of Hope for all French Canadians," a place to which many others had migrated already, it seemed clear to Sir John that the "Gentlemen as Martyrs will be amply supplied with funds and live like fighting cocks.

---

76. Ibid., pp. 199-204.

77. Ibid., pp. 205-213.

78. PAC, Macdonald Papers, Letter Books, vol. 17, pp. 320-323, Macdonald to Rose, 5 March 1872.

79. He told the same story in Parliament that he presented to the Select Committee the year before. At that time, according to Taché, "Macdonald lied (excuse the word) like a trooper"(Stanley, *Riel,* p. 206).

Meanwhile they will infest the frontier—keep up the discontent in Manitoba and have petitions annually before Parliament praying for pardon. In fact there is no end of the nuisance."[80] He added a special note of outrage when he exclaimed, "this is the punishment for murder!"

The five-year exile did defuse the Riel issue for the present, and, when Louis Riel did finally re-enter the Canadian political scene, Manitoba was not his field of combat. Too angered by Riel's small victories between 1869 and 1874, the former Prime Minister did not see that in the larger battle the victory was already his.

---

80. PAC, Macdonald Papers, Transcripts, vol. 584, Macdonald to T.C. Patteson, 16 February 1875.

Survey Party, ca. 1875
(Provincial Archives of Manitoba)

Gilbert McMicken, 1880
(Provincial Archives of Manitoba)

"McMicken . . . subverted Archibald's arrangements. . . ."

Chapter 6

"Unlocking" the Territory for "Actual Settlers"

While the denial of an amnesty to Louis Riel amounted to a denial of responsible government to Manitoba, the opening of the Métis land base to newcomers between 1870 and 1874 was probably even more important in the defeat of the Métis as a people. Macdonald hinted that such an objective might be pursued when he intimated to his old friend John Rose in February 1870 that "these impulsive half breeds have got spoilt by their emeute [riot], and must be kept down by a strong hand until they are swamped by the influx of settlers."[1] The inundation he contemplated was a flood of newcomers reducing the Métis to minority status. The "strong hand" for the interim included denial of community control of land claims.

In the midst of the negotiations with Ritchot, Macdonald made plain to Sir Clinton Murdoch and the Governor General that local control of land was as "inadmissible" as the amnesty. At the same time, "for the sake of peace," the delegates were led to believe that their accord with Canada included a pattern of self-government extending to the administration of the Métis homeland in the District of Assiniboia. Sections 30, 31, and 32 of the Manitoba Act (and Cartier's explanatory memorandum to Ritchot on May 23) indicated that the ownership of the occupied territory was conceded. The Old Settlement Belt was not Dominion land. Similarly, Section 31 of the act (and the same memorandum from Cartier) asserted that the Lieutenant Governor would set aside another 1.4 million acres, confirming selections by heads of families for their children. The two territories together meant that a Métis homeland of approximately two million acres would not count in the territory to be "administered by the Government of Canada for the purposes of the Dominion."[2]

---

1. PAC, Macdonald Papers, Letter Books, vol. 14, pp. 24-28, Macdonald to Rose, 23 February 1870.

2. Section 30 of the Manitoba Act is usually interpreted as Canada's authority for Dominion control of natural resources, a control that was exercised in Manitoba until 1930. But the clause appeared to contain an implied exemption of certain portions of the new province from such control: "All ungranted or waste lands [all territory except occupied land] shall be, from and after the date of the said transfer, vested in the Crown, and administered by the Government of Canada for the purposes of the Dominion. . . ."

Since the Métis expected to select their childrens' shares of the 1.4 million acres from the vacant, wooded territory fronting on the rivers and streams near the occupied land on the Red and the Assiniboine rivers, few among the people of Manitoba imagined that the remaining bald prairie would attract many newcomers. "Locking away" the best land from new settlers was, therefore, a primary reason for the Legislative Assembly of the provisional government to be jubilant when Father Ritchot and President Riel explained the provisions of the "Manitoba Treaty" to the public on June 24, 1870.[3]

Two months later, Archibald's instructions[4] appeared to acknowledge that the river-frontage had been pre-empted for use by the native population. At least Archibald understood the requirement that he ascertain what might be opened for immediate settlement in that light. Even when Macdonald wrote the Lieutenant Governor later in the year on the importance of dispelling the notion that Manitoba was a "half breed" reserve, he did not seem to challenge the more basic principle that some significant other portion of the land of the province was to be distributed pre-emptively to the original settlers.[5]

As a result, when Archibald prepared his report, he estimated the acreage that would be left after accommodating claims to the occupied land and the 1.4 million acres to be selected by parents for their children. In this way, he made the access of newcomers conditional on the resolution of native land claims; he believed firmly that the Métis land rights had priority over those accorded to emigrants from Canada,[6] and arrived at the number of acres that were likely to be available for the "considerable emigration" that Macdonald expected in the spring of 1871 by deducting all of the Old Settlement Belt (409,600 acres in Archibald's estimate), plus another 1.4 million acres for the children's claims. Then, after making allowance for the land that was covered by lakes and swamps, he deducted another million acres for the Hudson's Bay Company reserve, land for schools, and other religious institutions. Finally he arrived at the figure of 5.25 million acres of prairie that might be opened to immigrants, and recommended adoption of the American grid system of sectional survey, with 160-acre free grants for homesteaders.

---

3. The same point was a lingering cause for resentment by newcomers to Manitoba. "All the world believes that it was done to hinder settlement and lock up the country against development," the *Manitoba Free Press* reported on 11 January 1873.

4. Order in Council of Canada, 2 August 1870.

5. PAC, Macdonald Papers, Letter Books, vol. 14, pp. 422-425, Macdonald to Archibald, 1 November 1870.

6. PAC, Records of the Department of the Interior, RG 15, vol. 229, file 1/1871, Archibald to Joseph Howe, 20 December 1870; vol. 228, file 796, Archibald to Howe, 27 December 1870.

At first, the government appeared unperturbed by Archibald's forthright approach to the land question. At the end of January 1871, Macdonald acknowledged receipt of Archibald's "very interesting dispatches as to the mode of survey and also as to the settlement of the half breeds." But since he was making preparations for his diplomatic mission to Washington, D.C. — treaty negotiation that kept him out of the country from late February to mid-May — Macdonald turned the Archibald reports over to his old law partner, the former Minister of Crown Lands and Surveyor General for Ontario, Alexander Campbell. Macdonald assured Archibald that Campbell would make a "good report. He has already told me that he agrees in the main with your ideas as to the surveys."[7]

It was Alexander Campbell, nominally the Postmaster General in 1871, who revised Archibald's recommendations into a policy for disposing of the "public lands in the province of Manitoba," a policy the Cabinet approved on March 1, 1871. The leading statement in the Order in Council adopting Campbell's report was an endorsement of the American pattern of columns of "ranges" of square "townships" in uniformly numbered rows, each township containing thirty-six numbered "sections" (one mile on a side), with the basic unit of subdivision being the "quarter-section" of 160 acres available as free grants in return for five years of settlement duties by "homesteaders." In Manitoba, the sectional system would open 43,200 quarter sections, or 8.3 million acres by Campbell's reckoning.

The discrepancy of three million acres between Campbell's and Archibald's estimates derived in part from a different measure of the total area of the province (Manitoba was still defined only in terms of latitude and longitude, and the distance covered by a degree of longitude at 49 degrees north latitude was uncertain). Campbell believed that the total area of Manitoba was 9 million acres; Archibald's estimate was 7.7 million. The rest of the discrepancy resulted from Campbell's placing the children's 1.4 million acres, the Hudson's Bay Company's allotment of one-twentieth of the area, and the school lands in the basic sectional survey, reflecting the Cabinet's rather smug confidence that all of that land would be open to "actual settlers" almost as soon as it became available for anyone.[8]

Instead of affirming that sixty-eight townships adjoining the Old Settlement Belt were areas from which heads of families might select their

---

7. PAC, Macdonald Papers, Letter Books, vol. 15, pp. 161-164, Macdonald to Archibald, 25 January 1871.

8. Whereas Archibald had predicted that Canada would have to "tie it up for a long time" because nearly half of "these half breeds are under ten years of age: for eleven years to come you withdraw 490,000 acres from the market" (PAC, Records of the Department of the Interior, RG 15, vol. 229, file 796, Archibald to Howe, 27 December 1870).

children's land, and that such territory was guaranteed to the intended recipients for at least one generation — what Cartier promised Ritchot and Taché — Campbell's regulations called for distribution by lottery, and stated that there would be no federal restrictions concerning the sale of such territory after allotment.[9]

Still, the statements on the distribution process were sufficiently general to seem to accommodate Cartier's old assurances. For example, there was nothing in the wording of the regulations to prevent small groups from selecting river-frontage in certain "townships or parts of townships," petitioning the governor to designate such locations as their land, and having the same official make a drawing of "location tickets" for distribution to individuals just as lands were distributed in Upper Canada among companies of Loyalists in the 1780s. Similarly, on the matter of trusteeship, the regulations did not seem to preclude the Province of Manitoba from enacting "Infant Estates" legislation forbidding the sale of lands granted to minors.[10]

It would appear that the Order in Council proclaiming the first Dominion Land Policy was carefully crafted to avoid infuriating groups with opposing interests. Campbell did not want to give Taché and Ritchot the impression that the Manitoba Act was being ignored, and he was even more anxious to impress Ontario members of Parliament with the modest amount of land "locked up" — temporarily unavailable for immediate settlement. Yet he failed in his primary objective because it was the Ontario opposition (the same group that was so adamantly opposed to the Manitoba Act in the first place), who saw through the government's dual purposes.

The Opposition objected, in the first place, to such an important matter being enacted by Order in Council, rather than by Parliament after full debate of details. Secondly, critics objected to the substance of what was established. They opposed, for example, the concession that the river-frontage of nearly one-half million acres was already pre-empted, while requiring five years of settlement duties from incoming homesteaders. The Opposition wanted no more than a three-year trial period for newcomers and stringent examination of the claims of "half breeds" before giving them the valuable river-frontage of virtually the whole province.

Campbell brought the Order in Council of March 1 back before Cabinet on April 25. In the amended version of the Dominion Land Policy,

---

9. Nor did Archibald. While admitting that the "French, or their leaders, wish the land to be so tied up . . . to prevent them . . . for a generation from passing out of the family of the original grantee," he recommended against too much protection, arguing that the "effect would be to lock up a large portion of the land of the country, and exclude it from the improvements going on in localities where land is unfettered" (ibid.).

10. The language of the regulation was "there shall be no . . . restrictions as to their power of dealing with their lands when granted than those which the laws of Manitoba may prescribe" (Order in Council of Canada, 1 March 1871).

the paragraph that admitted that some land was already occupied was dropped entirely; a penalty clause for newcomers attempting to establish claims by fraud disappeared; more persons became eligible for military bounty[11] grants; and the homestead period was reduced to three years.

Probably the most important change was the total disappearance of any admission that there was "occupied land" in Manitoba at the time of the transfer. Indirectly, that deletion was equivalent to dropping section 30 of the Manitoba Act, the clause that distinguished between "ungranted or waste lands" and the surveyed lots of the Old Settlement Belt. The first belonged to the Crown in the right of Canada, to be "administered by the Government of Canada for the purposes of the Dominion," while the territory that was already occupied fell by implication under the jurisdiction of the Crown in the right of the province.

The April 25 designation of all land as Dominion land had the immediate result of interrupting a process that Archibald proposed for confirming the titles of river-lot occupants. Early in April he had proposed the enactment of

> a local statute whereby a party applying to be enrolled and treated as owner of a defined lot, should be required to put up certain public notices of his intended application.
>
> In case no opposition to his claim should be made within a prescribed time, he would be considered as entitled.
>
> If opposition were made, an inquiry should be held, the facts reported, and the title declared according to the evidence.
>
> This preliminary inquiry would settle the right to a Grant of the land if applied for.[12]

Archibald believed that such local adjudication of the question could settle all the claims to the occupied land perhaps in one year, or two at the most. And the Lieutenant Governor appears to have thought that adjudication of native land claims had to be a priority of the Macdonald government, even though Sir John A. Macdonald himself had written Archibald that all he wished to accomplish quickly was the settlement of as many Canadians as possible in Manitoba. "You know how industriously the Opposition have attempted to disseminate the idea that Manitoba is to be a Popish Preserve and this impression will be confirmed unless there is evidence of energetic action in the way of provision for a general immigration."[13] That overriding consideration became even more clear once the

---

11. A free grant of 160 acres was included in the original regulations as a bonus to people who were still serving with the Red River Expedition. The amended regulations provided the same benefit for men already discharged from service.

12. PAC, Records of the Department of the Interior, RG 15, vol. 229, file 1437, Archibald to Howe, 9 April 1871.

13. PAC, Macdonald Papers, Letter Books, vol. 14, pp. 422-425, Macdonald to Archibald, 1 November 1870.

Prime Minister returned from Washington in May, and the Cabinet approved yet another Order in Council concerning Dominion Land Policy on May 26, 1871.

The defect found in the previous orders was the assumption of completed surveys before new settlement would take place. The latest order solved that deficiency by giving newcomers the right to settle in advance of the surveys, to establish themselves wherever they found "vacant" land, assuring them that they would be "protected" so long as they filed their claims within three months of being found by the surveyors. Significantly, the Old Settlement Belt was not specifically excluded from the territory in which vacant land might be taken.

As soon as Riel learned of the intent to promote emigration before recognizing existing settlement (or Métis preferences in the location of the 1.4 million acres), he predicted that severe conflicts were likely to arise between newcomers and the people native to the country. Since June 1870 many Métis families had been staking claims to land that they expected to receive as their childrens' allotments.[14] Consequently, Riel urged Dubuc and Royal to pressure the Lieutenant Governor to resolve native land claims before a flood of immigration poured into the province in the summer.[15] Archibald readily agreed that quick action was necessary and that he had authority under the Order in Council of April 25 — at least to move tentatively towards setting aside the townships from which the 1.4 million acres would be drawn. On June 17 he proclaimed in the newspapers:

> the fairest mode of proceeding will be to adopt, as far as possible, the selections made by the Half breeds themselves.
>
> Whenever, therefore, any parish of Half breeds shall have made choice of a particular locality, and shall have publicly notified same . . . so as to prevent settlers entering upon the tract in ignorance of the previous selection, I shall, if the duty should fall to me . . . , be guided by the principle I have mentioned, and confirm the selections so made. . . .[16]

At the same time, Archibald wrote a long letter to Joseph Howe explaining his action, writing as Riel had written Dubuc and Royal,

---

14. "They worked with wonderful alacrity and unanimity. Since '62 or about that time they had been in the habit of wintering stock along the Seine, Rat and La Salle [sic] Rivers. These lands naturally offered the favorite playground for the staker who in short order had the entire river-front neatly staked off. A man didn't confine himself to 1 claim. He frequently had 2 or 3. Sometimes for children, present or in expectancy, he would have the riverside dizzy with blazes and stakes" (Provincial Archives of British Columbia, Archer Martin Papers, Add. Mss 630, box 1, file 5, [R.A. Ruttan] to Archer Martin, 11 July 1894).

15. PAM, Riel Papers, item 498, Riel to Dubuc [June 1871].

16. Printed in *The Manitoban,* 17 June 1871. Clipping appears as enclosure in PAC, Records of the Department of the Interior, RG 15, vol. 230, file 167, Archibald to Howe, 17 June 1871.

stressing the probability of severe conflict if newcomers had unimpeded entry to the province without resolution of the claims of the old settlers first. The particular difficulty, in Archibald's view, was the Canadians' asserting that they were "free to go where they choose, to take possession of any land that suits them." Archibald agreed with Riel that the "half breeds" were the group with the "right of first selection," and settlement of their claims was the prerequisite for preventing "dangerous collisions."[17]

Howe perceived that Archibald's action was inconsistent with the "rules and regulations, first confidentially printed and carefully reviewed, and then sanctioned by Order in Council."[18] Referring the matter to Macdonald, he urged the Prime Minister to correct Archibald's misplaced priorities with "definite instructions." In Howe's assessment, "the point is very important and ought not to be left in doubt."[19]

In the circumstances, Macdonald had to agree that "definite instructions" were apparently necessary. Yet the kind of document that Howe thought necessary would probably have contravened section 32 of the Manitoba Act.[20] At the minimum, such instructions would have amounted to a denial of the interpretation of section 31 that was promised the delegates the year before. Perhaps because he feared the repercussions with Taché, Macdonald did not send the memorandum or scolding that Howe recommended, but he did send a suitable instrument for achieving the same result. Macdonald found a man in Ottawa who would put the Order in Council of May 26 above the "fancied" land rights of "half breeds," and he would go to Winnipeg with the title of Dominion Lands Agent, knowing that the Lieutenant Governor had contrary views, agreeing to watch him on that account—and for the variety of other ways that "old Archibald's conduct and policy towards the Canadians" was likely to cause embarrassment at the next election.[21]

Macdonald's man was a former magistrate and policeman who knew nothing about land surveys or adjudicating land claims but a great deal

---

17. Ibid.
18. PAC, Joseph Howe Papers, MG 24, B 29, vol. 9, Howe to Archibald, 26 December 1871.
19. PAC, Macdonald Papers, Incoming Correspondence, pp. 46907-46909, Howe to Macdonald, 20 August 1871.
20. The preamble to the section stated that the intent was "For the quieting of titles, and assuring to the settlers in the Province the peaceable possession of lands now held by them...." For such a purpose to have had any practical effect, the claims of original settlers would have to be dealt with as the first determination of what was "vacant."
21. The political problem with Archibald is indicated by PAC, Macdonald Papers, Incoming Correspondence, pp. 157223-157230, J.Y. Bown to Macdonald, 3 September 1871; the view that Métis rights were unreal appears in pp. 110681-110686, McMicken to Macdonald, 22 December 1871.

about espionage, particularly spying on conspirators against the state, such
as Fenians. Indeed, that was the guise under which Macdonald introduced
the new Lands Agent to Archibald once the concern about Fenian raids
began to brew in Manitoba in the autumn of 1871. At the close of a long
letter to Archibald about the danger, Macdonald announced that
"McMicken will shortly be with you. . . . We are sorry to lose him here, in
fact I do not know what to do without him. You will find him of the
greatest use to you from his judgement & discretion, and the good faith
with which he will act."[22]

Gilbert McMicken's arrival in late September was timely, and he did
help Archibald through the crisis with O'Donoghue in the first week of
October. Then and later, however, McMicken was even more useful to
Macdonald with his constant flow of detailed correspondence reporting on
Archibald's activities.[23] At the same time, it was McMicken who faced the
awesome task of accommodating newcomers at the Dominion Lands Office
without seeming to repudiate the understanding that Cartier had with Taché
about where and how the 1.4 million acres were to be allotted.

From November 1871 until the spring of 1872, it was the impression
of Taché and Archibald that their major problem was getting Macdonald to
recognize that the time was right for conceding the amnesty and settling
land claims. Neither Taché nor Archibald seemed to realize that there was
more to both matters than the question of timing. On the eve of Archibald's
bidding bon voyage to the Métis cavalry, for example, Archibald wrote
Macdonald that the public peace depended upon speedy resolution of both
issues. He stated that the "resolution in council relative to their lands" of
May 1871, must have been inadvertent because it gave the impression that
"the promises relative to the lands . . . were not to be kept."[24] Archibald
said that was why he had been so conciliatory with his own promises and
had publicly thanked the Métis for their joining in the defence of the province.

Macdonald replied rather blandly that "their feelings, & prejudices
and rights are to be respected," but he was deeply concerned about the
unhappy aspects of the handshaking for the electoral prospects of the Tory
party in Ontario. There was not one word further on the land question.
Macdonald had passed the burden of giving the official critique of

---

22. Ibid., Letter Books, vol. 16, pp. 236-238, Macdonald to Archibald, 24 September 1871.

23. Typical of McMicken's spying assignments was Macdonald's demand at the end of
November for McMicken to "quietly collect all the information you can as to Riel's
connection with the [Fenian] rising & his sudden change [to aid Canada] on finding
that the raid had ended in a fiasco." Moreover, Archibald was not to know about the
investigation. "It is no affair of his" (ibid., vol. 16, pp. 522-523, Macdonald to
McMicken, 29 November 1871).

24. Ibid., Incoming Correspondence, pp. 77972-77976, Archibald to Macdonald, 7 October
1871. See also ibid, pp. 24960-24967, Archibald to Macdonald, 9 October 1871.

Archibald's land policy to Joseph Howe.[25]

Howe told his fellow Nova Scotian that he "very much regretted" the information that the Lieutenant Governor was "giving countenance to the wholesale appropriation of large tracts of country by the Half breeds." He said "all the lands not in actual occupation are open to everybody," and urged his compatriot to "leave the land Department and the Dominion Government to carry out their policy without volunteering any interference."[26]

Howe's scolding had such an authoritative tone that Archibald responded with a letter to Macdonald asking the Prime Minister if Howe was his official messenger.[27] Once again, Macdonald did not respond directly to the Governor. He spoke to Howe, and Howe sent another letter to Archibald saying he had met "several times" with Macdonald and other ministers who were concerned with the subject of Dominion lands. The message was that a "million and a half acres ... were to be surveyed and set apart by the Government, and until this was done the settlement of the country was not to be obstructed. Emmigrants and volunteers going into the country had a right to occupy and pre-empt vacant lands anywhere." The Government of Canada wished to avoid large concentrations of native people. "If any of these classes staked off and claimed *en bloc,* large tracts of land in favourable situations, in my judgement they violated the instructions and their claims cannot be sustained."[28]

One more time Archibald responded to Howe with a letter to Macdonald informing him that he was unhappy with Howe's position on the land question and wondered if Howe's opinions were official policy.[29] On the occasion of Archibald's last letter on the subject, Macdonald would neither confirm nor repudiate the Lieutenant Governor's position. Instead, he emphasized the need to delay any action on "half breed" matters until after the general election of 1872.[30] In the meantime, he refused to pursue the land issue as a matter of abstract principle. By January 1872, Macdonald knew that such a pursuit was beside the point. He knew that McMicken had already subverted Archibald's arrangements of the previous summer.

McMicken's first letter to the Prime Minister from Winnipeg was dated October 5, 1871 — in the midst of the Fenian crisis. His message was that he had talked to local people about the land question and readily

25. Ibid., Letter Books, vol. 16, pp. 537-42, Macdonald to Archibald, 30 November 1871.

26. PAC, Howe Papers, vol. 9, pp. 729-745, Howe to Archibald, 4 November 1871.

27. PAC, Macdonald Papers, Incoming Correspondence, pp. 78062-78065, Archibald to Macdonald, 2 December 1871.

28. PAC, Howe Papers, vol. 9, pp. 746-760, Howe to Archibald, 26 December 1871.

29. PAC, Macdonald Papers, Incoming Correspondence, pp. 78124-78130, Archibald to Macdonald, 19 January 1872.

30. Ibid., Letter Books, vol. 17, p. 301, Macdonald to Archibald, 4 March 1872.

persuaded them that their Dominion Lands Agent was a "good fellow and that all was being rightly and well done." No commitments were made; "it was all palaver and nothing else." Soothing words gave Ritchot the impression that "the selection of Lands may be as they wish and Riel and Lépine be subjects of an amnesty." Trouble was likely in the future, however, and there were not enough Canadian troops at Red River to deal with it effectively. Having sent the 400 British home in September 1870 and having reduced the remaining contingent of 800 Canadians to a mere corporal's guard of 80 in the spring of 1871, a minimum of 200 reinforcements was needed at once. According to McMicken, the occasion of the Fenian crisis was the "most desirable opportunity to augment the force here. Let them not come as opposed to the half breed, but to keep out the Fenians."[31]

Macdonald appeared to respond at once to McMicken's suggestion. In fact, the troops had been recruited already from among the veterans of the first expedition to keep the reinforcement of the army secret. As Macdonald had explained the ruse to one political friend, "strictly speaking there is no new Expedition going to Red River. The two companies that are now there are to be strengthened by two additional ones ... chosen from those who had served there before."[32] After the Fenian crisis, few people in Manitoba questioned the militia's return, and McMicken's continuing to play the role of "good fellow" at the Lands Office appeared to satisfy newcomers and old settlers alike. He reported in mid-November that there were no difficulties of any kind. He believed that "even the Half breed claims ... can all be acceptably and quietly arranged." McMicken believed that the more clever of their "class" had begun to see the wisdom of selling out and moving on, "the more interested amongst the French half breeds already begin to see that their true interests will be served other than in adhering rigorously to their first conception of what was their rights." The important point for the moment was getting the land allotted quickly so that it might be patented and pass to "actual settlers" without further delay.[33]

Even into the new year McMicken continued to write optimistically to Macdonald that he was "A No. 1 with the very Grit settlers" and, at the same time, he believed he had found the ideal way to deflect the "French half breeds" from their "fancied rights." The scheme that attracted him would "require explanations and consideration which can only be properly given through a personal interview." On that account, McMicken proposed a return to Ottawa in February 1872 for meetings with the relevant ministers, including Macdonald, of course.[34]

---

31. Ibid., Incoming Correspondence, pp. 24934-24941, McMicken to Macdonald, 5 October 1871.

32. Ibid., Letter Books, vol. 16, p. 342, Macdonald to J.J. Burrows, 17 August 1871.

33. Ibid., Incoming Correspondence, pp. 110657-110672, McMicken to Macdonald, 12 November 1871.

34. Ibid., pp. 110681-110686, McMicken to Macdonald, 22 December 1871.

Early in January, McMicken reported by coded telegram that he had completed a memorandum on the "half breed" land question. "Have prepared scheme for settling . . . claims." He asked Macdonald if he should solicit some local reaction to the proposal: "Would it answer to evoke expression upon it here?" Macdonald's immediate reply was negative. "I await your scheme by mail. Do not discuss it beforehand in Manitoba."[35]

Unfortunately, from Macdonald's point of view, secrecy was impossible, in part, because McMicken could not resist sharing his thoughts with the "loyal Métis"[36] and also because the French-Canadian clerk in the Land Office, A.A.C. Larivière, told everything he knew to Bishop Taché.[37] Consequently, the McMicken scheme that was treated so confidentially[38] in Ottawa was well known to Taché before the plan reached Macdonald's desk, and the Bishop did not hesitate to launch a campaign against the plan before McMicken's departure for Ottawa. He complained to Archibald, and he wrote a blistering letter of protest to Macdonald.[39]

What Taché preferred was the Archibald plan, the scheme that the Métis believed had already been implemented, at least partially. In Taché's view of Archibald's proceedings, bands of Métis, groups of about 150 people (roughly twenty-five families), had selected their townships (23,040 acres per block) in accordance with the custom of the country, choosing townships that straddled rivers and creeks that were tributaries of the Red and Assiniboine rivers — streams such as the Sale, the Rat, and the Roseau. The land was to be held en bloc; none could be sold to outsiders.[40] Questions of distribution and individual occupancy would be settled in the same way that such matters had been dealt with in the Red River Settlement over

---

35. Ibid., p. 110687, McMicken cypher telegram to Macdonald, 9 January 1872; p. 110688, Macdonald cypher telegram to McMicken, 11 January 1872.

36. The loyalists were probably James McKay and Pascal Breland, see ibid., pp. 110691-110694, McMicken to Macdonald, 13 January 1872.

37. The discovery that Larivière was a pipeline of information to Taché and the "Rielites" did not occur until 1873, see ibid, pp.114004-114009, Morris to Macdonald, 20 January 1873.

38. So secret was McMicken's memorandum that all copies appear to have been either destroyed or retained in files still closed by the relevant departments. No copy has been found in the Macdonald Papers or in the records of the Department of the Interior in the Public Archives of Canada. The copy used here was found by Dale and Lee Gibson in the Archives of Ontario, J.C. Aikins Papers, with a covering letter to Aikins from McMicken, 8 January 1872.

39. PAC, Macdonald Papers, Incoming Correspondence, p. 78135, Archibald cypher telegram to Macdonald, 24 January 1872; and ibid., pp. 41548-41551, Taché to Macdonald, 23 January 1872.

40. See, for example, the petition of 23 families (150 claimants) led by John Grant. They wanted Township 3, range 4 East on the Roseau River, submitted by Henry Clarke to Archibald, 7 August 1872 (PAC, Records of the Department of the Interior, RG 15, vol. 229, file 1937).

the last half-century (by staked claims and community consent).

So attractive was the idea of small groups of families finding their own reserves in townships that many heads of families in parishes such as St Norbert had already sold their old land, staked claims on the new, and petitioned Archibald for confirmation of their claims with Taché working as the go-between in the negotiations for the location of larger groups. Then all such preliminaries were overturned by the McMicken scheme. Only the overall appropriation of 1.4 million acres remained. To establish an individual entitlement close to 160 acres per head, Macdonald's man in Winnipeg proposed a new census, something to diminish the total number of recipients from the 10,000 cases evident in the 1870 enumeration (a figure that yielded an individual share of 140 acres per head) to a number closer to 8,750 (the magic total for making an individual entitlement one-quarter section). With that number, quarter sections of prairie could be drawn randomly from all 408 Manitoba townships. Since no one native to the country had ever settled on bald prairie before, there was every reason to think that nearly all of the "half breeds" would sell such grants at their earliest opportunity. To expedite sale

> let 'scrip' be issued to each for their respective shares — representing at the standard rate at which the public lands are held for sale. . . . Such scrip to be receivable . . . in payment for lands [in the sections randomly designated as "half breed" lands]. . . . Scrip shall be transferable.[41]

None of the land was to be held in trust.

Clearly, McMicken had the ideal formula for "unlocking" the territory for "actual settlers" without repudiating the letter of the law in section 31 of the Manitoba Act. Incredible though it may seem, McMicken actually believed that his plan was a "very fair way of meeting the difficulty." Moreover, he believed that the time had come for such "generosity," if only for the sake of political expediency. Elaborating the point for Macdonald's consideration, McMicken reported:

> The Metis are very uneasy at present. They are expressing themselves greatly dissatisfied with the Canadian Gov't — chiefly in regard to the Lands not being given to them and alleging that injustice has been done to Riel, that good faith has not been kept. . . .
> There has been something said about a number of them having intentions of moving up on the Saskatchewan and the plains of the NW.
> It is an undeniable fact that Riel is an object of the strongest regard with them and for him they would do almost anything especially if incited to it on grounds affecting their common interest or touching their feelings. The North West already contains elements of apprehension and with any considerable party of excited Metis with Riel at their head retelling the

---

41. Archives of Ontario, J.C. Aikins Papers, "Memorandum Re Dominion Lands, Manitoba," Gilbert McMicken, 5 January 1872.

story of their rising, etc., great difficulties . . . would be more than possible.[42]

McMicken had no idea that his concept of generosity would be denounced as a gross injustice by the self-appointed guardians of the best interests of the Métis, critics such as Bishop Taché, who wrote Macdonald at the end of January objecting in the boldest phrases imaginable. Taché told the Prime Minister that the McMicken scheme was "unjust to our people, impolitic to yourselves, and unfair to Governor Archibald" because it repudiated the notion that the Métis should make "selections and distributions of their lands in such a way as they please." The inevitable dissatisfaction was bound to be troublesome, and the immediate gratitude of the Orange party in Manitoba would not last. How long, Taché asked, "is this province to be governed especially with the view of pleasing a party which in fact it is impossible to please?"[43]

The challenge to Macdonald and McMicken was softening the scheme while keeping the essential feature of distribution by random selection from bald prairie. The result was a policy proclaimed by Order in Council on April 15, 1872, with all of the apparent emphasis upon settling the question quickly, authorizing the Lieutenant Governor to "make selections of townships in such number as is necessary to make up 1,400,000 acres. . . ." From Archibald and Taché's standpoint, the order had no more effect than sanctioning what had already been done. But since the order was silent on the distribution issue, the door was still open for the key aspect of the McMicken scheme. Taché, though, was satisfied; and that satisfaction pleased Archibald who was anxious to leave the province on a point of harmony. Consequently, Archibald congratulated Macdonald for the policy that "quieted all apprehensions" and asked to be relieved from his office at once. The Order in Council of mid-April 1872 was precisely the kind of break for which he had hoped.[44]

Having submitted his resignation earlier, Archibald packed his belongings in May and awaited permission to make his exit on a moment's notice. With "only one suit of clothes and a Bag of Paper Collars to fall back on," he made it clear to Macdonald that his continuation on the scene was a personal hardship of the first degree.[45] Macdonald, though, continued to dither in naming a replacement and put his captive Lieutenant Governor through several more crises arising from Macdonald's own indecision and delay. In addition to the tortuous ebb and flow of the amnesty promise, Archibald had to weather a renewal of conflict between newcomers and old settlers

---

42. PAC, Macdonald Papers, Incoming Correspondence, pp. 110691-110694, McMicken to Macdonald, 13 Jaunary 1872.

43. Ibid., pp. 41548-41551, Taché to Macdonald, 23 January 1872.

44. Ibid., pp. 78181-78183, Archibald to Macdonald, 8 May 1872.

45. Ibid.

for the same reason that strife had developed the first time in 1871: Canadians were settling on "half breed lands" and the Lands Office was confirming their occupancy. Evidently, the promise that the Lieutenant Governor had power to set aside townships was just another hollow affirmation. Trouble seemed imminent.

Even McMicken was frightened by the renewal of conflict in 1872. He reported to Macdonald early in July: "Half breeds are annoyed that their claims have not been adjusted and settled — the arrival of strangers here, some of whom settle upon what they consider their claims, exasperates them very much." Moreover, the resentment was "not confined to the French Half Breeds alone." As usual, however, the Métis were taking a more advanced position in protest, going so far as to force homesteaders off their land. McMicken's explanation to Métis petitioners at the land office was that nothing could be done until the new governor arrived: "his first duty would be distribution of the land." In the meantime, everyone should be calm. Privately, however, McMicken was frantic, fearing "great danger." The most frightening development he reported to Macdonald was the possibility of an alliance of the Métis and native English to promote their mutual interests against newcomers.[46]

McMicken's letters to Macdonald brought instant results. Within ten days of McMicken's alarm, Archibald had instructions to finish the designation of "half breed" townships so that the Lands Office might withdraw them from further entry by homesteaders. By the end of July, the task was finished.

"It was easy," Archibald reported on July 27, "in a general way to select a number of townships." Altogether, he reserved thirty-nine for the Métis and twenty-nine for the native English. That still left 340 Manitoba townships for newcomers. According to Archibald, "This quite satisfied Half breeds; and meets, I think, general approval. Everybody wishes question settled."[47]

The apparent settlement was barely a beginning, however, towards resolving the land issue in its larger complexity because there were two other aspects of the matter that the designation of sixty-eight townships did not approach, indeed, that it ignored. Eventually, that neglect rendered the designation process Archibald thought he had completed quite useless. One facet was the hay question, the other was recognizing the occupancy of land that had been taken up for settlement before the transfer. In his first reports, Archibald had called the right to hay lands extending an additional two

---

46. Ibid., pp. 110704-110707, McMicken to Macdonald, 12 July 1872; pp. 110723-110728, McMicken to Macdonald, 17 July 1872; and PAC, Records of the Department of the Interior, RG 15, vol. 228, file 940, McMicken to J.C. Aikins, 6 July 1872.

47. PAC, Records of the Department of the Interior, RG 15, vol. 228, file 1091, Archibald to Aikins, 27 July 1872; Archibald telegram to Aikins, 29 July 1872.

miles back from the river lots "only an easement" that might be commuted easily with compensation in land elsewhere.[48] But the settlers claimed that their hay privilege was an "exclusive right" and without it their use of the inner lot was nullified. The two strips were two together or nothing at all. The wooded river-front part gave them their shelter, fuel, and patches for gardens (sometimes as extensive as thirty or more acres), while the marshy back part gave them the winter fodder they needed for their livestock. Denial of the right to one amounted to a denial of the right to the other. That, however, is exactly what occurred when Archibald designated the hay lands part of the "half breed reserve" and when Gilbert McMicken gave the land to homesteaders.

Once Alexander Morris became the acting Lieutenant Governor (in his role of "Administrator" in the autumn of 1872), he was fairly stupefied by the mess that had developed from the open land policy for newcomers and the closed claim process for old settlers. In the context of Riel's quest for the premiership in November, Morris found the policy of calculated delay to be particularly unfortunate. On November 16 he telegraphed Macdonald for permission to give at least the appearance of comprehensive action:

> Authorize me at once to announce that plan of allotment of half breed lands has been adopted and allotment will be made forthwith, & that hay privilege will be settled this winter under statute, and on completion of survey the 32nd section of the Act will be carried out. Need this to meet attempt of Riel. Agreed on at secret meeting to combine both races of half breeds. Have warned Royal that if Riel persists, warrant will inevitably be issued by some magistrate, & that then civil force must be employed to effect arrest. Reply at once. If Riel persists in being a candidate what do you advise?[49]

Macdonald resisted the appeal for hasty action on the land question merely to head off Riel's rising popularity. He did not reply with an immediate authorization along the lines Morris demanded. Macdonald's position apparently had not changed from what he had written to Morris a month before when he indicated that the preferred way to deal with Riel's candidacy was to arrest him or to ignore the election because Orangemen could be relied on to "dispose" of the Métis leader should he make an appearance at the local legislature. In Macdonald's words: "If Riel is such a fool as to poke his nose into that mess he must abide the consequences on his person. I have little doubt that the mob will soon dispose of him."[50]

Morris persisted. He followed his telegram to Macdonald with a letter

48. Ibid., file 796, Archibald to Howe, 27 December 1870.

49. PAC, Macdonald Papers, Incoming Correspondence, p. 113901, Morris cypher telegram to Macdonald, 16 November 1872.

50. Ibid., Letter Books, vol. 18, pp. 702-703, Macdonald to Morris, 14 October 1872. The arrest advice had been offered several days before. See pp. 681-682, Macdonald to Morris, 11 October 1872.

on the same subject to the minister responsible for lands.[51] After a prolonged period of inaction by Ottawa, and after the attempt to arrest Riel
sent the shadow premier back into hiding, Macdonald did take one small
step towards conceding the assurances Morris had sought in mid-
November. Late in December, he authorized the Lieutenant Governor to
begin making allotments from the townships designated by Archibald. The
process he contemplated was a drawing of 10,000 tickets, each with the
legal description of a parcel of land, and at the time of the drawing, entering the name of a particular "half breed" (as indicated by the 1870 census)
in a register. On this basis, it was theoretically possible that all 10,000
"location tickets" could be drawn and become available to applicants for
patent as early as the spring of 1873.

To get the maximum political effect from the apparent move towards
resolution of at least one aspect of the land question, Macdonald announced
the decision to Taché on Christmas eve, but in general terms (avoiding any
reference to the random rather than self-selection process of distribution).[52]
The two other thorny facets of the land question remained, and no one in
Manitoba was prepared to see either the "hay privilege" or the river-lot
claims delayed much longer. Meetings occurred in nearly every parish
early in January 1873. All demanded that the multifaceted land issue had to
be settled before immigration could resume in the spring. Even the Winnipeg press, usually the voice of the Ontario party, united in support of the
old settlers' demands — at least to the extent of admitting that the claimants
had a legal right to such claims; the newspapers asserted that the sooner all
land promises were resolved the sooner the whole province would be open
for cultivation and would contribute to the more rapid development of the
North West.[53]

The newfound support of the Ontario party for comprehensive resolution of Manitoba land matters was in fact little more than thinly disguised
sympathy for some of the more enterprising Winnipeggers who were gam-
bling in claims of all kinds, but especially in allotments of the 1.4 million
acres. By 1873 it had become fairly common knowledge that the "half
breed heads of families" were not going to get the kind of reserves that
they had expected in 1870 or as laid out on the rivers in 1871-72. Those
lands would have to be claimed under the occupancy clauses in section 32
of the Manitoba Act, or perhaps as homesteads in accordance with what
was contained in the codification of the Orders in Council on the subject
enacted in 1872 as the Dominion Lands Act.[54] All was not lost. But what

51. PAC, Records of the Department of the Interior, RG 15, vol. 229, file 1721, Morris to
    Secretary of State for the Provinces, 20 November 1872.

52. PAC, Macdonald Papers, Letter Books, vol. 19, pp. 427-429, Macdonald to Taché, 24
    December 1872.

53. *Manitoba Free Press*, 11 January 1873.

54. For the Department of the Interior's view that the Dominion Lands Act, Statutes of
    Canada (1872), Chapter 23 was nothing more than a codification of the land provisions
    of the Manitoba Act and the Orders in Council of 1 March, 25 April, and 26 May 1871,
    see PAC, Macdonald Papers, Incoming Correspondence, pp. 45076-45087,

was expected from the 1.4 million acres was likely to be section land stripped of river-frontage and distributed by lottery. Consequently, hundreds of "half breed heads of families" responded positively to offers to buy such shares, frequently taking as little as $25 for an assignment of rights to a claim.[55]

Taché fought both developments. On the one hand, he continued to insist that the townships that had been chosen through his mediation "were selected merely and solely to secure the wood and the land along the rivers."[56] Thus, he protested withdrawal of the woodlands and river-frontage from the townships to be divided into allotments just as he vigorously opposed the method of distribution by lottery. Once it became evident that he had lost both of those battles, he set up a next line of defence on the issue of trusteeship.

Early in February 1873 Morris telegraphed Macdonald that a bill was in preparation to forbid heads of families from selling their allotments of the 1.4 million acres. "Pretension is that only actual children have rights, therefore, heads are trustees." Morris doubted that a province had the power to enact a law of special application affecting land reserved in recognition of Indian title. The question was not academic and the problem was urgent. "Reply," he demanded.[57] Macdonald referred the matter to his former law partner, Alexander Campbell, still the Postmaster General. Campbell concurred with Morris, saying such a law would violate section 91(24) of the British North America Act. As he put it, "No law dealing exceptionally with the rights of the half breed heads of families and preventing them from making conveyances which any of Her Majesty's subjects can make, would be constitutional."[58]

In the end, Morris had a different measure for the Governor General to veto because the movement to have the lands of the "half breed" heads of families "entailed" was resisted by the very people who were the intended beneficiaries of the action. In fact, it was a "deputation from St Norbert" that led the opposition to the trusteeship proposal and killed the measure in mid-February.[59] What followed was a "land grant protection act" that was a sale-cancellation scheme enabling vendors to repudiate any and all such sales but leaving purchasers with the power to "recover the price which is

"Memorandum on Regulations for Disposal of Agricultural Lands in the West," A.M. Burgess to Macdonald, 7 March 1882.

55. Ibid.

56. PAC, Records of the Department of the Interior, RG 15, vol. 229, file 1992, Taché to Morris, 14 January; and PAC, Macdonald Papers, Incoming Correspondence, pp. 113996-113997, Cypher Morris telegram to Macdonald, 15 January 1873.

57. Ibid., pp. 114035-114036, Morris telegram to Macdonald, 10 February 1873.

58. Ibid., p. 114041, Campbell telegram to Morris, 12 February 1873.

59. Ibid., pp. 114054-114059, Morris to Macdonald, 14 February 1873.

made a lien on the land when allotted.'' Though not as burdensome as an outright prohibition on sales, Morris still thought that the measure ''sins against sound principle'' and recommended disallowance. On that account, he withheld assent pending more detailed consideration by officials in Ottawa.[60]

In the meantime, Taché's suggestion that the intent of section 31 was to convey a land base to the children through their parents sent legal advisors back to the previous Orders in Council and the Manitoba Act. They concluded in March, to Taché's great relief, that the parents were indeed outside the class of persons to receive shares of the 1.4 million acres, and a new Order in Council was proclaimed on April 3 excluding the heads of families from allotments. Since the number of persons entitled to share was instantly reduced by about 4,000 cases, the whole allotment process undertaken to date was rendered obsolete and inoperable.

At almost the same time, the location of the townships from which allotments were supposed to be drawn was made equally meaningless by a confidential, quasi-judicial opinion that the only equitable resolution of the hay question was concession of the outer two miles, since the recognized tenure of the inner lot would be robbed of all its benefit by the loss of the outer half of the estate.[61]

By the end of March 1873, it had become clear that the entire question of land claims under the Manitoba Act was in total chaos. Three years had passed. Not one promised patent to a river lot had emerged. Not one of the 1.4 million acres was allotted. Most important, the little that had been accomplished to date suddenly had to be redone. To put the best possible face on the chaotic situation, the inner two miles of the Old Settlement Belt was closed to further sale or homestead on March 21,[62] and at the end of May a Dominion statute laid out procedures for adjudicating claims to river lots as soon as the government saw fit to hear them.[63] But the personnel on the inside, Lieutenant Governor Morris, for instance, knew that the ''multi-form'' land question had become loaded with nearly insoluble difficulties.

Yet another spring passed into summer, and one more time the native population set out to cut their hay in July. For the third year in succession, a frantic Lieutenant Governor telegraphed for help: ''Cutting

---

60. Ibid., pp. 114092-114095, Morris to Macdonald, 5 March 1873.

61. Morris had been authorized to appoint a commission of inquiry into the hay privilege by Order in Council of Canada, 13 January 1873. The confidential report of Judges Betournay and McKeagney, assisted by the Surveyor General, J.S. Dennis, was submitted to Morris in March and appears in the Morris Papers, Provincial Archives of Manitoba.

62. The closure date of 21 March 1873 is cited in Order in Council of Canada, 20 April 1876, section 4.

63. Statutes of Canada (1873), Chapter 6: An Act respecting claims to Lands in Manitoba for which no Patents have been issued.

commences ... what course do you advise? Collisions between the conflicting interests are threatened."[64] One more time the response from Ottawa was that the Métis and the native English had to give way to the newcomers. Only the terminology varied. In the messages of 1873, the "old settlers" became "former occupants."[65] In yet another dimension, inaction appeared to be inviting disaster.

Was delay a deliberate strategy of discouragement? It is possible that, since the government had so many other important matters under consideration, the Cabinet, by innocent inattention, found it easy to let questions of native land claims drift.[66] But there were so many occasions when Archibald or Morris had outlined a clear approach to the complex problem, only to have their suggestions rejected by Sir John A. Macdonald, that it seems more likely that delay was intentional. The stated policy between 1870 and 1873 was to "unlock" the territory for newcomers and that objective had come close to fulfillment. In the spring of 1873 Macdonald informed the Lieutenant Governor that future conflicts between "actual settlers" and "former occupants" ought to be handled by local militia. He encouraged Morris to "stir up the people to form volunteers or active militia corps . . . to protect themselves," and intimated that the army of occupation was to be removed in May 1874.[67] If the overriding goal of the preceding several years had been to govern the "unruly" Métis with a strong hand until they were swamped by the influx of new settlers, that was within sight of achievement and a matter of some consolation to Macdonald even if Louis Riel had not yet "stood his trial." Yet there is little evidence that Macdonald gave Métis matters any consideration one way or another in the last months of 1873. In the autumn he faced a more disturbing problem over other indiscretions, a crisis that forced the resignation of his ministry on November 5, 1873.

---

64. PAM, Morris Papers (LG Collection), Morris telegram to Alexander Campbell, 18 July 1873.

65. Ibid., Campbell telegram to Morris, 22 July 1873; and letter, Campbell to Morris, 31 July 1873.

66. Incapacity is the official interpretation, the one that appeared in the annual reports of the Department of the Interior after it was created in 1873. That interpretation, with some evidence of incompetence, reappeared in the work of professional historians in the 1950s following Douglas Kemp's assertion that the "need to do many things quickly and, what is more, to do them simultaneously, despite conflict and confusion, would account for many of the problems which faced the administrators." There is no suggestion of deliberate delay in Kemp's work, "Land Grants under the Manitoba Act," Historical and Scientific Society of Manitoba, *Transactions,* series 3, No. 9 (1952-53), pp. 33-52.

67. PAC, Macdonald Papers, Letter Books, vol. 20, p. 157, Macdonald to Morris, 19 May 1873.

Archbishop Taché, ca. 1870
(Provincial Archives of Manitoba)

"Taché suggested that if they did amend the Manitoba Act somebody would probably launch a legal action contesting the constitutionality of the legislation."

Chapter 7

Amending the Manitoba Act

Sir John A. Macdonald's embarrassment over public disclosures that he appeared to have traded the presidency of the Canadian Pacific Railway for campaign contributions in the elections of 1872 and the subsequent resignation of his government late in 1873 were the prelude to an important test of the former Prime Minister's political substance for at least two reasons. The first was his acquiring the luxury of being the opposition. He was free to attack anything, everything, with all the rhetorical cunning and biting wit he had learned over the previous thirty years of his political career. Secondly, and more importantly, since Macdonald was an aging politician, in thorough disgrace, with no hope of recapturing his former power (and determined to retire from the Conservative leadership as soon as possible), he was more free to show his true political colours.

Concerning the Métis, it has already been shown that Macdonald vehemently opposed Mackenzie's amnesty for Riel when that was conceded (conditional on five more years of exile starting in 1875). Macdonald's position was that murder was a capital crime; Riel was a murderer; he ought to hang. Consequently, notwithstanding the widespread support for unconditional clemency in Quebec, and despite the importance of Quebec's sixty-five seats to the Conservatives' strength in Parliament, Macdonald struck a high profile of opposition to Mackenzie's conditional amnesty, and urged the editor of the Toronto *Mail* to stir up reaction in Ontario. "The changes should be rung on the names of the Ontario men who voted for the resolutions," he wrote T.C. Patteson on February 16.[1]

> They amount to an absolute pardon. Riel and Lepine are French. The US is the haven of Hope for all French Canadians. The people of Quebec won't stay at home, but flock in crowds to the US and the Quebec Gov't proposes bonuses to get them back in vain — and this is the punishment for murder! The Gentlemen as Martyrs will be amply supplied with funds and live like fighting cocks for 5 years. Meanwhile they will infest the frontier — keep up the discontent in Manitoba and have petitions annually before parliament

---

1. PAC, Macdonald Papers, Transcripts, vol. 584, Macdonald to T.C. Patteson, 16 February 1875.

praying for pardon. In fact there is no end of the Nuisance. . . . Burn this.

Three days later, Patteson printed Macdonald's words as his own, repeating all the key phrases with only minor rhetorical embellishment:

> Edward Blake and his fifty seven associates from Ontario voted the equivalent of an absolute pardon to the murderers of Thomas Scott. They voted that two more French Canadians should go across the line into the haven of hope, whereas the Quebec Government is offering large bonuses to get back the truant population of *Bas Canada*. Fifty-eight Upper Canadians thought it enough to send Riel and Lepine to live in clover among the old friends of their childhood, amply supplied with funds, and revelling . . . in one five years spree! They will infest the frontier, keep alive discontent in Manitoba, have petitions placed yearly before Parliament praying for pardon, and be and remain a nuisance, the mainspring of social, political, and religious agitation. But they will all the while be paying the Parliamentary penalty for *murder*, a murder of which the cruelty, the highest authorities assure us, can claim no indulgent mitigation whatever from the complexion of contemporaneous events.[2]

Macdonald's incitement of Patteson for rekindling anti-Riel sentiment to embarrass the new government in Ontario may have indicated more of the former Prime Minister's political cleverness than his true sentiments, but the absence of any evidence of simultaneous exploitation of the issue in Quebec suggests not. Macdonald used Patteson to "inflame sectional jealousy" in Ontario; he did not instruct Quebec editors to denounce Mackenzie for stopping short of unconditional amnesty and "inflame the worst passions" of the people there.[3] Moreover, Macdonald had done nothing to exploit the Liberals' significant transformations of the Manitoba Act before — or after — the amnesty controversy of 1875.

Mackenzie's initial amendment had appeared in the first session of the new Parliament in the spring of 1874. A bill introduced in the Senate on May 13 (and brought into the House of Commons three days later) acknowledged that section 31 set aside land "towards the extinguishment of Indian Title" of families of part aboriginal ancestry by reserving 1.4 million acres for the children, and observed there was "no provision . . . for extinguishing the Indian title to such lands as respects the half-breed heads of families." The proposed remedy was to grant each parent "one hundred

---

2. Toronto *Mail,* 19 February 1875. The next day, Patteson repeated the substance of the same editorial, adding a special note of sarcasm about Riel's comfort in his escape from punishment: "For once across the border and his place of residence known, . . . his French Canadian friends will see that he lives in a luxury commensurate with the extra halo of heroism which his banishment will in their eyes throw around him."

3. Ironically, in ringing the changes on the names of the Ontario men who supported the resolutions, Patteson suggested they were the group who excited "sectional jealousy" and "inflamed passions" on the Riel question originally. For his part, Patteson asserted: "We have been at pains . . . to avoid the saying of a word that was likely to inflame sectional jealousy, religious animosity, or rouse a spirit of vindictive retaliation." Toronto *Mail,* 19 February 1875.

and sixty acres of land or . . . scrip . . . to be receivable in payment for the purchase of Dominion Lands.''[4]

A critical observer of the proceedings might have wondered how the Liberals had become such sudden converts to the recognition of the aboriginal title of ''half breeds'' and might have asked them if they were taking a first step towards establishing ''scrip,'' a form of personal property, as a legal equivalent to real property, meaning land. A watchful guardian of the Manitoba Act would have asked if the commutation in scrip that was being proposed for the parents was contemplated for the children as well.

The same defender of native rights might have raised an equally embarrassing question concerning the proposed changes to section 32. The part of Bill 51 amending rights to the river lots declared that the old clause giving the Métis, the native English, and other original settlers pre-emptive right to land beyond the Old Settlement Belt was ''hereby repealed'' and substituted new language that implied a right to consideration, but no guarantee of recognition. An interested critic of the change might have attacked the proposed amendment on at least two levels. First, one might have observed that the new language amounted to a denial of rights because the onus of proof was shifted from the government to the claimants. Then a defender of the Manitoba Act could have taken up a second line of criticism with the argument that the statute in question was not within the power of Canada to alter since the the original act had been confirmed by the Parliament of Great Britain in 1871.

Macdonald, the parliamentary champion of the Manitoba Act in 1870, was not prepared to defend his creation in 1874, or later. He did not object to any provision of Bill 51, nor did any other member of the official Opposition. In fact, the matter went back to the Senate after having passed all three readings in the House, virtually without debate. But before the bill came up for consideration by the Upper Chamber, someone had apparently spoken with the amendment's senatorial sponsor, R.W. Scott (Secretary of State in the Mackenzie ministry), about the possible constitutional difficulties that might arise from declaring one of the clauses of the Manitoba Act ''hereby repealed.'' The result was that Scott proposed somewhat altered language to reach his original intended objective. Instead of declaring that subsection 4 of section 32 was repealed, the revised text appeared merely to provide some procedures for administering the rights in subsections 3 and 4:

> Whereas it is expedient to afford facilities to parties claiming lands under
> the third and fourth subsections of the thirty-second section of the Act
> thirty-third Victoria, chapter three, to obtain letters patent for the same, —

---

4. Statutes of Canada (1874), Chapter 20: An Act respecting the appropriation of certain Dominion Lands in Manitoba, preamble.

> Be it enacted that persons satisfactorily establishing undisturbed occupancy of any lands within the Province prior to, and being by themselves or their servants, tenants or agents, or those through whom they claim, in actual and peaceable possession thereof on the eighth day of March, One thousand eight hundred and sixty-nine, shall be entitled to receive letters patent therefor, granting the same absolutely to them respectively in fee simple.[5]

The original purpose of the amendment was achieved in the sense that the earlier pre-emptive right was reduced to an opportunity to prove a satisfactory level of improvements, while appearing to maintain the fiction that the fuller, unqualified right was undisturbed.[6] After the change, the bill went back to the House. Once again, the matter passed without objection, and the revision of the land-promise provisions of the Manitoba Act received royal assent on May 26, 1874.

The Conservatives' acquiescence in the first set of changes invited other, bolder adjustments to the offending land promises to "half breeds." The Liberals were especially anxious to eliminate the "tremendous obstacle to the speedy settlement of the region" that they found in section 31 of the Manitoba Act, the "curse" of the reservation of the 1.4 million acres for the children.[7] With a view towards making the distribution as soon as possible, officials devised a scheme for making allotments immediately among the children enrolled in the 1870 census with lists of allottees to be published in every parish. It was expected that "this plan would at once give the rights of the Métis a marketable value, . . . a feeling of ownership in the land" even though no Métis child would be eligible to claim a patent or make use of the soil until reaching eighteen years of age.[8] A

---

5. Ibid., section 3.

6. The text of subsection 4 promised: "All persons in peaceable possession of tracts of land at the time of the transfer to Canada, in those parts of the Province where the Indian Title has not been extinguished, shall have the right of pre-emption of the same, on such terms and conditions as may be determined by the Governor in Council." Ritchot was promised an Order in Council confirming the "most liberal interpretation" of the clause, and the promise did appear to be fulfilled by an Order in Council of 11 November 1872 providing a "free grant" to any claimant outside the Old Settlement Belt (squatters within the two-mile limit of the rivers were already protected by the occupancy provision of subsection 3 of section 32 given the meaning of the clause in relation to the homestead policy of the Council of Assiniboia since 27 February 1860).
   An important legal point is that section 33 provided that the Orders in Council giving final shape to the incomplete rights defined in sections 31 and 32 were to have "the same force and effect as if . . . a part of this Act." Consequently, the issue of alteration of 32(4) by SC (1874), cap 20 would appear to be not simply how the amendment compared with 32(4), but how 32(4) in conjunction with OC 11 November 1872 was affected by the alteration of terms.

7. PAC, Alexander Mackenzie Papers, MG 26 B, General Correspondence, pp. 599-605, E.B. Wood to Mackenzie, 3 July 1874; and pp. 801-808, Wood to Mackenzie, 25 May 1875.

8. PAM, Morris Papers, Ketcheson Collection, Alexander Morris to David Laird, 11 February 1874.

complicating historical reality was that at least six per cent of the original population had left the province already. If the land allotted to absentees were never patented, it would be argued that a full 1.4 million acres had not been divided among the children as the act required. Consequently, the same bill provided for a distribution of scrip covering the residual amount of land.

In late March 1875, the *Manitoba Free Press* received a garbled version of the proposed bill and announced all problems were solved. The paper indicated that the sixty-eight townships making up the 1.4 million acres were to be thrown open for immediate settlement and the children, like their parents, would receive scrip instead of land. The paper praised the government for correcting a gross injustice. "We do not think that it can be reasonably asked on behalf of the minor participants that the whole country should be kept back, until they are of age. Another advantage of the scrip system is that it will speedily put the lands of those who are not disposed to utilize them into the hands of those who will."[9]

Subsequent developments showed that the Liberals' long-range intention was indeed to commute all "half breed claims" with scrip, but the proposal of the moment was certainly less grandiose than what the *Free Press* reported. The wording on the scrip provision was to cover only "an amount equal to the sum total of the acreage of allotments the right of which may fail to be proved" (to be distributed among the persons whose claims were confirmed in order to bring the total up to 1.4 million acres). Another section of the bill offered a refinement of the meaning of the word "children" in section 31, but the overall package fell far short of what was hoped for by Manitoba's Ontario party.

Still, Macdonald and his fellow Conservatives did support the measure when the Minister of the Interior, David Laird, moved second reading of the new "Bill to amend" the Manitoba Act on March 27. Unfortunately, the maverick leader-in-waiting of the Liberals, Edward Blake, saw an opportunity to impress the House with his knowledge of constitutional detail while reinforcing Macdonald's disgrace by reminding Parliament that the former Prime Minister had stuck them with a statute they could not alter. Blake observed that the "Bill was to amend the Act creating a constitution for Manitoba." Citing section 6 of the BNA Act (1871) he asserted that such a step would be "beyond the powers of this House."[10]

Macdonald responded with lame agreement that the Parliament of Canada could not alter the provisions of the Manitoba Act, but the former Prime Minister "fancied" that the substitution of scrip for land was "quite consistent" with the original act; therefore, he saw no reason to obstruct the

9. *Manitoba Free Press*, 23 March 1875.

10. House of Commons Debates, 27 March 1875, pp. 931-932.

measure's passage through second reading. As for the redefinition of children, Mackenzie agreed to look into the matter in more detail over the next several days. On that reflection, he and his legal advisors decided it was better to abandon legislative action — to Laird's disgust, who wrote Morris a few days later complaining that the "bill was dropped, as it was supposed in some way to amend the Manitoba Act." Laird stated that he thought Blake had raised a "false objection" because, in Laird's view, the Manitoba Act "has been amended already two or three times almost as far as I proposed."[11]

The amendments to which Laird referred had arisen from the Liberals' continuing refusal to recognize pre-emptive rights in the original statute. Macdonald's way of coping with the same difficulty had been to delay consideration of claims to river lots while opening "vacant lands" to new settlers despite reports from one official in charge of the surveys that "the complaint of encroachment by newcomers is universal."[12] It was not until May 1873 that an apparatus for receiving claims had been established even in principle, and the actual opening of the application process was delayed for another season of immigration put off until mid-September 1873.[13] Then, when applications came forward without proof of title from the Hudson's Bay Company, and without any acknowledgement of occupancy in the field reports of the Dominion land surveyors, officials in Winnipeg asked for authority to refuse to consider such "weak" claims.

Two civil servants who pursued the issue like terriers after a rat were McMicken's successor as Agent of Dominion Lands, Donald Codd, and the new Inspector of Surveys, A.H. Whitcher. Both reported to the Surveyor General, John Stoughton Dennis, the same J.S. Dennis who had tried to rally the counter-insurgents against the Métis in December 1869. As if to make the world even smaller than that coincidence implied, Donald Codd had been on the scene at the same time serving as a draughtsman and aide-de-camp to Dennis until he too was forced to flee Red River on foot to Minnesota.[14] Later, from 1870 to 1873, Codd worked as a clerk in the Dominion Lands Branch when it was part of the Department of Secretary of State. Then, with the creation of the Department of the Interior in 1873, and after the decision to begin to entertain claims to river lots in the autumn of the

---

11. PAM, Morris Papers, Ketcheson Collection, Laird to Morris, 27 April 1875.

12. PAC, Records of the Department of the Interior, RG 15, vol. 227, file 155, Lindsay Russell, Assistant Surveyor General, to J.S. Dennis, Surveyor General, 21 September 1871.

13. For claim adjudication see Statutes of Canada (1873), Chapter 6: An Act respecting claims to Lands in Manitoba for which no Patents have been issued. A sample notice of intent to receive claims, dated 10 September 1873, appears in *Manitoba Free Press*, 3 January 1874.

14. Donald Codd, "Some Reminiscenses of Fort Garry in 1869-70," *Great West Magazine* 13 (1899), pp. 294-299.

same year, it was Dennis who nominated Codd for the vacancy at the Lands Office in Winnipeg, notwithstanding Taché's objections that Codd despised the Métis as much as he was ignorant of the French language.[15]

The persistence of Dennis in the position of overall authority and the emergence of Codd in the important role of first-level consideration of claims[16] may have illustrated nothing more than the cronyism that characterized so much of the public service in the nineteenth century. But the placement of Codd may have been an indication of a desire for revenge[17] inasmuch as Dennis had found officials who could be trusted to exploit the surveyors' field reports for maximum discouragement of "half breed" claims.

It is clear that some of the surveyors were prejudiced,[18] and may have intentionally misrepresented the actual pattern of occupancy. For others, the haste to finish the settlement surveys as quickly as possible prompted them to be less than conscientious about their instructions to "search and note all farm lines, . . . note all fences, the several buildings and reputed owners."[19] The oversight appears to have caused little inconvenience for newcomers to the province. Codd and Whitcher investigated their requests for another look at the land with prompt courtesy.[20] It was the overlooked Métis and native English that Codd and Whitcher suggested were "not entitled to any consideration at all."[21] Immediately after the change of government late in 1873 they recommended referral of sample cases to the Department of Justice, urging that "the sooner they are stopped the better,

---

15. PAC, Macdonald Papers, Incoming Correspondence, pp. 96892-96895, H.L. Langevin to Macdonald, 5 October 1873.

16. The role of the Agent of Dominion Lands is set forth in a memorandum of J.S. Dennis to the Minister of the Interior, 5 September 1873. Later, the same set of procedures was reiterated, and reapproved "for the information of the Minister of Justice" in 1876. Both memoranda are in PAC, Records of the Department of the Interior, RG 15, vol. 164, MA file 7390.

17. Taché and Royal believed such was the case. See PAC, Macdonald Papers, Incoming Correspondence, p. 8884, J. Royal to Macdonald, 2 November 1880.

18. William Pearce, for example, considered the Dominion Government "prodigal in dealing with these claims." In Pearce's opinion, "The grants did not do the half breeds any good. As a class they would have been better had they received neither land nor scrip, it only demoralized them." See his manuscript, "Lands Obtained Under the Manitoba Act in Manitoba, and Surveys Incidental to the Granting of Titles Thereto" (15 December 1913). Archives of the University of Alberta, Pearce Papers, MG 9/2, series 6, vol. 4, file 9.

19. Letter of instruction from J.S. Dennis to George McPhillips, 10 June 1871, in Survey Field Book #562, Provincial Archives of Manitoba.

20. See Table 1 and supporting documentation in P.R.J. Mailhot and D.N. Sprague, "Persistent Settlers: The Dispersal and Re-Settlement of the Red River Métis, 1870-1885," *Canadian Journal of Ethnic Studies* 17 (1985), pp. 1-30.

21. Department of Justice, Central Registry Files, file 13/1873, Codd to J.S. Dennis, 19 November 1873.

or they will pour in from every direction.''[22]

Over the winter of 1873-74 officials in the Justice Department did consider the matter, apparently deciding that the claims Codd and Whitcher wanted disallowed would have to be entertained, unless the words of section 32 of the Manitoba Act were altered. Such was the background to the repeal of subsection 4 in May 1874, the amendment that required claimants to establish occupancy that was first satisfactory to Codd and Whitcher, before referring the matter for action in Ottawa.

Unfortunately for the officers in the Dominion Lands Office at Winnipeg, many of the 800 vulnerable families were reluctant to take refusal of their cases quietly. On the chance that some might take their claims to the judicial body created for such matters by Canadian statute in 1873, the act was amended in 1875 to remove disputes against Canada from the jurisdiction of the ''court of claims,'' leaving that body to adjudicate nothing more than the conflicts between settlers (newcomers versus old settlers, most typically). At the same time, another of the amendments Laird had in mind in his protest letter to Morris changed the date on which occupancy had to be sworn from March 9 to July 15, a time of year when the largest number of Métis and native English were likely to have been out of the province at work in the production of pemmican or freighting supplies for the HBC.[23]

Macdonald supported both measures. No one in his party observed that the conflicting claims bill amounted to the denial of due process to persons whose land rights had already been reduced merely to consideration by the Department of the Interior. Nor did anyone on his side of the House object to the second measure by quoting H.Y. Hind's observation that ''about the 15th of June they [the Métis] start for their summer hunt of the buffalo''[24] as Hind had been quoted in the House of Commons before (in 1867 and 1869) to excite enthusiasm for annexation of Rupert's Land.[25] In 1875 no one seemed interested in the obvious implication that the routine of the hunt meant absence from occupation at the time required under the new act. Later, with the same acquiescence, Macdonald's Conservatives did not object to the provisions of the defunct Bill 110 when they reappeared as an appendage to an Order in Council dated April 26, 1875.

Bill 110 as an Order in Council began reasonably enough; it provided nothing more than a set of regulations for distributing the 1.4 million acres

---

22. Ibid., A.H. Whitcher to J.S. Dennis, 19 November 1873.

23. The date-change appeared in Statutes of Canada (1875), Chapter 52: An act to amend 'An Act respecting the appropriation of certain Lands in Manitoba'; the amendments to the court of claims legislation were in Statutes of Canada (1875), Chapter 53: An Act respecting Conflicting Claims to Lands of Occupants in Manitoba.

24. Hind, *Narrative*, I, p. 179.

25. See, for example, the speeches of Alexander Morris, collected and reprinted in 1884 as *Nova Britannia*.

to the children and scrip for their parents. Lists were to be posted in every church announcing "the names from the census" and inviting all such persons to appear before special commissioners sitting in each locality at various times over the summer of 1875. At each sitting, sworn affidavits were to be collected for establishing each claimant's right to an allotment of land (for the children) or an issue of scrip (for heads of families). The amending part of the Order in Council came at the end. There were the abandoned clauses of Bill 110 refining the definition of children, excluding, for example, any child resident at the time of the transfer if his or her parents were absent from the province on July 15, 1870. A searching critic of the government would have seized upon such provisions the moment they appeared in the *Canada Gazette* in May 1875 and asked the government (while Parliament was still in session) whether it was Liberal Party policy to pursue by Order in Council that which they thought was illegal by statute of Parliament. No one asked.

Nor did the Opposition oppose yet another erosion of the land-promise provisions of the Manitoba Act in 1876 when the government proclaimed a more precise definition of what was meant by "satisfactory occupancy" in claims to land under section 32 and its amendments. Here as well, the amending instrument was an Order in Council, not an Act of Parliament, despite the sweeping nature of the policy and its conflict with the Manitoba Act. The document distinguished three categories of claims to river-frontage: one was land occupied "in accordance with the custom of the country" before January 15, 1870; a second was unimproved land "alleged to have been taken up" before the transfer; and the last was land "resided upon and cultivated continuously . . . as homesteads under the Order in Council of 26 May, 1871." Under the new regulations, claims arising from categories one and three were admissable, those in class two were "not entitled to consideration."

The difficulty created for potential claimants was that many families who ought to have been included in class one automatically fell into the second category because the document incorrectly asserted that the customary method of taking up land before the transfer was "to employ one of the two surveyors in the colony to survey and lay out the land." In fact, such proceedings were rare and exceptional occurrences. The normal practice of intending occupants was simply to plant stakes at the corners of a chosen area; if no one objected, no survey was needed. In the event of a dispute one of the two surveyors was called in. If he found that the property was no more than twelve chains wide and did not encroach on the land of any prior, neighbouring occupants, no objection could be sustained.[26] In

---

26. Minutes of the Council of Assiniboia, 27 February 1860, quoted in Department of the Interior Memorandum, 19 April 1876 (PAC, Records of the Department of the Interior, RG 15, vol. 235, file 5537).

effect, the new Order in Council barred all claims where occupancy was unrecorded by the Hudson's Bay Company or overlooked by Dominion surveyors after 1870, and took the entire history of the region back to October 1869 in the sense that hundreds of Métis claimants became suddenly uncertain that their hold on the land was secure. The order of April 1876 seemed to confirm the original "rumour" that everyone without HBC title might be "driven back from the river and their land given to others."[27]

Sir John A. Macdonald knew that land loss was the central anxiety of the "half breeds" in 1869-70. He knew the issue of "squatters' claims" was one of the most important topics to be dealt with in the negotiations with the delegates. He was there. He knew what Ritchot wanted in the Manitoba Act, and why. He had appeared to agree. Yet six years later, Macdonald uttered not one recorded whisper to challenge the Liberals' completion of the elimination of that assurance. One possible explanation was that Macdonald had no interest in maintaining a promise that he himself had not wished to keep. Another was his preoccupation with more opportune bases of opposition.[28]

By the spring of 1876, Canada was moving into the third year of a severe economic recession. National revenue, for the most part derived from the tariff on imports, was down fifteen per cent, and the Finance Minister, Richard Cartwright, refused any increase in his budget of February 25, calling "every increase in taxation a positive evil" at the best of times, but particularly inappropriate during present circumstances. "This is no time for experiments," he explained.[29]

Macdonald seized upon Cartwright's declaration with an endorsement of the opposite position. Asserting that a stiff tariff increase would boost the national revenue, he claimed such a rise would also promote Canadian industrial development. Then Canada would be in a better position to finish the Pacific Railway and see a tide of settlement pour into the West. Calling his panacea the "National Policy," he began to spark enthusiasm outside of Parliament as well as among his own colleagues; he began to feel that he was riding a wave of returning popularity. The perception of political recovery convinced the old leader (he was sixty-one in 1876) that he ought to abandon recent plans for retirement. Apathy turned to more vigorous opposition, but Macdonald and his party did not discover any newfound dislike of the Liberals' administration of Manitoba land claims.

Archbishop Taché became increasingly worried. Earlier he had

---

27. PAC, Macdonald Papers, Incoming Correspondence, pp. 40751-40758, William McDougall to Macdonald, 31 October 1869.

28. Macdonald's opportunism is fully described by P.B. Waite, "Depression, Protection, and the Resurgence of Sir John Macdonald, 1874-1878," in *Canada, 1874-1896: Arduous Destiny* (Toronto, 1971), pp. 74-92.

29. Creighton, *Old Chieftain*, p. 211.

watched and waited, hoping the Liberals would soon pass from political power, and with Macdonald or his successor back where the Conservatives belonged in the Prime Minister's office, he might resume his patient wheedling, believing the Tories were the lesser of two evils (if only because they saw the expediency of having a Cartier or, after Cartier's death, a Langevin, at the Prime Minister's right hand). In 1876, however, with Macdonald's new, seemingly reckless advocacy of a high tariff, his renewed commitment to rapid completion of the Pacific Railway regardless of cost, and his statements about completely unrestricted immigration to the West, together with the recent boldness of the Liberals' bypassing of the Manitoba Act, Taché appears to have decided that it was unwise to observe further innovations with quiet contempt. He would have to protest, even if that meant face-to-face meetings with the "Protestant fanatics"[30] governing in Ottawa.

In the autumn of 1876 Taché met David Mills, known to the Archbishop earlier as the most outspoken opponent of the Manitoba Act when it was debated in 1870 and 1871. In October, Mills became the new Minister of the Interior. Taché hoped to impress him with his distress at what had been done to date and took special exception to the recent Order in Council, which presumed that every settler had been required to have a survey of his lot before 1870. Taché informed Mills that "staking was the customary way of proclaiming intent to settle." He contended that denial of that fact would jeopardize the only home of the claimants and, contrary to reports of Dominion surveyors, the lands in question were far from vacant. Mills promised an investigation.[31]

Responding to ministerial instructions late in November, Dennis asked Codd for a confidential report on the number of cases in which land was claimed but surveyors indicated there were no improvements. He wanted to know whether such claims conflicted with other potential patentees in Manitoba and whether there was "any reason to believe that similar claims are likely to be preferred to land on the Saskatchewan, or elsewhere in the Territories...."[32]

If Codd had answered consistently with his previous memoranda on the same subject, he would have indicated that there were hundreds of cases in which land was allegedly occupied in 1870, but not covered by any kind of Hudson's Bay Company grant, and quite unimproved according to the

---

30. " 'I don't like French,' often was the only answer obtained to legitimate requests"; clipping of article by Taché appearing in *Montreal Herald and Daily Commercial Gazette* (15 December 1885) in PAC, Macdonald Papers, Incoming Correspondence, p. 43928.

31. The substance of the meeting between Taché and Mills is found in a letter from Dennis to Codd, 20 November 1876 (PAM, Morris Papers, LG Collection, item 1327).

32. Ibid.

Dominion survey. In many such cases, the claim would conflict with recent entries for homesteads or sales to newcomers, and it was important to discourage them on that account alone, as well as to prevent similar chaos from arising along the branches of the Saskatchewan River. Eventually, a full inventory of "doubtful claims" was prepared.[33] In the short term, however, Codd and Whitcher had to wait for a reply to test cases submitted in an earlier attempt to find the minimum of acceptability. In September they had pointed out that the amendments to the Manitoba Act required "undisturbed occupancy and actual peaceable possession, etc" and their understanding of the recent Order in Council was that without adequate improvements, a claimant needed to show authorization by the Hudson's Bay Company. To find the acceptable minimum, they had sent an assortment of examples, hoping for their return with "a Memo attached to each application, shewing the opinion in each case definitely as to whether they will or will not pass."[34]

An opinion was rendered quickly on many of the cases.[35] Some failed, some passed (although the Justice Department approved one in 1876 that the same officials rejected when the dossier was returned for immediate patent).[36] The test cases still not ruled upon in the late autumn of 1876 were referred by Dennis to his Minister, and from the Department of the Interior to Justice at the end of January 1877.[37]

The January referrals involved eighteen claimants in Ste Agathe whose homes and gardens were on the west side of the Red River, with the land immediately opposite used for timber and hay. Having asked the surveyors to take account of both parts of their lots at the time of the survey, the residents had learned that the government was not likely to recognize any such claims, so they filed a formal petition for the land on November 4, 1873, asserting that the east portions of their holdings were an "integral part of our first property and even the principal part" given the value of the land for fuel, building timber, and fodder.[38] Earlier, officials at the Dominion Lands Office in Winnipeg had advised against the claimants, suggesting

---

33. See "List of Lands in the parishes of Baie St Paul, Poplar Point, High Bluff and Portage la Prairie prepared in accordance with Instructions of the Surveyor General dated 17 November 1877" (PAC, Records of the Department of the Interior, RG 15, MA file 9683). Presumably there were other lists to cover the same subject in the other parishes but they have not been found.

34. Ibid., vol. 140, MA file 13, A.H. Whitcher to J.S. Dennis, 8 September 1876.

35. Ibid., Dennis to Whitcher, [23] September 1876.

36. Ibid., Whitcher to Dennis, 13 February 1878.

37. Department of Justice, Central Registry Files, file 21/1877, J.S. Dennis to David Mills, 30 January 1877.

38. PAC, Records of the Department of the Interior, RG 15, file 720 (petition in which eighteen claimants assert that the dominion survey does not reflect the boundaries they themselves had agreed to), 4 November 1873.

that if they succeeded "there will be little if any land in the Settlement Belt, or indeed in the Province which cannot be claimed in this way."[39]

While the dossiers moved from department to department in Ottawa, Taché became increasingly anxious for news about the general inquiry, and asked for a meeting with Mills in January 1877. But the Minister was not available. His letter of explanation, dated February 6, acknowledged Taché's concerns, promised the Archbishop that the government had "no intention to disturb anyone in actual possession of the lands," qualified the assurance with the warning that there would be no recognition of claims without significant improvements, and stated that nothing could be done for the moment because "certain papers" had not yet arrived from Winnipeg.[40]

If Mills had been more honest, he would have admitted that the matter was before the Department of Justice, and the issue under consideration was the legal limit of stringency, not generosity. After rulings in June, and more memoranda between Dennis and Mills, the policy that finally came down to Codd in October 1877 (the instructions for preparing the comprehensive lists of doubtful claims) was that all would fail "without some really valuable improvements." The specified minimum was a house and five acres under cultivation in every case where there was no HBC survey, and no indication of occupancy in the Dominion surveyors' field notes. Even then, what the claimant earned was the right to buy his land "in cash or scrip at the Government price of one dollar per acre." A final stipulation was a forty-acre maximum purchase.[41]

The impact of the policy concerning "staked claims" was horrendous from the standpoint of the Métis. At Rat River, for example, the implementation of the ruling in late December of 1877 meant that eighty-four of ninety-three families were told that they were vulnerable to eviction by "writs of ejectment."[42] Only nine of the claimants passed the "really valuable improvements" test establishing their right to buy the land they considered already their own. To be sure, the government had recently distributed $160 scrip to each "half breed" head of family, but that benefit had passed almost immediately to persons with powers of attorney alleging ownership of the right; and no head of family who did collect scrip was told that it would buy anything but vacant section land—bald prairie. The

39. Ibid., Whitcher to Deputy Minister of the Interior, 13 November 1873. The locations of the petitioners was illustrated by a map enclosed with the letter. The map is in PAC, National Map Collection, 54106.

40. Archives of the University of Western Ontario, David Mills Papers, Letter Book, Mills to Taché, 6 February 1877.

41. PAM, Morris Papers, LG Collection, Dennis to Codd, 24 October 1877.

42. PAM, Morris Papers, LG Collection, Fragment of "Memorandum on the subject of the so called 'Staked Claims' in Manitoba," [20 December 1877].

policy innovation that permitted occupants of "staked claims" to clear their titles with the scrip they had lost two years earlier was, therefore, an innovation that came two years too late.

From Mills' point of view, the solution to the "staked claims" issue was sensible and just. The formula did not please Taché, of course, but Taché's pleasure was none of his concern, even though the Archbishop was proving useful as a sounding board, particularly in testing the nature of opposition to innovations in the field of Métis land rights. The day after Taché had made his inquiry into the river-lot question in January 1877, J.S. Dennis wrote the Archbishop informing him that the minister was anxious to "confer" on another matter. Dennis indicated that the issue of the "lands granted to the children of Half Breeds in Manitoba" was something to which Mills had given "earnest consideration since assuming the office of Minister of the Interior" on October 24, 1876. According to Dennis, "The minister fears that the Grant, as proposed to be made, is not likely to realize the anticipated value to the recipients, while it is certain to operate greatly to the public disadvantage in retarding for an indefinite period the settlement of a very considerable area, say one-seventh, of the lands in the Province." From the point of view of the government, the appropriate remedy was to "commute the claim of each Half Breed child entitled to participate in the land grant *by a fixed cash payment. . . .*" Mills admitted through Dennis that an amending act of Parliament was needed. Taché's views were invited to set the just price. "What sum," Dennis asked, "would be a reasonable commutation for each claim?"[43]

The Minister of the Interior and the Surveyor General both knew that the Archbishop would probably refuse to consider their proposition. Neither Mills nor Dennis could have expected Taché to come up with a liquidation value. They both knew that he had stood firmly on the principle of trusteeship in the past. What Dennis and Mills probably wanted to learn was how far Taché might take his opposition. They could not have been surprised when he sent a critical reply to their proposal in mid-February 1877.

The letter began quietly enough. Taché expressed surprise that the government believed "the majority of claims . . . will pass from their owners for comparatively a merely nominal consideration," and suggested that if speculators were operating on such a vast scale "if there be any means of checking their efforts it would be advisable to do so. . . ." Taché agreed that it was futile to forbid grantees to sell their land after they came of age. Still, for those who should choose to sell, it would be well to have a legislated minimum price as a discouragement to fraud and speculation.

---

43. PAC, Records of the Department of the Interior, RG 15, vol. 236, file 7220, Dennis to Taché, 22 January 1877.

Indeed, Taché believed that the most effective approach to assuring fair value would be having the government itself "offering a fair price." Of course, that was not the commutation Dennis and Mills had in mind. Turning to their proposition, Taché suggested that if they did amend the Manitoba Act somebody would probably launch a legal action contesting the constitutionality of the legislation. He reminded Mills (who fancied himself an expert in constitutional law) that "the Manitoba Act having received the sanction of an Imperial Act, its provisions cannot be re-adjusted by the Canadian Parliament, and I am very doubtful as to the willingness of the Imperial Parliament to enact for the disposal of lands set apart for minors." Taché also doubted the wisdom of presuming to know the wishes of seven-year-olds, the youngest of the allottees, eleven years hence, when they would be eligible to receive patents to their allotments. "I would not feel justifiable in recommending any action which minors, when of age, might deem as having been prejudicial to their interests." Then, with clear reference to the losing battle he was waging over river lots, Taché concluded: "Scarcity of land in a few years . . . may render the children of Half Breeds better able to appreciate its value than their relatives do at present, and the preservation of their grant may be the only way to secure a footing for them in their native country."[44]

As Dennis and Mills learned that the legislation they were contemplating was likely to be challenged in the courts, the matter was dropped. At the same time, both officials should have perceived a remarkable change in Taché's pleading. He called their proposal unconstitutional, said he was afraid to be identified with it, and warned the government that champions of Métis rights might use the measure as a rallying point in the future. While defining coherent grounds of opposition, the letter lacked the cutting edge that was evident in his earlier writing concerning, for example, the amnesty. The letter seems to have marked a turning point in Taché's relations with the Métis, a change that Riel perceived as early as September 1874 when he began to complain that the Archbishop was a friend but one who was too "soft" in adversity.[45] By 1877, with Riel out of the country, with the Archbishop having little success on the river-lot question, and expecting the worst on the disposal of the 1.4 million acres, he appears to have decided that the Métis would have to be replaced by a French-speaking, Catholic population recruited from Quebec, or repatriated from the United States, to save his church and language from British-Protestant inundation.[46] He no longer believed, as had Ritchot and Riel in 1870, that

---

44. Ibid., Taché to Dennis, 5 February 1877.

45. *Riel Papers*, I, pp. 386-394, Riel to Dubuc, 10 September 1874.

46. See Benoit, *Vie de Mg. Taché*, II, pp. 295, 298-300; and Robert Painchaud, "French-Canadian Historiography and Franco-Catholic Settlement in Western Canada, 1870-1915," *Canadian Historical Review* 59 (1978), pp. 447-466. Both observe that Taché's recruitment effort was most emphatic in the later 1870s.

the Métis colony might be shaped into an "independent province in the Canadian Confederation."[47] They were swamped. Taché's new hope was to salvage some of the Métis homeland for acceptable replacements recruited from elsewhere.

The Archbishop's protest of 1877 discouraged Mills temporarily, but one year later the government achieved the desired end of immediate dissolution of the reserves by other means, and without significant opposition from anyone in Manitoba. On July 4, 1878, the Department of the Interior gained authority by Order in Council "for the issue forthwith of Patents to all claimants of Half-breed lands, irrespective of age." Suddenly, children as young as eight years became the legal owners of 240-acre parcels of section land, became responsible for its taxation, and were unprotected by legislation — federal or provincial — concerning their "Infant Estates."[48] In about eighty per cent of the cases, the land passed to new owners the moment the patent arrived in Winnipeg.[49]

Part of the reason that "half breed grants" passed so quickly to "speculators" was another Order in Council restricting the distribution of patents to individuals known personally to Donald Codd or to the agents of patentees with power of attorney "in proper form, duly executed in the presence of a Justice of the Peace."[50] The problem with the procedure was that it was open to fraud. Anyone could make up fraudulent documents by getting information from published lists of allottees, and determining whether the family had already left the province. Since the signatures of the patentee and the subscribing witness were rarely more than an X, and since the Justices of the Peace attesting to the validity of such legal instruments were leaders in fraud and speculation themselves, there was no obstacle to creating forged documentation that looked entirely proper in form and execution.[51]

Of course, the criminal behaviour that was easy for one "speculator" was just as simple for another. As a result, many "attorneys" sometimes descended on the patent for the same land. Codd's way of coping with the circling flock of "speculators" was to recognize powers of attorney on a

---

47. *Riel Papers,* I, p. 276, Riel to Royal, 2 August 1873.

48. See Gerhard Ens, "Métis Lands in Manitoba," *Manitoba History* 5 (1983), pp. 2-11.

49. See Table 1 in D.N. Sprague, "Government Lawlessness in the Administration of Manitoba Land Claims, 1870-1887," *Manitoba Law Journal* 10 (1980), pp. 415-441.

50. The words in the directive are taken from a form letter sent to patentees or recipients of heads of family scrip by Codd, a sample of which appears in PAM, E.L. Barber Papers, MG 14 C66, p. 2954, Donald Codd to Mrs. E.L. Barber, 10 May 1879. Codd's authorization for such a requirement was Order in Council of Canada, 23 March 1876.

51. A.G.B. Bannatyne, for example, was one of the most frequent signers of powers of attorney covering children's allotments (See PAC, Records of the Department of the Interior, vols. 1421-1423). His frauds were known to the Government of Canada, but never prosecuted (ibid., vol. 232, file 2447).

first-come, first-served basis.[52] It was against policy to investigate — or even to report — instances of fraud of any kind (either of patentees negotiating multiple sales of the land, or of agents claiming to act for persons they had never met).[53]

The overriding consideration stated by the Chief Justice of the Manitoba Court of Queen's Bench, E.B. Wood, was that the "half breed reserves, like other reserves of every kind . . . are a curse to the country and should be distributed without delay."[54] Wood profited personally in the distribution, as did most of the other members of the legal profession of Manitoba. No one voiced any squeamishness about the irregularities in the transfers of "half breed lands." According to one informed lawyer, "It was the opinion of nine out of ten of the profession that it was an improvident grant to the half breeds — in the first place — that it would bring them more harm than good — and that the sooner the whole of these lands was settled the better."[55]

In the same spirit of expeditious settlement, the Liberal government proposed one final statutory adjustment to the Manitoba land question in 1878. Having had three years experience with their own version of the "court of claims" for adjudicating disputed ownership of river lots, they decided that even the previously streamlined proceedings were too cumbersome and costly. Lieutenant Governor Morris, commissioned by Order in Council to hear the cases, reported that the requirement of several months notice, and the presence of both parties to the dispute before the case could be heard, led to unnecessary delay. Morris suggested reducing the notice period to thirty days, and permitting proceedings even if one of the parties to the dispute was absent. The two together would mean that all of the outstanding conflicts could be "speedily disposed of." Morris did not add that many of the claimants were absent from their lots for months or even years at a time in such work as freighting, fishing, or hunting. The more important consideration was speedy closure of outstanding claims.[56]

Mills agreed. The appropriate amending legislation appeared and passed through the House of Commons without debate in early April 1878. Then, as the matter reached the Upper Chamber, a Manitoba Senator, Marc

---

52. "I transmit . . . seventy three (73) receipts for said letters patent. The Powers of Attorney are retained in this office for reference" (ibid., vol. 238, file 9321).

53. Originally the policy was more of a tacit understanding between Codd and Dennis than a written rule handed down to every agent. See ibid. In 1913, however, the matter became the subject of a written rule (PAC, Records of the Department of the Interior, RG 15, vol. 21009, ruling 893).

54. PAM, Mackenzie Papers, General Correspondence, pp. 801-808, Wood to Mackenzie, 25 May 1875.

55. Heber Archibald quoted in Ens, "Métis Lands," p. 9.

56. PAC, Records of the Department of the Interior, RG 15, vol. 235, file 4666, Morris to Mills, 26 November 1877.

Girard, produced an amendment reflecting Taché's concern with the earlier dismissal of the so-called "staked claims." Girard's move was not a complete surprise; the Senator had declared only days before: "We hear of confiscation everywhere. The people are told that they cannot remain any longer on the lands on which they have been settled for years. . . ." Quoting a phrase in section 32 of the Manitoba Act, Girard stated that he could not understand "why so many improvements are requisite when the law merely requires *peaceable possession*." Hinting that the amendments of 1874 and 1875 and the Order in Council of 1876 were all unconstitutional, he asserted, "By an Order in Council you cannot over-ride the law of the land."

Senator Scott, still a minister of the Crown in the Mackenzie government, denied that any injustice had been done to "actual settlers." He asserted that "it is only in the case where there has been no expenditure of muscle" that patents were denied. Scott said it was "speculators that the Crown is not bound to recognize."[57]

Girard replied that, if the government were so confident of the facts, there was nothing to fear from people telling their stories in the "court of claims." Consequently, no one was shocked when Girard proposed an amendment on April 11 broadening its scope to include the disputes involving a claimant against the Crown.

Scott repeated his assertion that "no man . . . had been overlooked . . . . All well-founded claims had already been recognized." The disallowed claims had arisen from the question: "What occupancy gave possession? And that was a question which the Minister of Justice and the Minister of the Interior should agree upon." Later he suggested that "it would not do to give away the public property right and left," and asserted that serious delays and costs would arise from opening the court to all the claims that the department had refused to consider.

Macdonald's old law partner, Alexander Campbell, answered Scott with an appeal for a more compassionate regard for minority rights. "Of course the majority could say, 'You shall not be heard, because your possession is very slight, and your usages and customs are different from ours,' but that would be inflicting an injustice upon those people and wounding them in a manner from which they would not recover." A majority of the Senators seemed to agree with Campbell's appeal for fairness and voted twenty-two to eighteen in favour of the Girard amendment.[58]

Campbell's noble words about minority rights and due process of law did not stir Conservatives in the House of Commons one week later when Mills called for rejection of the proposal repeating Scott's point that

---

57. Senate Debates, 8 March 1878.

58. Ibid., 11 April 1878, pp. 559-563.

officials in his department could handle all such cases "more expeditiously, efficiently, and cheaply than can be done under this amendment." Sir John A. Macdonald did not rise from his seat to reiterate the sentiments of his old friend Campbell.[59] He sat quietly with the rest of the Opposition, silently supporting the latest denial of rights to the native settlers of Manitoba even though his party was in a full fury of anger over almost every other action by the government. By 1878 they sensed that Mackenzie's was a ministry in deep trouble and were serving up no-confidence motions for breakfast, lunch, and dinner. On the land rights of the "former occupants" of Manitoba, however, what one hand had done, the other had undone, and both hands of the two national parties quite contentedly washed one another.

---

59. Journal of the House of Commons, 20 April 1878.

Joseph Royal, ca. 1880
(Provincial Archives of Manitoba)

"Royal said that Codd and Dennis had been working in collusion to subvert the entire claims process since 1871."

Chapter 8

Completing the Dispersal of the Manitoba Métis

Continuing recession, unrelenting criticism of the Liberals' handling of economic issues, and clever use of political "picnics" by the Opposition led to a crushing defeat of Alexander Mackenzie's party in the federal election of September 17, 1878. The remarkable recovery of the Tories with Sir John A. Macdonald still leading was an unqualified triumph, except in one important detail. For the first time in his political career, Macdonald himself suffered defeat in Kingston. Under the cover and novelty of the new secret ballot, a majority of the city's 3,000 electors expressed a preference for Macdonald's opponent, the totally undistinguished Alexander Gunn.[1]

Macdonald might have become the outside leader of the inside party on September 17 were it not for his running in two other constituencies on the same day. He won by acclamation in Marquette, a predominantly native English riding in Manitoba, and by a comfortable plurality in Victoria, British Columbia.[2] Under normal circumstances, a politician probably would have accepted the compliment of the electorate that appeared to approve him most highly; at the same time, such a successful candidate might have shown his gratitude by pledging support for the special demands of his particular admirers. In the Manitoba case, Joseph Royal reminded Macdonald of the earlier rescue of Cartier, and pointed out that he considered the old promises all the more binding in view of the repetition of the courtesy for Macdonald himself. Among the items on Royal's list of nine requested favours were demands that the Prime Minister should intercede in Manitoba affairs for the maintenance of confessional schools and the two official languages; that he should concede a "complete and final amnesty to all persons implicated in the trouble of 1869-70"; and that Macdonald should finally guarantee the distribution of patents to river-lots in accordance with the original intended meaning of section 32 of the Manitoba Act.[3]

---

1. Canadian Sessional Papers (1879), no. 88, p. 44.
2. Ibid., pp. 220, 221.
3. PAC, Macdonald Papers, Incoming Correspondence, pp. 118172-118177, Royal to Macdonald, 28 September 1878.

Refusing to be snared in the defunct promises of his previous ministry, Sir John declined election in Marquette. All the Victoria electors demanded was a transcontinental railway, and the railway demand was consistent with Macdonald's own priorities. In his view, native issues were settled. As far as he knew, all 1.4 million acres had been alloted to the children of the "half breed heads of families"; the parents had received their scrip in 1876; and, at the same time, nearly all of the old settlers with land granted by the HBC had their titles confirmed by letters patent from Canada. Further west, the last of seven treaties had extinguished the aboriginal title of every Indian on the Prairies. The great work that remained was completing the railway to the Pacific, promoting the industrial development of metropolitan Canada, and pouring a flood of farmers into the "empty" West.[4]

Macdonald admitted that he was not fully familiar with the intricacies of the land policy which he himself had contrived with Campbell in 1871 and 1872, nor was he conversant with the details of the treaties.[5] Still, he recognized that the Department of the Interior was one of the most important arms of the government for promoting Canadian expansion. Consequently, when the Cabinet positions were announced in October 1878, Macdonald emerged as the Minister of the Interior and therefore also as Superintendent-General of Indian Affairs.

Macdonald's hope that he would be presiding over the transformation of the West rather than concluding dealings with aboriginal people was sustained by a welcomed freedom from Manitoba matters for nearly one full year until Taché resurrected the old land-claims issue in the autumn of 1879. Refusing to be stirred from his preoccupation with more important concerns, Macdonald referred Taché's inquiry to J.S. Dennis, the new Deputy Minister of his department. Dennis advised refusal of the Archbishop's appeal, saying that the government had already "erred" too much in the direction of "liberality." Dennis recommended an Order in Council proclaiming that all legitimate claimants had been accommodated and that the time had come for "all other persons" claiming land under the Manitoba Act to pay for their land at the government price of five dollars an acre or face eviction for illegal trespass.[6]

Macdonald's problem was Taché's continuing complaint that a case-by-case analysis would show that "Colonel Dennis" did not understand the custom of the country in staking claims. After the Archbishop appeared to convince Macdonald that Dennis suffered from narrow vision, Taché

---

4. Creighton, *Old Chieftain*, p. 246.

5. Ibid.

6. PAC, Macdonald Papers, Incoming Correspondence, pp. 88777-88784, Dennis to Macdonald, 10 October 1879.

received a promise in November 1879 that a thorough investigation of river-lot claims would follow, and recommended Joseph Dubuc (then a Judge of the Court of Queen's Bench) for the role of commissioner investigating outstanding claims in the French-speaking parishes. Unlike Chief Justice Wood (still charged with adjudicating conflicting claims in general), Dubuc had the advantage of knowing "all the people of the district"; and since he was "young and active," Taché believed that he was capable of making a "full investigation that would relieve us all of any further complaint with regard to that question."[7]

Macdonald preferred to leave matters as they were. The promised investigation was not followed by the nomination of an investigator. Weeks passed into months, and Taché prompted Joseph Royal (still prominent in Manitoba affairs and about to enter the federal scene under the Tory banner) to use his influence with the Prime Minister. Royal's action was a letter reciting the history of river-lot claims from 1870 to 1880, beginning with the statement that the "fears" of the Métis

> relative to the Land Question were one of the first causes of the outbreak in the Country. Among the means resorted to by the Government to quiet the people were the repeated assurances that the most liberal policy would be followed in that respect and that no one would lose an inch of land to which he had a claim.

Unfortunately, according to Royal, the law had been set aside, and replaced by administrative processes that meant "hundreds of claims are disallowed, *not having this or that,* which was never required by the Act of Manitoba."[8]

About the same time as Royal's appeal, the Legislative Assembly of Manitoba added the influence of the provincial government to the urging for a final disposition of land claims. A letter to the Government of Canada revealed that a final disposition of land claims. The Métis parishes of St Franois Xavier and Baie St Paul had been unaccountably left out of the process of allotting the 1.4 million acres that was completed elsewhere between 1875 and 1878. In the same communication, the legislature appealed for patents for any person who "staked out and pre-empted claims to certain unoccupied land, and were in peaceable possession of the same at the time of the actual transfer on the 15th July 1870. . . ."[9]

Surprised to learn that all of the children's allotments were not distributed already, Macdonald ordered completion of the process at once. At the same time, he thought it was expedient to make a final, declarative

7. Ibid., pp. 167897-167899, Taché to Macdonald, 25 November 1879.
8. PAC, Records of the Department of the Interior, RG 15, vol. 245, file 22638, Royal to Macdonald, 8 March 1880.
9. Quoted in Order in Council of Canada, 12 April 1880.

statement on the river-lot question. In the Order in Council that answered the formal address of Manitoba (and the private pressure exerted by Taché and Royal), the Government of Canada declared that "staked claims" were inadmissible by definition, reiterating the Liberal's position that "the mere fact of staking out the land, without entering into *bona fide* possession and occupation . . . did not bring that class of claims within the operation of the Manitoba Act, and therefore patents were refused."[10] Moreover, since Macdonald did not want the agitation on such matters to continue interminably, a final amendment of the Manitoba Act declared, in April 1880, that any claim not proved "to the satisfaction of the Minister of the Interior . . . [before December 1882] shall be barred as fully and effectually as if such claims had not been made."[11]

The two discouragements of denying "staked claims" and shutting out all other "claims by occupancy" in two years prompted Joseph Royal to seek fresh assurances that the general investigation Macdonald had promised Taché was about to proceed. A face-to-face discussion with Macdonald, during which the Prime Minister took sketchy notes on everything from the English-only effrontery of the Winnipeg Lands Agent (still Donald Codd) to the necessity of a case-by-case review of the river-lot question, prompted Sir John to tell Colonel Dennis, "We must talk over these matters."[12]

The result of Macdonald's subsequent discussion with his Deputy Minister was the decision to have a two-person delegation from Ottawa investigate affairs on the spot. Lindsay Russell, the new Surveyor General, was to look into the allegations against Codd. Robert Lang, the officer principally in charge of Manitoba Act cases at their last stage of consideration in Ottawa, was to investigate the "staked claims" issue.[13]

The conclusion of Russell's inquiry was that Codd was either incredibly lazy or intentionally negligent. As soon as Taché launched a fresh round of complaints about the Dominion Lands Agent's refusal to deal with anything French, Russell sought Codd's resignation.[14]

Lang's assignment was both more complicated and more time consuming. He took the entire summer of 1880 to examine literally hundreds of claims in Ste Agathe and St Norbert. Two patterns were readily evident in his case-by-case rendition of the facts. The first was that officials were

---

10. Ibid.

11. Statutes of Canada (1880), Chapter 7: An Act for the final settlement of claims to lands in Manitoba by occupancy, under the Act thirty-third Victoria, chapter three, Section 2.

12. PAC, Records of the Department of the Interior, RG 15, vol. 245, file 22638, Macdonald to Dennis, 11 May 1880.

13. PAC, Macdonald Papers, Incoming Correspondence, pp. 118191-118192, J. Royal to Macdonald, 11 June 1880.

14. Ibid., pp. 88868-88870, Russell to Dennis, 12 October 1880.

contemptuous of patterns of land use other than full-time farming. In the case of Jean Baptiste Jolibois, Jr., for example, Lang found a young man who claimed that when he was eighteen years of age he "staked out" an attractive point of land on the Red River several miles south of his father's farm on lot 41 in St Norbert. Jolibois built a log house on his claim in 1868, lived there until 1870, then decided that he had built his home in the wrong place. In the summer of 1870, Jolibois disassembled the first structure and moved the timber to a preferred corner of his claim. In the meantime, he lived with his parents when he was not working on the relocation of the first building. Later in the year, Jolibois accepted work freighting supplies from St Cloud to Winnipeg, then resumed construction of his new dwelling in the summer of 1871 (considerably discouraged in the task because over the winter someone carted off most of the logs from the partially completed structure of the previous summer). Still, Jolibois was able to complete a habitable home before freeze-up, and a second work-opportunity took him away to the North West, and kept him there for the next four years. When Jolibois finally returned in 1875 to resume the development of his land, he discovered that vandals had dismantled his house entirely, again probably for the firewood in the oak building timber. From 1875, however, Jolibois lived on his lot more or less continuously, and demanded a patent from Lang on the basis of the "peaceable possession" that had begun in 1868.[15]

The case of Jean Baptiste Jolibois, Jr., illustrates what Joseph Royal had called the principal reason for old settlers fearing the transfer. According to Royal, "They knew perfectly well that their right to the portion of the Settlement Belt regularly surveyed and occupied could not be disputed, but they apprehended that the same right to the land they possessed outside the surveyed Settlement Belt might be contested." They were afraid that "they would be more or less at the mercy of the New Government that might refuse to accept or understand the former conditions of this Country."[16]

Of course the process of delay and amendment after 1870 proved that their fears were justified. Notwithstanding the words in section 32 of the Manitoba Act, and the promises of liberal interpretation that accompanied the negotiation, Jean Baptiste Jolibois, Jr., — and hundreds like him — received "nil" consideration because they failed on three points. First, they did not exhibit the "continuous occupation" required by the amendments of 1874 and 1875. In the second place, they were not covered by the Hudson's Bay Company survey required by Order in Council in 1876. And finally, they did not show the "really valuable improvements" demanded

---

15. PAC, Records of the Department of the Interior, RG 15, vol. 1554, "Lang's Report on claims in the parishes of Ste Agathe and St Norbert [October, 1880]," Lot 267, Ste Agathe.

16. Ibid., vol. 245, file 22638, Royal to Macdonald, 8 March 1880.

by executive memorandum in 1877.

Hearing of Donald Codd's repeated refusals of their claims, many of the claimants had become increasingly suggestible in the late 1870s to the offers of newcomers willing to gamble in such matters. As a result, the other pattern that was readily apparent in the Lang report — indeed, the central tendency in the cases he described — was recent settlers obtaining their land at unspecified prices from unnamed "squatters." If newcomers paid less than five dollars an acre, their gamble was that they could obtain valuable river-frontage at less than the government price merely by improving the defective claim of the vacating "half breed." Simon Callum, for example, bought a claim to 242 acres from such a "squatter." Instead of paying the government price of $1,210, Callum admitted that he paid a mere $300 for the faltering claim of his predecessor. Since Callum had built a house, several substantial outbuildings, and had almost 100 acres of fenced land in crop by 1880, he was clearly serious about farming the land he had acquired by dubious means in the late 1870s. The marginal note beside the report of his claim was "yes."[17]

The two patterns together showed that the "staked claims" issue had acquired a new complexity with the passage of time and the transfers that were encouraged by the statutes and Orders in Council amending the Manitoba Act. Moreover, some of the Callum-type newcomers were repatriated French Canadians recruited by Taché to carry on a Franco-Manitoban presence after the Métis had begun to give up on their own unrecognized claims. Consequently, after Lang returned to Ottawa in September 1880, and a rumour began to circulate in Manitoba that the government was planning to auction all the unpatented river-lots, Taché and Royal mounted a campaign to discredit Lang's report, calling the investigation little more than a superficial and hurried visit.[18] Dennis replied to Macdonald that the inquiry was "minute" on every detail of each particular case.[19] Royal's continuing insistence that the report was defective, and his assertion that the one French-speaking surveyor in the province, Roger Goulet, had "refused to sign Lang's report" gave Macdonald some cause to consider more radical allegations.

Royal said that Codd and Dennis had been working in collusion to subvert the entire claims process since 1871. Their motive was that neither official could forget the opposition to their "odious conduct" in 1869. Warming to his theme with considerable passion, Royal asserted, "It is a fact that only in the county of Provencher [the Métis parishes] are found to

17. "Lang Report," Lots 317, 319, Ste Agathe.

18. PAC, Macdonald Papers, Incoming Correspondence, pp. 118196-118197 88884-88890, Royal to Macdonald, 25 October and 2 November 1880.

19. Ibid., pp. 88876-88878, Dennis to Macdonald, 29 October 1880.

exist such a large number of questions of delayed patents and disputed land claims.'' He thought the pattern of delay running to 1880 was clear enough proof of prejudice ''fixedly adhered to and persistently carried out.''[20]

After Macdonald passed Royal's letter to Dennis, and the Deputy Minister dismissed all charges against himself and his officials as a ''slanderous attack,'' Colonel Dennis did agree to meet with Russell and Taché to go over the outstanding claims. Subsequently, the threesome worked from November 6 through November 10 adjusting ''all outstanding claims except staked claims.'' On those, according to Dennis, ''I declined to have any discussion.''[21]

Of course Taché and Royal would not be satisfied until the entire collection was disposed of in accordance with the original intent of the Manitoba Act. At the end of December 1880, the Archbishop proposed, therefore, a two-class system of consideration. Class I would consist of claims with the ''original owners or their legal representatives'' living on the lots. In Class II, the claimant or new owner at least would have paid local taxes on the land. Taché suggested that everyone in Class I was entitled to patents without further delay, and the others should receive at least the right of purchase from the Crown at the price of one dollar per acre.[22]

Father Ritchot added his voice to the same appeal two weeks later in a letter that seems to have been the only direct communication he had had with Macdonald since 1870. The subject of his message of January 1881 was their negotiations in Ottawa. ''You will remember,'' he said with the firmness of a patient schoolmaster, ''I showed Sir George and yourself the localities where the lands had been taken possession of, among others, I showed you on the map, the Rat River, Sàle River, the Little Prairie de Chènes, and the Upper Red River, etc., etc.'' All, according to Ritchot, had been ''fully explained'' and it was freely admitted that there were but slight improvements on such lands. Indeed, some were ''not inhabited but marked only by posts, lines, ploughing, little houses or otherwise, and that this manner of taking up lands in the country had been respected, in fact, for ten, twelve, and fifteen years.'' That was what the delegates understood the ''peaceable possesion'' clause to cover. Pursuing the point as relentlessly as Royal, Ritchot asserted that section 32(4) was

> not intended to say that all persons having a good written title and duly registered, etc. etc. that he shall have continually resided and cultivated so many acres of land yearly and for so many years before the Transfer to Canada, and that he shall cultivate and continually reside during the period of ten years after the Transfer to Canada, so many acres etc. etc. to be

---

20. Ibid., pp. 88884-88890, Royal to Macdonald, 2 November 1880.

21. Ibid., pp. 88880-88883, Dennis to Macdonald, 10 November 1880.

22. Ibid., pp. 172990-172992, Taché to Macdonald, 28 December 1880.

entitled to Letters Patent for lands so cultivated and inhabited, [but] . . . this is what is required today by the Government through their employees.

That could not be the meaning of the words contained in the Manitoba Act; nor the meaning the Hon. Minister gave them, you told the North West Delegates in 1870 that the greatest liberality was meant by these words and that all lands thus taken were and would be the property of those who were in possession thereof.

Ritchot suggested that if another meaning were more strictly correct, then Macdonald and Cartier had deliberately "deceived" the Métis to "dispossess" them. "Was their intention then to add [a] few words to the phrases which would later deprive the Manitoba settlers of their rights?"[23]

Macdonald did not respond to Ritchot's letter, but a new Order in Council governing "staked claims" did appear to accommodate Taché's appeal by broadening the scope of consideration on February 25. Cases previously refused were to be considered if the land was still in the hands of the original claimant, or if the acreage had passed to new owners who subsequently took up residence on the land. Unimproved lots sold to someone who still did nothing "in the way of cultivation or improvement" were to be referred to a special commission consisting of Judges Dubuc and Miller.

If the claimants in the first category were given free grants, and if Miller and Dubuc granted pre-emption rights to persons in category two, the most that Taché and Ritchot could have said in objection to the policy was that the generosity was ten years too late. Unfortunately for the claimants, officials still clung to their stringent concept of "possession."[24] Persistent old settlers with improvements similar to those of Jean Baptiste Jolibois, Jr., won nothing more than the right to buy their land at five dollars per acre, while newcomers such as Callum received free grants. The rationale, of course, was that the new settlers were serious farmers.

The Order in Council of February 1881 was even less satisfactory for claimants referred to the special commissioners. Before the two judges began, Macdonald coached Miller with a confidential letter explaining that "all those claims that deserve to be settled had already been adjusted and disposed of." The only reason the commission had been appointed was that "Archbishop Taché is now kicking up such a row about the matter." Macdonald warned Miller that his "co-commissioner" will be "very apt" to lean towards generosity. On that account, the Prime Minister instructed the trustworthy judge to hold the line where it was meant to be held: "the parties must prove a claim which could be enforced in a court of Law or Equity."[25]

Naturally, Royal and Taché disliked the discriminatory treatment of old settlers. They were pleased that some of the newcomers whom they

23. Ibid., pp. 141514-141526, Ritchot to Macdonald, 15 January 1881.
24. Ibid., pp. 45051-45060, Royal to Mackenzie Bowell, 20 September 1881.
25. Ibid., Letter Books, vol. 21, pp. 411-412, Macdonald to Miller, 24 February 1881.

themselves had recruited would not have to buy land they had already paid for once, but they refused to see the justice in requiring persistent old settlers to pay for their land simply because their improvements were slight. Moreover, the perennial problem of delay continued.

No patents covering "staked claims" appeared in the spring of 1881, or in the summer of the same year. Instead, panic developed over the renewal of rumours that the government intended to auction unpatented river-lots, and when the list of lots for sale finally appeared late in September, it became clear that some unpatented claims were included.[26] Mainly, though, the government seemed determined to defeat inadmissible claims by delay.

On May 1, 1882, the clock began to run on the final six months allowed for the settlement of claims by occupancy. May 1 was the last day for filing applications; November 1 was the date by which the Minister had to be satisfied that the claim was legitimate. The clear implication was that the claims that were filed as many as nine years earlier—and still not acted upon—would be rejected if Macdonald were not persuaded of their legitimacy by the end of 1882. Royal panicked in August because there was still no action on the cases the government had agreed to recognize in February 1881. He complained that one promise had followed another, all "without any result." Royal estimated that over the last ten years he had personally written "50 memoranda on the subject." Royal admitted that his patience was at its absolute limit and begged Macdonald, "Now, for God's sake, let your government once and forever attend to and settle these land claims. . . ."[27]

The first result arising from Royal's emotional appeal for immediate resolution of the "everlasting question" was a blistering rebuke from the Prime Minister for the excessive "frankness" of the letter. Macdonald heatedly denied that any officer in his department was guilty of any gross "incapacity or prejudice." Still, Macdonald did hint that the entire package was about to be turned over to a recently created Lands Board that had been established by the Department of the Interior at Winnipeg to supersede the special commissions held by Governor Morris, followed by Chief Justice Wood, and most recently by Judges Dubuc and Miller.[28]

Increased efficiency was part of the reason for turning the "staked claims" over to the Lands Board. Another motive was secrecy in the investigation of scandal, the first suggestion of which came to Macdonald in

---

26. Ibid., Incoming Correspondence, pp. 45051-45060, Royal to Mackenzie Bowell, 20 September 1881.

27. Ibid., pp. 45061-45064, Royal to Macdonald, 11 August 1882.

28. The Lands Board was authorized by Order in Council of Canada, 31 October 1881. The content of Macdonald's private letter to Royal is inferred from the text of Royal's apologetic reply (ibid., pp. 118231-118232, Royal to Macdonald, 28 September 1882).

September 1882,[29] just before he wrote Royal with unqualified praise of the officials in his department. The first evidence of trouble was a letter from Codd's successor in the Winnipeg Land Office informing the Minister of the Interior that Robert Lang had been exploiting his position to extort land from claimants in Manitoba. Working through local accomplices (a ring that included A.G.B. Bannatyne and probably also J.C. Schultz) potential patentees were informed that "for a consideration . . . in which parties are in straits to obtain their Patents, he undertakes to put them through upon being well recompensed." Soon the allegations were discovered to be "well founded."[30] Then an Order in Council declared that the positions of Minister of the Interior and Superintendent General of Indian Affairs ought to be separated, and Macdonald withdrew from the affairs of his old department long before the scandal became public.[31] D.L. Macpherson was Minister of the Interior after October 1883, and by the time the "Lang conspiracy" first appeared in the pages of the Toronto *Globe* (in the spring of 1885) the country was in the midst of another controversy of infinitely greater interest to the Opposition.

In the meantime, the Lands Board dutifully worked its way through the hundreds of unresolved claims to river lots. In most of the cases the patentee was a newcomer claiming through an old settler who had long since departed. The original settlers who persisted in Manitoba were normally the people with nothing to fear from the process in the first place.[32] They were the claimants with HBC titles, or settlers with significant improvements recorded by surveyors (a house, outbuildings, and at least ten acres under cultivation — a group of about 800 families out of a total of nearly 2,000).[33] The others, the cases resembling that of Jean Baptiste Jolibois, maintained a tenuous hold on the land they believed they owned until they were evicted or sold their defective claim to newcomers like Callum (who received his patent in 1888; the land claimed by Jolibois was patented

---

29. Saskatchewan Archives Board, William Pearce Papers, Letter Book, Pearce to A.M. Burgess, 22 November 1883.

30. The earliest confirmation was reported to Macdonald in the spring of 1883 (PAC, Macdonald Papers, Incoming Correspondence, p. 134760, A. Walsh to Macdonald, 26 April 1883). The final report of the subsequent investigation did not arrive in Ottawa until March 1886 (see PAC, Records of the Department of the Interior, RG 15, vol. 232, file 2447).

31. The separation of the two ministerial offices was by Order in Council of Canada, 17 October 1883. The first public disclosure of the "Lang conspiracy" appears to have been in the Toronto *Globe*, 10 May 1885.

32. Compare "Table 4: Geographical Location and Children of Manitoba Families, 1870" with "Table 5: Recognition of Riverlot Occupants by the Government of Canada" in Sprague and Frye, *Genealogy of the First Métis Nation.*

33. See "Table 1: Ethnic Groups' Recognition by Land Surveyors and the Distribution of Patents for River Lots" in Mailhot and Sprague, "Persistent Settlers," p. 11.

to another newcomer, James Begg, in 1882).[34]

The dispersal of the Métis and native English from Manitoba[35] was gradual but perceptible between 1871 and 1876; it became remarkable from 1877 to 1880; and the migration increased to a rush of personnel between 1881 and 1884.[36] Overall, more than 4,000 persons participated in the exodus, mainly to Saskatchewan.[37]

The migration of Manitobans was not unnoticed by police. Nor did the clergy fail to appeal for aid in resettlement. To understand the government's reaction to the alarms from the one source, and the supplications from the other, it is necessary to see the complicated larger pattern of Canada's emerging settlement priorities in the early 1880s.

---

34. See Table 5 in Sprague and Frye, *Genealogy of the First Métis Nation.*

35. A parallel development occurred in North Dakota at the same time. In the case of the American Métis, the United States government had negotiated a treaty guaranteeing that every family would be secure on the land then occupied but the Senate refused to ratify the agreement and the area became "a part of the white man's farming frontier of the post-Civil War Period." The non-ratification of the North Dakota treaty would appear to be the analytical equivalent of the non-enforcement of the Manitoba Act in Assiniboia. Moreover, the American government's suspicion that the North Dakota Métis had abetted Sioux "renegades" in 1862 was an exhibition of resentment by newcomers analogous to Ontario's hostility towards the Manitoba Métis for their acts of "insurrection" in 1869-70. See N.L. Woolworth, "Gingras, St Joseph and the Métis in the Northern Red River Valley, 1843-1873," *North Dakota History* 42:4 (1975), pp. 16-27.

36. The periodization of the Manitoba exodus is neatly illustrated by the timing of new arrivals at new communities in the North West. At the largest settlement of displaced Manitobans, only 10 per cent emigrated between 1871 and 1876; 20 per cent from 1877 to 1880; and fully 70 per cent between 1881 and 1884. See Mailhot and Sprague, "Persistent Settlers," pp. 18-26.

37. See "Table 3: Métis and Native English Population of the North-West Territories (June 1884)," in ibid., p. 12.

George Stephen, ca. 1885
(Provincial Archives of Manitoba)

"Stephen hinted that he would resign before letting the government take over even part of his property."

Chapter 9

Reaching for the Commercial Value of the North West

The basic promise to newcomers in the statute that first proclaimed Canada's homestead policy in 1872 was that "any person, male or female, who is the sole head of a family, or any male who has attained the age of eighteen years," could claim a free grant of 160 acres, and a pre-emptive right to buy the adjoining quarter section at one dollar an acre. Such applicants had to pay a $10 registration or "entry" fee, and "occupy and cultivate" their homestead for three years before claiming patent, but where else could a person hope for 320 acres of some of the finest wheat land in the world for the paltry sum of $170?[1]

The United States had made no such offer to its settlers. By their earlier, competing legislation (enacted in 1862), "pre-emption" meant a "squatter's right" to claim land occupied before survey, and the settlement duties required of later arrivals extended to five years.[2] In principle, the intending settler who knew both laws should have found Canada more attractive than, for example, North Dakota. In practice, however, the more generous offer to Canadian homesteaders was almost as hollow as the verbal accommodation of the Métis in the Manitoba Act.

Throughout the early 1880s most of the land that ought to have attracted homesteaders was either closed or available only for purchase because of the overriding impact of section 125(b) in the 1879 revision of the Dominion Lands Act. The overriding clause empowered the Cabinet

> To reserve from general sale and settlement Dominion lands to such extent as may be required to aid in the construction of railways in Manitoba or in the Territories owned by the Dominion, and to provide for the disposal of such lands, notwithstanding anything contained in the said Act, in such manner and on such terms as may be deemed expedient. . . .

---

1. See "Homestead Rights or Free Grant Lands" covered by section 33(1-12) in Statutes of Canada (1872), Chapter 23.
2. Chester Martin, *"Dominion Lands" Policy* (Toronto, 1973), p. 16.

In July 1879, expediency seemed to dictate the reservation of every acre of vacant land for 110 miles on *either* side of the expected route of the Pacific Railway for the entire distance from Winnipeg to the Rocky Mountains. None of the 100 million acres within the 220-mile railway belt contemplated in 1879 was to be given away in 160-acre homesteads. All was for sale; the closer to the railway, the higher the price. Any quarter section in Belt "A" (five miles either side of the main line) was priced at six dollars an acre. Further out, homesteads up to eighty acres were permitted, if the settler agreed to buy the other half of the quarter section at twice the normal pre-emption price.[3] The rationale, Macdonald explained to the House of Commons on May 10, was that the railway was to be built on the value of the lands through which it passed.[4]

Critics, including the Lieutenant Governor of the territories, considered the scheme unworkable because they imagined that there were few individuals who would "spend a small fortune to reach the country and afterwards submit to pay two dollars [minimum] per acre for the land."[5] Of course Macdonald did not intend to restrict the pace of railway construction to the rate of collection of payments in land sales to individuals. His aim was to use the 100 million acres as collateral for $50 million to be recruited in 1879 from British capitalists buying Government of Canada railway bonds. As the railway advanced into new territory ahead of settlement, he expected that newcomers would cheerfully pay the required price, and that would provide the revenue to retire the bonds paying four per cent to investors in the interim.[6]

The Prime Minister went to London in August 1879 hoping that the British government would support his public works proposition for defence reasons, just as the imperial authorities had taken an interest in earlier railway and canal schemes that were initially uneconomic — sensible only from the standpoint of imperial defence.[7] In the case of the Pacific Railway, the Canadian prospectus boasted that once the system began sea-to-sea operations about 1890 it would provide a safe, reliable, all-British route across North America, a vital "Imperial link" between the Atlantic and Pacific oceans. Moreover, if the British government supported the concept through the construction phase, Macdonald assured Prime Minister Disraeli that Canada's railway would cost Great Britain nothing. "Not only will the credit of Canada be pledged for, and all its revenue charged with, the

---

3. See the memorandum on regulations for the disposal of agricultural lands in the West in PAC, Macdonald Papers, Incoming Correspondence, pp. 45076-45087, prepared by A.M. Burgess for Macdonald, 7 March 1882.

4. Martin, *"Dominion Lands" Policy*, p. 42.

5. PAC, Mackenzie Papers, Letter Books, pp. 2282-2287, David Laird to Alexander Mackenzie, 1 July 1879.

6. W. Kaye Lamb, *History of the Canadian Pacific Railway* (New York, 1977), p. 65.

7. Creighton, *Old Chieftain*, p. 267.

redemption of the bonds,'' Macdonald asserted, the ''tracts of land to be assigned and the railway itself with its earnings will stand as additional securities, and these . . . will be found eventually sufficient of themselves to redeem the debt. . . .''[8]

In other words, Macdonald and his colleagues were quite prepared to ignore the declared policy of free land for homesteaders in the interest of securing the capital to build the transcontinental railway that the Cabinet agreed was indispensable if Canada was to become more than ''merely a geographical expression.'' To their credit in 1879, they did at least contemplate a trade of one public property for another. The Pacific Railway envisioned then was to be a public work, not a private enterprise paid for by the public.

As the British government seemed less than enthusiastic about endorsing Macdonald's public works scheme in August, the next alternative was to attract private investors with a large cash subsidy and land grant, as in 1872. Fifty million dollars was the estimated total cost of the work to be done in British Columbia, the Prairies, and over the north shore of Lake Superior. An offer of the sections completed to date plus $20 million in cash and 30 million acres in land was the subsidy agreeable to Cabinet, but Macdonald's old friend and President of the Bank of Montreal, George Stephen, insisted that $26.5 million subsidy and a 35 million-acre land grant were the minimum he would need to build the rest of the railway as a private undertaking.[9]

The anomaly of the Government of Canada providing the capital to a private company troubled some senior members of the government. As a result, a second attempt to recruit support from the British government was undertaken in London in the summer of 1880 — with the same result as the year before. Once more, Macdonald and company entertained an offer from Stephen and associates, conveniently on hand in London.

On September 4, Macdonald telegraphed the information back to Ottawa: ''Best terms can be got are twenty-five million cash, twenty-five million acres. . . .'' He added that four colleagues with him in England agreed that they could do no better for the moment. Macdonald asked for concurrence from the rest of the Cabinet in Canada. ''Absolute secrecy. Answer quick.''[10] They concurred, and the preliminary agreement on the award of the most lucrative patronage plum in Canadian history was signed on the same day.

The contracting parties then recrossed the Atlantic, and pursued the

---

8. See the Cabinet memorandum on the Pacific Railway scheme in PAC, Macdonald Papers, Incoming Correspondence, pp. 52521-52529, attributed to J.A. Macdonald, S.L. Tilley, and Charles Tupper, 20 August 1879.

9. Lamb, *CPR*, pp. 66-67.

10. Macdonald quoted in Creighton, *Old Chieftain*, p. 299.

terms of their arrangement through more meetings before signing the formal agreement on October 21, 1880. The final accord called for several special tax exemptions, monopoly rights, and specified how the cash and land grant were to be paid. A portion of the money was to be claimable after the completion of each 20 miles of the main line,[11] and the fiction that the cost of the railway was to be born by the value of the vacant land through which it ran persisted in the implication that a new 48-mile belt from Winnipeg to the Rocky Mountains was going to yield 25 million acres in the odd-numbered sections reserved for the CPR, with a similar quantity of land to be sold for at least $25 million by the Government of Canada from the even-numbered sections of the same 48-mile belt.

A particularly important aspect of the land subsidy was the railway's right to claim its 25 million acres from outside as well as within the 24-mile belt on either side of the route. The justification for the "indemnity" promise was ostensibly nothing more than the reasonable recognition that some of the sections along the railway's main line were likely to be unsuitable for agriculture, therefore, unsaleable. The full story of the privilege for taking the land grant from within or beyond the railway belt was, however, more complicated and reflected the political artistry of its authors as much as the geographical imperatives. In the first place, it was mathematically impossible for the CPR to have found 25 million acres of odd sections in the 48-mile belt even if every acre were "fairly fit for settlement." If every inch were the Garden of Eden the most that could be located in the 48-mile belt was 10 million acres.[12] The second consideration was that from the beginning the directors had contemplated[13] a radical change from the surveyed route through the Saskatchewan Valley (then following Yellowhead Pass to the Pacific), preferring a flatter, shorter run close to the American border through near desert (using as yet undiscovered passes through the mountains). Selecting their grant from a 48-mile belt of that territory would mean most of their land would be unsaleable at any price.[14] The "indemnity" clause gave the CPR the benefit of flexibility in choosing its route without jeopardizing the railway's claim to a full share of the best 25 million acres of farmland to be served later by its own branch lines running north. The pretence that nearly all the land was likely to come from the 48-mile belt only made the contract look more palatable to Parliament.

---

11. Lamb, *CPR*, pp. 70-74.

12. Martin, *"Dominion Lands" Policy*, p. 49.

13. The change in route was on the minds of the directors as early as August of 1880, according to Lamb, *CPR*, p. 79.

14. The proportion is the CPR's own estimate, based on the rejected quantity in preference for acreage elsewhere. See James B. Hedges, *Building the Canadian West: The Land and Colonization Policies of the Canadian Pacific Railway* (New York, 1939), pp. 38-39.

But the other lucrative aspects of the contract (the tax concessions and the monopoly clause) were not so easily disguised, and received an unusually rough passage through the House of Commons when the matter was debated between December 13, 1880, and February 1, 1881. The Opposition hurled its greatest denunciation at the monopoly and tax benefits, questioning the apparent ease of the relationship between Macdonald and Stephen, wondering if other businessmen without similar access to the Prime Minister had received equal consideration for their proposals. And even if Stephen's group was the only Canadian syndicate capable of taking on the enormous project, Liberals asserted that the alternative of building piecemeal along with demand, rather than extravagantly in advance of settlement, was more sensible. Winnipeg had acquired a north-south railway connection to the outer world in 1878; soon its east-west link was expected to be in operation (no later than 1882) with the completion of the line that they had started from Thunder Bay. Later, no doubt, other lines would serve Winnipeg and points west as well.[15]

Macdonald answered the Opposition by exploiting nationalist sentiment, insisting that the country could not afford a continuation of the slow construction pace of the previous years. Canada faced a national emergency, he said. A railway had to be running from sea to sea within ten years or the Dominion would likely perish; the issue was, therefore, a matter of "patriotism." Macdonald claimed that the Canadian Pacific Railway he proposed was the only "arrangement which will give us all we want, which will satisfy all the loyal, legitimate aspirations, which will give us a great, a united, a rich, an improving, a developing Canada, instead of making us tributary to American laws, to American railways, to American bondage...."[16]

For saving Canada, Stephen expected to gain a great deal personally. His private estimate of costs was $45 million. He and the other directors were putting up $5 million of their capital. With the expected cash subsidy and another $15 million raised from other "resources," the original investors would still enjoy exclusive ownership if they avoided a public issue of stock or bonds. Stephen guessed that shares would sell at miserably low prices until the railway proved itself. A bond issue was abhorrent because he dreaded mortgaging the company's future. Stephen's intention in 1881 was to depend mainly on the cash subsidy, revenue from the portions of the line that were already in operation, and from land sales.[17]

The desire to generate millions from real estate was potentially in

---

15. For the most balanced brief account of the debate of the CPR bill, see P.B. Waite, *Canada, 1874-1896*, pp. 108-112.

16. Macdonald quoted in Creighton, *Old Chieftain*, p. 308.

17. Lamb, *CPR*, p. 88.

conflict with the traffic-generating, large-scale influx of newcomers which might have followed the distribution of free grants of land.[18] Stephen's hope was that he might exploit Macdonald's often-repeated notion that the railway and the government were partners co-ordinating the distribution of government land for maximum benefit to the railway. At first, that meant having the Department of the Interior sell the government's even-numbered sections near the main line for a higher price than the railway's odd-numbered sections in the same vicinity. With a government price of $6 per acre, there was a strong incentive for settlers to prefer CPR lands that were $3.50 per acre cheaper, and even more attractive in terms of payment — installments over five years with a fifty per cent rebate if the land came under cultivation within four years.[19]

By the end of 1881, however, Stephen realized the absurdity of competing against the Americans' free-land policy with a cheap-land scheme in Canada. Stephen's solution was for his country to give its land away free. A return to the free-homestead system would encourage a more rapid influx of newcomers, sustain heavy traffic on the completed sections, and as soon as the free land showed the slightest development, the CPR acreage would look attractive at $2.50 per acre for the later arrivals. Consequently, late in December, Stephen advised Macdonald that "it is a mistake charging more for the land near the railway" and urged his partner to consider that it might be "better to give that advantage away to the first comers." In Stephen's view, "that attraction if speedily set forth will be more potent and immediate in its effect upon emigration than anything else we can offer."[20] Macdonald agreed and persuaded the Cabinet to open all even-numbered sections for settlement as homesteads on January 1, 1882.[21]

The restoration of the free-homestead policy contradicted the frequently repeated assertion that the cost of the subsidy was to be born by the value of the land through which the railway passed. Still, the announcement did accord with Stephen's request, and was timely as well in the election campaign that Macdonald was leading at the same time. His "national policy" of tariff protection for the industrializing east and rapid settlement of the Prairie West — the central thrust of 1878 — was reiterated in January 1882, when he announced that the railway was going to be completed, not in 1890, but four years earlier than the contract required. Macdonald said he was proud to think that he might be able to ride a train from sea to sea

---

18. If the conflict proved insurmountable, Stephen confided to Macdonald in May of 1881, "It is *settling*, not *selling* that we must aim at . . . if our lands won't sell we will give them away to settlers" (quoted in Lamb, *CPR*, p. 216).

19. PAC, Macdonald Papers, Incoming Correspondence, pp. 53186-53189, Dennis to Macdonald, 9 May 1881.

20. Ibid., pp. 121297-121302, Stephen to Macdonald, 20 December 1881.

21. Martin, *"Dominion Lands" Policy*, p. 43.

before he was "quite an angel" (and, he might have added, before the next election anticipated in 1886).[22]

The reason for the unexpectedly rapid completion of the line was not entirely attributable to the engineering skill of Stephen's construction chief, Cornelius Van Horne, or the alleged financial wizardry of George Stephen. Two other important factors were the nearly unlimited support of the Government of Canada and a new, more easily constructed route which was many miles shorter than the line previously surveyed through the rolling agricultural lands along the Saskatchewan River. Of course, the change to the south tended to belie the assertion that the CPR was a "settlement railway," but that problem was addressed by Stephen and his directors who met in May 1881 with a Canadian botanist, John Macoun, finder of flowers in the desert wilds west of Moose Jaw Creek.[23] The owners of the CPR encouraged him to publicize his notion that the flora he had just collected were nothing in comparison with the bountiful yield of wheat that might be expected from the same area.[24] It made no perceptible difference later when other experts, including H.Y. Hind, declared that Macoun's "meteorological tables are all faked." The CPR and the Canadian Geological Survey had the report they wanted, and Stephen could claim that the cause of settlement was just as well served by running the main line south of the "fertile belt."[25]

In fact, the real settlement emphasis was still on the fertile belt where Hind and Palliser had placed it originally. Consequently, the emphasis in land distribution remained on land sales in that area rather than on free-homesteads along the main line. In March 1882, the first row of sections in the relatively arable land east of Moose Jaw Creek was withdrawn from homestead entry,[26] and Macdonald invited applications from syndicates for wholesale purchase of settlement tracts twenty-four miles north of the railway.[27]

New regulations permitted land sales on an unlimited basis. Promoters could approach the government for almost any quantity and acquire

---

22. Macdonald quoted in Creighton, *Old Chieftain,* p. 326.

23. Lamb, *CPR,* p. 79.

24. The work that completed Macoun's mission as publicist was *Manitoba and the Great North-West* (Guelph, 1882).

25. PAC, Macdonald Papers, Incoming Correspondence, pp. 186562-186566, H.Y. Hind to Macdonald, 8 March 1883 and PAC, Records of the Department of the Interior, RG 16, vol. 295, file 61147, "The Corruption of the Geological Survey" by Henry Hind [May 1883]. See also the chapter on Macoun in Owram, *Promise of Eden,* pp. 149-167.

26. March 11, 1882 is the withdrawal date mentioned in a subsequent Order in Council of Canada (30 April 1884) that reopened the "mile belt reserve" for homestead and pre-emption.

27. See A.N. Lalonde, "Colonization Companies in the 1880s," *Saskatchewan History* 24 (1971), pp. 101-114.

millions of acres for half the normal price by "placing two settlers on each section in the tract." Macdonald envisioned a total distribution of perhaps 10 million acres for 10 million dollars. As a land boom developed in Winnipeg in 1881 and continued into 1882, hundreds of other speculators applied for good positions in what they hoped would be an extension of the same land rush further west. Over 250 applications crossed Macdonald's desk between February and April 1882, many stressing long and loyal service to the Conservative Party among the reasons why their proposals should receive prompt and favourable consideration. By June 1882, 106 applications had received the approving initials of "JAMD" and 6 million acres of the best agricultural land in central Saskatchewan were designated "colonization tracts."[28]

A typical prospectus of the emerging companies was that of the Land and Colonization Company of Canada, nominally headed by the Duke of Buckingham and two Liverpool "capitalists"—though the real leaders were a group of Montreal Tories that included Thomas Cram, John Rankin, F.W. Henshaw, and J.J.C. Wurtele. Their award was one million acres on the North Saskatchewan River near Prince Albert. Like the others, they promised to perform a great philanthropic service by assisting the surplus population of England to make new homes for themselves in the Little Britain of the Canadian North West. "It is well known," the prospectus asserted, "that a large portion of the industrial population of Great Britain are unable to avail themselves of the liberal offers of land by the Canadian Government, as . . . it requires at least 500 dollars (100 pounds) to commence farming operations and they cannot provide themselves with that amount." The remedy was to back the newcomers with the resources of a company, "so that the Settler will at once be enabled to begin farming operations without having to undergo the preliminary expenses. . . ." In time, newcomers might accumulate a large enough surplus to challenge their status as share-croppers or tenant farmers and buy their land outright. But either way, the promoters were confident that the "sources from which the company will obtain the large profits expected from its operations will be as follows: A) Sale of improved farms B) Letting farms on lease C) Farming on the sharing system D) Sale of Town lots E) Cattle Ranches F) General trading."[29]

No such proprietorial regime succeeded, however, because the

---

28. The most important record of such patronage is in PAC, Records of the Department of the Interior, RG 15, vol. 277, file 44447. There one finds the full "Schedule of Colonizaton Tracts proposed to be granted." Each entry contains the names of the grantees, the area to be granted, the legal description of the land, and the approving initials of Sir John A. Macdonald.

29. Ibid., vol. 273, file 42819, "Prospectus: Land and Colonization Co. of Canada," [1882].

Winnipeg land boom collapsed in the summer of 1882, and investors developed second thoughts about the North West at the same time. Consequently, of the 106 applications approved, only 27 paid the first installment of one-fifth of the total purchase price.[30] Moreover, officials in the Department of the Interior and the CPR reacted adversely to allowing so many latecomers into the land business on such a vast scale. A.M. Burgess (soon to be the Deputy Minister of the Department of the Interior) warned Lindsay Russell in September that so much land was reserved for one company or another, "we practically deny the intending settler an asylum" on free land.[31]

As Macdonald began his withdrawal from the affairs of the Department of the Interior in the spring of 1883, the pressure to abandon his colonization company scheme increased. His successor as Minister, D.L. Macpherson, recommended outright abolition in May,[32] but only a discreet halt was declared in June when an Order in Council announced that enough land had been allotted "to test the plan . . . [therefore] no new grants or allotments should be made . . . to colonization companies."[33] By that time, the CPR was recovering its commanding lead in the wholesale land market.

Early in 1881 CPR officials estimated that the entire 48-mile railway belt through the southerly route was not likely to yield more than 6 million acres acceptable to the company. They advocated reservation of a vast tract of land in the Saskatchewan Valley early in 1882 before all the best acreage were alloted to colonization companies. They were particularly anxious to secure all the land between present-day Saskatoon and Edmonton. From such a vast northerly tract they were certain of finding at least 19 million suitable acres.[34]

Anticipating the closure of the arrangement at any moment, Stephen arranged for a colonization company of his own in the summer of 1882. A syndicate calling itself the Canada North West Land Company emerged as the CPR's prime customer, agreeing to buy 5 million acres of the expected Saskatchewan property with $13.5 million of its own bonds, negotiable paper that Stephen might sell in his turn to realize cash for construction purposes.[35]

When Macdonald seemed reluctant about setting aside the northerly tract, the railway president reminded the Prime Minister that he was a

30. Lalonde, "Colonization Companies," p. 103.
31. PAC, Macdonald Papers, Incoming Correspondence, pp. 45574-45584, Burgess to Russell, 11 September 1882.
32. Ibid., pp. 112596-112597, Macpherson to Macdonald, 4 May 1883.
33. Order in Council of Canada, 4 June 1883. See PAC, Records of the Department of the Interior, RG 15, vol. 277, file 44447.
34. Hedges, *Building the Canadian West,* p. 38.
35. Lamb, *CPR,* p. 92.

"senior partner in the outside wing of our co-partnership," and repeated that "it is of utmost importance that we get all the lands we have earned located at once...."[36] Subsequently, Macdonald did as he was told, and moved as quickly as he dealt with anything to complete the arrangements. The required Order in Council reserving the entire western two-thirds of the Saskatchewan River Valley was approved in October, by which time the land boom had collapsed, the Canada North West Land Company was refusing to purchase all the land originally negotiated, and a new estimate of the inferiority of the land in the 48-mile belt prompted Stephen's people to inform the Department of the Interior that another million acres had to be located in a second vast reserve elsewhere.[37]

The reservation of yet another tract amounting to 2.5 million acres in the Qu'Appelle Valley in November 1882 appeared to resolve the question of locating the last of the CPR's 25 million acres, but the disappointing outcome of the Canada North West Land Company left Stephen cash poor at the end of the year. His solution in December was a $30 million stock issue to be sold to a New York brokerage firm at a 48 per cent discount. The resulting $15.5 million would take him most of the way through 1883 but left him doubly determined to find more effective means for recruiting land buyers in large volume.[38]

Early in the new year he went to England with two purposes (other than capital recruitment) in mind. One was to persuade the Hudson's Bay Company to pool its land resources with the Canada North West Land Company to reduce overhead costs and co-ordinate recruitment of immigrants. In February, John Rose (representing the HBC in the negotiations) reported to Macdonald that the "scheme, or rather idea is still in embryo, and might not meet with the approval of the shareholders...."[39] Still, the idea continued "simmering" and Stephen was hopeful late in March when he reported to Macdonald that Rose and the railway president were still pursuing their "land pooling project." Stephen believed that he was extremely close to creating "one great powerful colonization agency ... which will have a great influence in promoting the Settlement of the North West."[40]

Ultimately, however, pooling was not possible because the interests of the two largest companies proved irreconcilable. Stephen wanted to sell his land at comparatively low prices to generate a quick cash return for the

---

36. PAC, Macdonald Papers, Incoming Correspondence, pp. 121437-121440, Stephen to Macdonald, 16 July 1882.

37. Hedges, *Building the Canadian West*, p. 39.

38. Lamb, *CPR*, p. 93.

39. PAC, Macdonald Papers, Incoming Correspondence, pp. 117699-117703, Rose to Macdonald, 1 February 1883.

40. Ibid., pp. 121992-121994, Stephen to Macdonald, 22 March 1883.

construction of the main and branch lines, while the HBC was more prepared to wait for an unearned increment. The Hudson's Bay Company feared that dumping too much land on the market at once would depress prices even further.[41]

Unable to persuade the directors of the Hudson's Bay Company that they could not afford to wait for a profit in a region that would not develop in the first place, Stephen pressed all the more firmly on his second objective, which was selling an assisted emigration scheme to the British. In mid-May, Gladstone did agree to invest 1 million in resettlement loans for impoverished Irish, if Canada would guarantee repayment. Stephen cabled his coup to Macdonald on May 11. The Prime Minister replied the same day that the timing was less than ideal: "No legislation possible this season. Government favourably inclined. Await details."[42]

Subsequently, however, nothing developed in what might have been Canada's first experiment in foreign aid. Macdonald tried to console Stephen with the apology that the proposal was simply unworkable: "If we endorsed the first million for the Irish, we couldn't stop when asked to assist Settlers from England, or Scotland and there would be no end to it."[43] In fact, Macdonald's real objections concerned the proposed beneficiaries, as he confessed to Tupper later in July: "*Entre nous, we don't want the Western Irish emigration. They are bad settlers and thoroughly disloyal. It won't do to have a little Ireland in the North West.*"[44]

Although Stephen (who was Scots Protestant by birth) agreed that the Irish were "a doubtful lot at best," he preferred any kind of European settlement to the impoverishment of his railway. Consequently, the CPR president scolded his "senior partner" late in August for his apparently half-hearted attitude towards settler recruitment. "I have a feeling," Stephen confided, "that the co-partnership between us & the government for the settlement of the country is not so active and efficient as it should

---

41. The clearest evidence of the conflict of interest between the two companies was the discrepancy in the average price at which their lands were sold: gross average of $12.10 per acre for HBC lands, $7.63 for CPR land (Martin, *"Dominion Lands" Policy*, p. 144). Still, it must be admitted that the HBC did face a dilemma. On the one hand, the Company wanted an immediate land revenue and feared the possible political consequences of being regarded as too speculative. Both of those considerations called for quick sales. On the other hand, the directors were equally determined to reap the largest possible profit from their land resources and did not hesitate to criticize persons in charge of the land department for selling the company's real estate too cheaply (See J.E. Rea, ed., *The Letters of Charles John Brydges, 1883-1889*, Publications of Hudson's Bay Record Society, 33 (Winnipeg, 1981).

42. Macdonald quoted in Creighton, *Old Chieftain*, p. 351.

43. PAC, Macdonald Papers, Transcripts, vol. 584, Macdonald to Stephen, 23 June 1883.

44. Macdonald quoted in Lamb, *CPR*, pp. 218-219.

be."[45] If the government balked at assisted emigration, the least that might be done was releasing some of the government-held even-numbered sections near the railway main line for immediate occupancy by homesteaders. "We must in some way make it easier for emigrants to get on to homesteads." Stephen asserted that "good settlers" had looked at opportunities for free land in Canada, found nothing, and "left our country annoyed at the difficulty of finding homesteads."[46]

Shamed by previous timidity, Macdonald did agree to that small concession. Late in 1883, the "mile belt reserve" of even sections immediately alongside the railway main line (withdrawn from settlement in March 1882) was opened again from Winnipeg to Moose Jaw after January 1, 1884.[47] At the same time, Stephen hoped for another favour in the form of an infusion of financial support beyond the $25 million in the contract.

The scheme Stephen devised in October 1883 was for the Government of Canada to guarantee current and prospective CPR stockholders a minimum five per cent dividend on their investment. Part of the dividend guarantee was to come from $15 million to be deposited by the railway with the federal treasury. The remainder would flow from the public credit.[48] Stephen's gamble was that the promise of a certain return would exert an upward pressure on the value of stock already issued, and attract new buyers for a fresh block to go on the market early in the new year. In mid-December, however, the value of CPR stock moved unexpectedly in the wrong direction, suggesting that knowledgeable buyers interpreted the guarantee as nothing less than the last desperate attempt to save an overextended enterprise before the railway passed into receivership, or suffered a worse fate.[49]

On December 15, Stephen informed Macdonald that "things have gone to the devil in New York" and pleaded for "something . . . at *once* to put the company out of discredit or we better give up and let the government step in and carry on the business of the company."[50] Stephen's "something" was to make a new arrangement for expediting the dispersal of the $25 million cash subsidy, $12 million of which had yet to be earned

45. PAC, Macdonald Papers, Incoming Correspondence, pp. 121711-121714, Stephen to Macdonald, 13 August 1883.

46. Ibid.

47. Order in Council of Canada, 29 November 1883. See also PAC, Records of the Department of the Interior, RG 15, vol. 275, file 43449.

48. Lamb, *CPR*, pp. 107-108.

49. According to Creighton, the falling price of CPR stock was clear proof of a conspiracy to destroy the railway. In his interpretation, "Macdonald had known from the beginning . . . that there were powerful interests in the world which had deliberately determined to effect the ruin of his railway." Creighton, *Old Chieftain*, p. 362.

50. PAC, Macdonald Papers, Incoming Correspondence, pp. 122029-122030, Stephen to Macdonald, 15 December 1883.

by the requisite miles of completed railway. At the same time, he demanded a $15 million low-interest loan. With that $27 million, Stephen believed "the road can be completed by the spring of 1886" — well before the next general election. He asserted that "nothing short of this will do any good."[51]

Macdonald hesitated. His first impulse in any crisis was to wait and see. Time and again he had learned that inaction would make some of the most complicated problems apparently dissolve; the unforeseen consequences of a quick fix often made a touchy situation even more complicated. The CPR financial crisis of 1883-84 was the kind of problem he hated most. It was not a matter of placating an angry colleague with pleasant assurances of future action, or soothing the electorate by climbing the fiscal oak tree to shake loose a few acorns to the swine below.[52] The issue called for bold strategic action, a make-or-break decision that had to be taken at once.

One set of colleagues in the Cabinet, a small group headed by J.H. Pope (the Minister of Railways) informed Macdonald that the matter was uncomplicated and clear. Stephen knew his business. They had to follow his instructions. "The day the Canadian Pacific busts," Pope predicted, "the Conservative party busts the day after."[53] Other Tories agreed that the national railway was an economic and political necessity, and agreed as well that the campaign promise of 1882 had to be fulfilled before the next general election in 1887. Yet a group of Cabinet ministers around D.L. Macpherson and Sir Alexander Campbell had become increasingly resentful of Stephen's imperious attitude towards the "partnership" sealed with Canada in 1880-81.

Macpherson reasoned that if Canada and the CPR were partners in any meaningful sense, it was inappropriate to shoulder yet more of the risk without acquiring a tangible interest in the railway they were paying for without buying. Macpherson proposed a stock purchase that would give the company the needed capital for an 1886 completion date, and leave Canada with a 48 per cent interest in the national railway forever after.[54]

Stephen's reaction was horrified opposition. When he first heard a preliminary verbal rendition of Macpherson's late-December written proposal, the railway president advised Macdonald that "our friend Macpherson has not grasped the situation, or he would not talk as he does." Then, moving from condescension to indignation, Stephen hinted that he would resign

---

51. Ibid.
52. Macdonald's swine model of democratic politics is discussed in Carl Berger, *The Writing of Canadian History* (Toronto, 1976), p. 225.
53. Pope quoted in Lamb, *CPR*, p. 109.
54. PAC, Macdonald Papers, Incoming Correspondence, pp. 112498-112504, Macpherson to Macdonald, 26 December 1883.

before letting the government take over even part of his property. Canada was suddenly no longer the partner he wanted, but a threatening "*outside pressure*."[55]

Fearing he would lose his CPR president if he followed Macpherson's and Campbell's advice, and fearing he would lose control of his majority if he agreed to Stephen's demands, Macdonald tried doing nothing a little longer. Increasingly excited notes and telegrams from Stephen finally convinced Macdonald in January 1884 that he had run out of time. He turned his back on the Macpherson-Campbell proposal and called his friend Charles Tupper home from Britain to take the heat of the parliamentary fury which was certain to erupt when the railway-aid bill was introduced to the House of Commons in February.

When the aid package did come before the House, Opposition members claimed that the proposal was clear confirmation of their earlier warnings against the original bill in 1881. Opposing the matter even more furiously in 1884, they claimed that the new route would leave the company teetering on the edge of bankruptcy indefinitely, that it would constantly require fresh assistance and perennially receive it from the corrupt intimacy between Stephen and Macdonald. That prompted Stephen to demand a speech from his Ottawa partner. "The pretension that the line cannot pay for many years to come is an invention of the enemy which it is absolutely necessary to correct." As asserted in his letter to Macdonald on February 10, "If the North West succeeds, the CPR cannot fail." But he also said, "if the CPR should prove to be a commercial failure, it will be because the North West is a delusion — nothing in it."[56]

Macdonald preferred to leave the speech-making in Parliament to Tupper. Occasionally the Prime Minister spoke on procedural issues or in personal defence of his old friend for returning to work for the salvation of the railway.[57] Tupper performed well, as did the rest of Macdonald's obedient majority. There were no public utterances by opponents in Cabinet. Nor did any other Conservatives oppose the aid package in the House. Yet Macdonald knew that party discipline was strained to the limit. A significant portion of his colleagues opposed aid in the form Stephen had demanded. As a personal favour to their "Old Chieftain" they had not rebelled openly. They voted with their leader to the last division. As Macdonald slumped back into his seat after the final vote late on the evening of February 28,[58] he must have known that he had reached the limit of normal

---

55. Ibid., pp. 122029-122030, Stephen to Macdonald, 15 December 1883.
56. Ibid., pp. 122037-122040, Stephen to Macdonald, 10 February 1884.
57. House of Commons Debates, 18-19, 21, 26 February 1884, pp. 373, 376, 460, 468, 524.
58. Ibid., p. 569.

parliamentary manoeuvring. If there were any more crises in the construction of the Pacific Railway before the expected completion date in 1886, such matters would have to be resolved by something beyond normal parliamentary manoeuvring.

Lawrence Clarke, ca. 1880
(Provincial Archives of Manitoba)

'' . . . the Métis reacted to Clarke's news as the final provocation.''

156

Chapter 10

Confronting Riel and Completing the CPR

As the construction of Stephen's railway proceeded across the Prairies, the largest exodus of Red River Métis moved from Manitoba towards Saskatchewan. The most frequent destination was the district of Prince Albert, attractive because of employment by the Hudson's Bay Company (distributing freight to or from nearby Fort Carlton) and because the vacant land fronting the south branch of the Saskatchewan River closely resembled that of the old Red River colony. As positive reports from the first migrants reached discouraged relatives and former neighbours still in the large Métis parishes of St Norbert, St Franois Xavier, and Baie St. Paul, one relative followed another with increasing frequency in 1882 and 1883.[1]

In the new colony, called St Laurent, the many settlers of the early 1880s were careful to avoid trespassing on the claims of their countrymen,[2] but normally they paid little attention to the settlement status of particular parcels as designated by the Department of the Interior. The Métis were not concerned with the grid pattern of townships, sections, and ranges, and whether the parcel on which they landed happened to fit into an even-numbered section (potentially open for homesteading) or was odd-numbered (reserved for some system of sale).[3] And even if they had been careful to settle exclusively on even-numbered sections fronting on the river, they would still have encountered difficulty with the Dominion Lands Branch because, although the basic sectional survey had been completed in 1879 (and in the normal course of events would have been open to homestead entry within one year), there was an inexplicable delay in the case of

---

1. See Mailhot and Sprague, ''Persistent Settlers.''
2. There were no ''Class 16'' claims (land disputes) in the detailed report upon St Laurent submitted by the Lands Board to headquarters in the autumn of 1884. See University of Alberta Archives, William Pearce Papers, MG 9/2/4-4, vol. 4, pp. 224-275.
3. For the system of sectional survey adopted by Canada see Chester Martin, ''Dominion Lands'' Policy.

157

St Laurent.[4]

Part of the delay is attributable to the effect of Macdonald's land policy: on the south branch of the Saskatchewan, portions of several townships amounting to more than 50,000 acres had been reserved for the Prince Albert Colonization Company in April 1882; and the area underwent an inspection nearly equivalent to resurvey in 1883 before the final reservation occurred in November 1883.[5] Homestead entries became acceptable in February 1884.[6]

In the interim, almost 300 Métis families had come into the territory and settled mainly on river lots they laid out for themselves. Periodically, the Métis settlers asked George Duck, the Dominion Lands Agent at Prince Albert, to record their claims and to recognize the emerging river-lot pattern. Of course all such requests were frustrated, at first because the land was not open to entry of any kind; then, after February 1884, the Métis found their claims were complicated by the distinction between river lots and section land, and whether the land was odd or even-numbered in the sectional survey.[7] A few residents complied with the legal complexities; more than ninety per cent of the population held out for their own pattern of settlement and for the demand for patents immediately. What made claimants all the more persistent was seeing that approximately one-fifth of the area of new settlement had been laid out as river-lots as the Métis had wanted (in 1878 to take account of the observed pattern of occupancy at the time of original survey),[8] but even the occupants of the regularly surveyed river lots were deemed to be "squatters" until they made legal entry and completed the settlement duties that would make them eligible for patents.[9]

The Minister of the Interior might have recommended use of the sweeping powers in section 125 of the Dominion Lands Act to cut through the complexities depicted on Map 2. He might have exempted the St Laurent Métis from the odd circumstances that made their case so complicated, but there was no political advantage to be gained by moving boldly on the matter. Sir John A. Macdonald preferred continuing doing nothing,

4. Flanagan, *Riel and the Rebellion*, pp. 30-33, 37-40.

5. PAC, RG 15, vol. 277, file 44447, p. 19; and House of Commons Debates, speech by Edward Blake, 6 July 1885, p. 3100.

6. The report of William Pearce, "All Claims to land ... on the South Saskatchewan" (University of Alberta Archives, Pearce Papers, MG 9/2, series 5, vol. 1, file 6 and series 4, vol. 4, pp. 888-901) states that some of the land was open for entry as early as 1881. But in response to a question on the subject in the House of Commons on June 8, 1885, Macdonald admitted that much of the district was not open for homestead entry until February 15, 1884 (House of Commons Debates, 8 June 1885, p. 2358).

7. PAC, Records of the Department of the Interior, RG 15, vol. 336, file 84478, George Duck to Commissioner of Dominion Lands, 15 June 1884.

8. Flanagan, *Riel Reconsidered*, p. 33.

9. Pearce, "All Claims to Land," p. 6-8.

Map 2:
Conflicting Claims to the Colony of St. Laurent

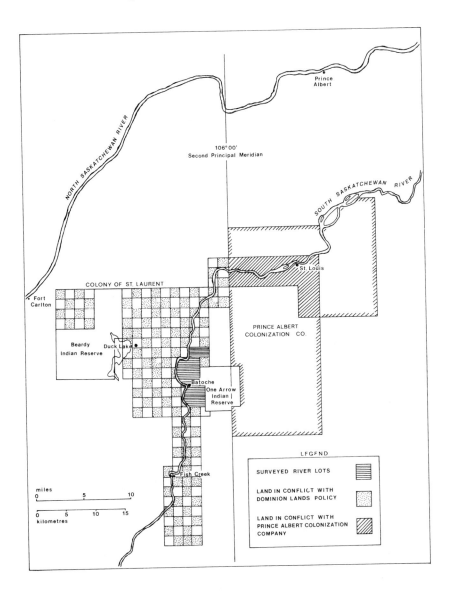

a position he had chosen deliberately in the spring of 1879 after Métis land claims first came to his attention as the Minister of the Interior following the Conservatives' return to power in September 1878.

Early in 1878, the North West "half breeds" had petitioned for land, seed grain, and implements to ease their transition to farming as the extinction of the buffalo became more and more evident in the late "1870s."[10] But none of the pleas for assistance had found favour with Macdonald's predecessor, David Mills, who dismissed all such appeals with a peculiar contradiction that was frequently evident in the utterances of officials writing on the subject of "half breeds." On the one hand, they denounced the allegedly inherent aversion of the Métis to field agriculture. On the other hand (in response to explicit requests for aid to make the transition to the way of life for which priests and certain government officials seemed to have prayed so fervently), they were told that non-Indians need not apply. In Mills' case, a letter went to the territorial governor explaining that the Métis were either Indians or not. If non-Indian, Mills could "not see upon what grounds the half breeds can claim to be treated in this particular differently from the white settlers in the territories."[11]

But the North West Territorial Council (the appointed committee advising the Lieutenant Governor) saw the matter rather differently. In its view, all native people previously dependent on the buffalo were entitled to aid. Council members recommended an assistance programme in August 1878 that was remarkably similar to the scheme adopted by the British for the resettlement of Loyalists in Canada after the American Revolution. They proposed that a "non-transferable location ticket" entitling the recipient to 160 acres should be issued to every "half breed" left without land in the North West. Once located on plots of their own choosing, each family could then make free use of government supplied seed-grain and farm implements for up to three years, just as the British had resettled their displaced persons in North America a century before. Then the Métis settlements would be carefully monitored in their agricultural development. The council members recommended a ten-year period of probation for each assisted claimant of a free grant. It was not recommended that they should receive their land automatically. The "half breeds" would have to perform settlement duties in their first three years, then continue in residence for seven more years before they would be eligible to claim patents for their farms.[12]

---

10. PAC, Macdonald Papers, Incoming Correspondence, pp. 42053-42056, 42067-42070.

11. Ibid., pp. 42048-42050, Mills to Laird, 18 March 1878. Later, Macdonald told the House of Commons that Mills had given the appropriate response. See House of Commons Debates, 6 July 1885, p. 3112.

12. PAC, Macdonald Papers, Incoming Correspondence, pp. 42067-42070, Minutes of the Council of the North West Territories, 2 August 1878.

Such was the policy recommended by the persons closest to the scene. Since the North West was a kind of crown colony ruled from Ottawa, one delay followed another. After Sir John A. Macdonald replaced David Mills in the Interior Ministry, he neither accepted nor rejected the advice of the Territorial Council, preferring instead to refer the matter to his Deputy Minister, J.S. Dennis, for more study. Dennis, in his turn, did draft a broader range of alternatives, adding two other possibilities to the council's proposal late in December 1878. One was extending the provisions of the Indian treaties to the Métis and native English, to "treat them as wards of the Government . . . and look forward to their remaining for many years in their present semi-barbarous state." The other possibility was giving them an issue of scrip as had been done with the Manitoba "half breed heads of families" with the same doubtful benefit to the nominal recipients in the North West. Reluctantly, Dennis recommended the package proposed by the North West Council.[13]

Macdonald still hesitated. He disliked rewarding the Métis for what he considered their own improvidence — it was they who spoiled their opportunities in Manitoba, and they as well who killed most of the buffalo.[14] Not worrying about further delay, the Prime Minister instructed Dennis to send his memorandum on the subject to the three bishops most acquainted with the Métis. The two Roman Catholic consultants added their endorsements to the Territorial Council's scheme, saying, "the half breed cannot compete with the White man in the discharge of the duties of civilized life unless some steps are taken at the outset to equalize the conditions on which they start." They admitted that the appropriate affirmative action would be expensive, but the first costs were expected to be fully returned by the prosperity of future generations of Métis.[15] Later, the Anglican bishop contributed more muted approval to the growing chorus of promoters of aid, saying that he thought that the free land, seed grain, and implements would be "necessary at first." Still, because he believed that fear of starvation was God's way of teaching respect for civilization, Bishop Machray added that "the less of such gifts the better. They are apt to do mischief."[16]

The result of Macdonald's fruitless quest for a cheap and simple alternative to the proposal of the North West Council was the addition of a few phrases to the Dominion Lands Act in the spring of 1879. The new words

---

13. Ibid., pp. 138984-138987, "Confidential Memorandum: Remarks on the Condition of the Half Breeds of the North West Territories, 20 December 1878."

14. See Macdonald's sketch of the history of Manitoba land claims reported to the Governor General in August 1884 (ibid., Transcripts, vol. 585, Macdonald to Lansdowne, 5 August 1884).

15. Ibid., Incoming Correspondence, pp. 42072-42083, Bishop Grandin to Dennis, 18 January 1879.

16. Ibid., pp. 42084-42091, Bishop Machray to Dennis, 15 February 1879.

appeared to recognize that the North West "half breeds" had a claim to a share of the Indian title to the territory and that the Cabinet was empowered to set aside land "to such extent, and on such terms and conditions, as may be deemed expedient" to satisfy such claims.[17] But in 1879, 1880, 1881, 1882, and 1883 nothing was done towards implementing the new authority to deal with the Métis. Not surprisingly, Macdonald was no more inclined to respond favourably to the new demands of the Métis reinforced in number and resolve by the large migrations from Manitoba. Consequently, the St Laurent claims underwent the same rigour of evaluation as those of any other group of complaining homesteaders. Of the more than 250 persons demanding patents in 1884, less than 10 were considered legally entitled to what they claimed.[18] Then a new factor suddenly caused Macdonald to reassess his sense of political profit and loss in "half breed" claims. He received an alarming assessment of the situation in June 1884.

Lawrence Clarke, Chief Factor of Fort Carlton, had informed James Grahame (Clarke's superior officer in Winnipeg) that a pattern of escalating discontent was reaching a point of crisis; "repressive measures" were needed. Clarke explained that as "half breeds" in the District of Saskatchewan were losing freighting employment to the railway and steamboats, they were becoming poorer and poorer, and were pressing extravagant claims on the government in the hope of getting something they might readily sell for cash. As their first appeals were failing, they were on the point of taking extreme action — threatening to repeat the events of 1869-70. A delegation had gone to Montana intending to bring Louis Riel back. The repression Clarke proposed was arresting Riel at the border if he accepted the offer of leadership. Otherwise his presence among hundreds of armed Métis and native English might involve the Indians and even some of the disgruntled white settlers who resented having been bypassed by the CPR. Clarke admitted that taking Riel prisoner would anger some people, but he said a "strong detachment" of police near St Laurent could deter the most militant. The others would be calmed by judicious use of the "influence" at Clarke's disposal and that of the Catholic priests in the area.[19]

Receiving the alarm via Grahame,[20] Macdonald reacted immediately by seeking more information. On the one hand, he asked his man on the spot, Edgar Dewdney, for his assessment. The Lieutenant Governor replied in a matter of days that the "half breeds" had been "ventilating their

---

17. Statutes of Canada (1879), Chapter 31: "An Act to amend and consolidate the several Acts respecting the Public lands of the Dominion," section 125(e).
18. Pearce, "All Claims to Land," p. 6.
19. PAC, Macdonald Papers, Incoming Correspondence, pp. 42244-42250, Clarke to Grahame, 20 May 1884.
20. Ibid., pp. 42242-42243, Grahame to Macdonald, 29 May 1884.

grievances" in secret meetings, and Dewdney also agreed that the principal reason for their discontent was economic because the Hudson's Bay Company had drastically cut both the volume and the rate of pay for overland freighting. But Dewdney added that a little group of Prince Albert speculators (including Clarke) had suffered from the collapse of the recent land boom. They welcomed the idea of a larger police garrison for the money it would bring into the district. Indeed, Lawrence Clarke was playing a double game. Having goaded the "half breeds" to bold protest, his "very sensational" letter now played to his speculator's interest more than to a real crisis.[21]

Dewdney's reassuring letter was not confirmed by the result of the police inquiries that Macdonald requested at the same time. He wanted to know the overall number of "half breeds" in the North West, how many were disaffected Manitobans, where they lived, and their probability of following Riel in the event of his attempting to form a second provisional government. Macdonald had also asked the Deputy Minister in charge of the police, Fred White, to go west for his own first hand impressions.

Before his departure, Comptroller White ordered Superintendent Crozier and Commissioner Irvine (the field officers in the North West Mounted Police with military ranks of major and colonel, respectively) to collect the statistical data. On June 10, White ordered Irvine to make discreet inquiries while travelling from community to community under some improvised purpose — "with some object . . . other than the real one."[22] On the same day, White sent identical instructions to Crozier, ordering him to "visit the settlements and . . . form an opinion which you can communicate to me confidentially."[23]

Thus, Macdonald did not ignore Clarke's warning. He moved quickly for a comprehensive view and from diverse sources, even though he rejected the appeal for immediate "repressive measures." Riel and the delegation were not arrested when they reached the Canadian border in late June, but the police did "shadow" the progress of Riel and his entourage closely, and kept the Prime Minister fully informed of what followed.

While Dewdney continued to report that Riel's return was a political nuisance but no threat (not unless the Métis leader "tampered" with Indian discontents),[24] White's report was remarkably consistent with the original alarm sounded by Clarke. Canada's most senior policeman was certain that, despite peaceful appearances, Louis Riel did aim for something like a

---

21. Ibid., pp. 42767-42778, Dewdney to Macdonald, 14 June 1884.

22. Ibid., pp. 42251-42253, White to Irvine, 10 June 1884.

23. Ibid., pp. 42254-42255, White to Crozier, 10 June 1884.

24. See, for example, the letter from André to Dewdney, 7 July 1884, that the Governor forwarded to Macdonald (ibid., pp. 42277- 42280).

second provisional government. "I am convinced that there is an illegal movement of some kind in contemplation."[25] A detailed statistical report substantiating the danger of such a development suggested that, of the 5,400 "half breeds" in the North West, 4,400 were Manitoba emigrants. Although they were found in twenty-one separate localities, almost half were settled near the forks of the Saskatchewan. There Riel could expect support from an estimated force of 600 men capable of bearing arms in the event of trouble. St Laurent was the true centre of "disloyalty" because its population was "chiefly from White Horse Plains, Baie St Paul, etc. in Manitoba. A hard lot, were Riel's supporters in 1869."[26] Other communities were either too small or too far away from St Laurent to pose any serious difficulty. "They would take no steps unless Riel's party was fairly certain of being successful," or "not . . . mixed up, but if Indians were once on the warpath they would likely join them."[27]

On July 10, Macdonald reported the disturbing news to the vacationing Governor General, Lord Lansdowne, saying that the situation was serious but manageable. He believed land was the key. "Some of the Half breeds have land claims which are in the process of adjustment. The claims are for the most part invalid, but they will be liberally treated."[28] Then, as the news continued to be "disquieting," Macdonald outlined a broader programme of conciliation in more correspondence with the absent representative of the Queen. On August 5, the Prime Minister repeated the idea that he was prepared to honour the land claims of Riel's followers, and something special might be offered to Riel himself:

> In his answer to the invitation sent him which was a temperate and unobjectionable paper, he spoke of some claims he had against the Gov't. I presume these refer to his land claims which he forfeited on conviction and banishment, [but] I think we shall deal liberally with him and make him a good subject again.
>
> If I don't mistake his character, he will make a good Moral Agent or Detective for the Gov't and keep the metis in order.[29]

Lansdowne replied the same day with a note stating that the idea of conciliating the leader was the key factor, and urged Macdonald to "make every endeavour to 'obtain touch'" with Riel and offer him a bribe; "it might be intimated to him that you were prepared to deal generously with him in so far as his private requirements seem concerned, and that you were

---

25. Ibid., pp. 134906-134916, White to Macdonald, 7 July 1884.

26. Other sources tend to corroborate the police report. See "Supplement 2: The Settlers of the Colony of St Laurent," in Mailhot and Sprague, "Persistent Settlers," pp. 18-26.

27. PAC, Macdonald Papers, Incoming Correspondence, p. 148567, "Estimated Number of Half Breeds."

28. Ibid., Transcripts, vol. 585, Macdonald to Lansdowne, 10 July 1884.

29. Ibid., Macdonald to Lansdowne, 5 August 1884.

ready to consider in a general conciliatory spirit the demands put forward by the half breeds.''[30] In the arrangement envisioned by Lansdowne, the people would get their land, and Riel could receive at least an appointment to the North West Council if not to the Canadian Senate.

In Macdonald's opinion, the contemplated patronage for Riel was excessive. Macdonald protested that Louis Riel had "committed a cold-blooded murder in '69, which will never be forgotten by the whites either in Manitoba or Ontario.''[31] A less extravagant offer was more appropriate, but the rest of Macdonald's answer did make clear that he was still committed to conciliation in principle. Emissaries of good will would see Riel and his lieutenants as in 1869 and "encourage them to specify their grievances in Memorials and send them with or without delegations to Ottawa.'' Such a course would "allow time for the present effervescence to subside — and on the approach of winter — the climate will keep things quiet until next spring.'' Meanwhile officials in the Department of the Interior could use the respite bought by the promise of conciliation to go over the land claims and concede patents to any with "a semblance of foundation.''[32]

Lansdowne approved. He appreciated that the problem of Riel and his people was "intricate,'' and Macdonald's proposed method of handling Riel would make him "understand that he has more to gain, personally and as a public man, by confining himself to the legitimate ventilation of the grievances of his clients, than by leading a disorderly movement.''[33]

The first person recruited to have a private word with the Métis leader was C.B. Rouleau, a French-Canadian lawyer recently appointed to judicial responsibilities at nearby Battleford, Saskatchewan. A second, more prominent prospective emissary was Sir Hector Langevin, the Minister of Public Works in the federal Cabinet and already committed to tour the West on other errands. Here as well the Governor General gave unqualified approval. On August 13, he agreed that Rouleau could "gauge the situation pretty accurately''[34] and on August 23 Lansdowne expressed special satisfaction that Langevin was going on his errand to "set Riel's head the right way.''[35]

All was arranged by the end of August for avoiding the political liability of Riel leading several hundred families into a second provisional government. Macdonald had reliable intelligence from diverse sources that

---

30. Ibid., Incoming Correspondence, pp. 32872-32879, Lansdowne to Macdonald, 5 August 1884.

31. Ibid., Transcripts, vol. 585, Macdonald to Lansdowne, 12 August 1884.

32. Ibid.

33. Ibid., Incoming Correspondence, pp. 32884-32887, Lansdowne to Macdonald, 13 August 1884.

34. Ibid.

35. Ibid., pp. 32893-32895, Lansdowne to Macdonald, 23 August 1884.

such a development was possible, and he had a plausible plan for undercutting the basis of the "foolish plot"[36] and for buying Riel's loyalty. Should conciliation fail, the safety of the government was still assured by a planned expansion of police power. Macdonald told Lansdowne that he intended to increase the police force in the West by thirty per cent with a flying column of 100 to be garrisoned at Fort Carlton.[37] If there was a second "Riel rebellion," it could be checked quickly by a mounted constabulary already on the scene. Still, timely conciliation was expected to prevent such a development.

The policy Macdonald described to the Governor General in July and August flowed from the obvious calculation that an "outbreak" in the North West was an avoidable political liability. The cost would be land that the Métis already occupied and money or patronage to be invested in Riel with the expectation of larger dividends in more general native pacification. In this sense, Macdonald had to agree with Lansdowne that Riel's return was "anything but a misfortune."[38] Yet Macdonald appears to have decided near the end of August 1884 that an angry Riel could be even more useful in the broader field of Canadian politics. For some reason, the Langevin visit was mysteriously[39] cancelled; the land claims were

---

36. Ibid., Letter Books, vol. 23, pp. 33-34, Macdonald to J.C. Aikins, 28 July 1884.

37. Ibid., Transcripts, vol. 585, Macdonald to Lansdowne, 12 August 1884; and Letter Book, vol. 23, pp. 56-57, Macdonald to Donald A. Smith, 5 September 1884.

38. Ibid., Incoming Correspondence, pp. 32872-32879, Lansdowne to Macdonald, 5 August 1884.

39. Why Langevin failed to fulfill the mission is a problem of considerable complexity. The conventional explanation (See Stanley, *Riel*, p. 285; and Bob Beal and Rod Macleod, *Prairie Fire: The 1885 North-West Rebellion* [Edmonton, 1984], pp. 117-118) is that Langevin's change of itinerary represented his own independent alteration of plans. Having arrived at Regina in the last week of August, he is supposed to have been so fatigued by the earlier part of his journey that he could not face travelling 200 miles over muddy cart trails to St Laurent just to suffer the harangues of political malcontents. Thus he cancelled the trip despite the consequences. Langevin proved later that he was indeed capable of foolish initiatives. But the cancellation of the Riel mission was more than foolhardy. Once Riel had been informed that Langevin was visiting in 1884 — in the role Smith had played in 1869-70 — and once it became known that Riel regarded the meeting as "marked proof of good will towards the North West" (Riel quoted in Beal and Macleod, *Prairie Fire*, p. 118), cancellation without justification or notification of regret was equivalent to provocation.

The difficulty with assigning sole responsibility to Langevin is evidence of earlier communication with Macdonald. The day of Langevin's departure from his home, August 18, Sir Hector sent a brief note to the Prime Minister inviting last-minute instructions (PAC, Macdonald Papers, Incoming Correspondence, pp. 97438-9743). There is no record of Macdonald's response, but on August 19 a telegram went from Langevin to Judge Rouleau at Battleford informing him that Sir Hector would not be making the digression to Batoche (Stanley, *Riel*, p. 285). Subsequently, Rouleau either forgot or was instructed not to report the news to Riel, with the result that the Métis continued an unsatisfying vigil, constantly watching the roadways to Batoche for some face resembling Langevin's.

If the change was Langevin's mistake, Macdonald had an opportunity to correct it on August 29 when his good-will ambassador sent him a message before leaving

handled more in conformity with the Dominion Lands Act than with what the "half breeds" demanded; and none of Riel's personal claims received favourable consideration. In the context of escalating discontent the Métis did become more militant; Riel did lead them into an illegal government; and the Government of Canada did respond with force — with the mobilization of militia from as far away as Halifax, as well as with the police power already on the scene. What were the political advantages of the sequence of events as they actually occurred?

The political problem that made provocative inaction ultimately worthwhile was renewed difficulty with Stephen's railway. At the time that Macdonald was first thinking about his programme of Métis conciliation, Stephen had begun to hint that he might need more assistance from Canada.[40] Macdonald's reaction was so swift and completely discouraging on July 18[41] that the railway president promised not to say another word on the subject, then violated his own promise in the same letter: "I will only say here that I cannot under the existing condition of affairs, any longer, look forward to the land grant as affording an available asset . . . and our 35 million capital is equally useless. . . ."[42]

Concurrent with Macdonald's corresponding with Lansdowne, Macdonald and Stephen exchanged eight letters[43] (which have survived) and held at least two meetings (mentioned in the correspondence). The Prime Minister fretted about the "many threads" of crisis he had to attend to personally and showed the railway president the papers documenting developments in the North West.[44] Stephen assured Macdonald that the railway construction was proceeding better than expected but continued to complain about a serious deficiency of capital for other needs. Macdonald could not agree to what Stephen thought essential, but he did agree to help in

---

Manitoba for Regina (PAC, Macdonald Papers, Incoming Correspondence, pp. 97441-97442). Langevin reported that the train had taken him as far as Brandon. After a brief visit with Dewdney he expected to continue on to the end of the railway: "In a week I will have reached the end of the road and be on the return." Obviously, that itinerary precluded the errand to Batoche. If Macdonald's previous plans were still in effect, it was important to intercept Langevin before his return. No record of attempted interception has been found. Nor did Macdonald complain later about a unilateral upset of his conciliation scheme.

40. PAC, Macdonald Papers, Incoming Correspondence, pp. 122328-122331, Stephen to Macdonald, 17 July 1884.

41. Ibid., Transcripts, vol. 585, Macdonald to Stephen, 18 July 1884.

42. Ibid., Incoming Correspondence, pp. 122340-122347, Stephen to Macdonald, 22 July 1884.

43. Macdonald's letters to Stephen were dated 24 and 30 July 1884 (both in ibid., Transcripts, vol. 585). Stephen's to Macdonald were 27 July, 2 August (two letters), and 13, 16, 19 August (all in ibid., Incoming Correspondence, pp. 122353-122419).

44. Ibid., Transcripts, vol. 585, Macdonald to Stephen, 30 July 1884.

recruiting $5 million from private bankers in London and to accompany the railway president on his Atlantic crossing.

Unfortunately for Stephen, neither a letter of recommendation[45] from Canada's Prime Minister nor Macdonald's presence in London was sufficient to persuade Baring Brothers that the railway was a safe risk, and Stephen's need for the additional $5 million from Parliament matured before anything else to convince Macdonald's colleagues (or the country) that additional legislative assistance was warranted. Then, once Macdonald returned to Ottawa, Sir David Macpherson complained that Langevin had returned from the West as the perfect champion of "dead beats."[46]

Langevin's position even without seeing Riel was that the Métis leader was too dangerous to ignore. "We must take care not to make a martyr of him and thus increase his popularity." The solution was "good treatment of the half breeds." Langevin believed even a little would "go a long way to settle matters."[47] Macpherson tried to convince Langevin that every land claim had been "fully considered and equitably disposed of," but Sir David believed Sir Hector remained unconvinced. A meeting with Sir John was needed.[48] That appears to have ended the matter. At least there were no more memoranda advocating concessions such as Langevin had proposed early in November.

Macdonald's greater difficulty was calming Stephen. By mid-January the railway president was insisting that the survival of his company absolutely depended on aid from the government, but Macdonald insisted that the proposition was still "hopeless." A telegram from the Prime Minister on January 20 urged Stephen to "postpone matter to eighteen eight six can carry it in Council."[49] Stephen replied that postponement was "impossible" and begged for a meeting the next day to "decide finally on course am forced to take."[50] They did meet, but the only surviving record of what was apparently agreed to was a letter from Stephen in mid-April alluding to maturing obligations that "three months ago were postponed till now on the faith that by this time we should be in a position to meet them."[51] Further contextual evidence that something had been agreed to in late

45. Ibid., Letter Book, vol. 23, pp. 59-60, Macdonald to Baring Brothers, 6 September 1884.

46. Ibid., Incoming Correspondence, pp. 112802-112805, Macpherson to Macdonald, 31 December 1884.

47. Ibid., pp. 97452-97456, Langevin to Macdonald, 6 November 1884.

48. Ibid., pp. 112802-112805, Macpherson to Macdonald, 31 December 1884.

49. Ibid., Letter Book, vol. 23, p. 101, Macdonald cypher telegram to Stephen, 20 January 1885.

50. Ibid., Incoming Correspondence, p. 122608, Stephen cypher telegram to Macdonald, 20 January 1885.

51. Ibid., pp. 122818-122821, Stephen to Macdonald, 15 April 1885.

January was a more optimistic tone and shift in Stephen's correspondence on the subject in February and early March as he devoted most of his letters to the terms of the rescue he was clearly expecting.[52] Conversely, Macdonald seemed more depressed than ever. On January 24 he reported to his old friend Tupper that the situation was nearly as bad as the worst the two had imagined in the previous autumn. "Geo Stephen says the CPR must go down unless sustained," and he enumerated the key personnel in Cabinet who were adamantly opposed to any such additional aid. "How it will end I don't know."[53]

Nothing had happened to change "the thing"[54] in Ottawa. Yet the abandonment of straightforward conciliation had meant that Métis discontent was maturing into an exploitable crisis. Riel had spent the entire autumn and early winter writing—and rewriting—the draft of a comprehensive statement of grievances covering claims. The most preliminary statement specified: territorial self-government; land rights similar to the assurances in section 32 of the Manitoba Act; a 2-million-acre trust (the income from which would provide long-term development capital for the Métis); 64,000 acres of "swamp lands" to be reserved for the children of Métis heads of families (to be distributed every eighteen years over seven generations); reconsideration of the land rights of the Manitoba Métis; and preferential consideration of "half breeds" for "works and contracts" in the Territories.[55]

After consulting Bishops Taché and Grandin, Riel dropped some of the demands that the clerical consultants and his own close advisors considered "extravagant."[56] The petition that the St Laurent Métis finally mailed to the Governor General on December 16 was more limited in its focus upon land titles, home rule, and compensation for alleged maladministration of the Manitoba Act. Considering the last point, it was not surprising that the document was addressed to the Governor General with a covering letter requesting that the Queen's representative should forward the document directly to England in the hope that the British would compel Canada to act as in 1870.[57]

Given the direct parallel that the Métis drew between their present

---

52. See Stephen's letters of 3, 8, 9, 12, 13, 19 February and 2 March in ibid., Incoming Correspondence, pp. 122643-122704.

53. Ibid., Transcripts, vol. 585, Macdonald to Tupper, 24 January 1885.

54. Ibid.

55. Ibid., Incoming Correspondence, pp. 42935-42937, Riel to Bishop Grandin, 7 September 1884.

56. See PAM, Riel Papers, item 414, Taché to Riel, 4 October 1884.

57. Lansdowne did not forward the petition as requested. See Lansdowne to Derby, the Colonial Secretary, 21 April 1885 (PAC, Records of the Governor General, RG 7 G 10, vol. 8).

situation and the events of 1869, the alarms that kept streaming in from the North West might have led Macdonald to expect the formation of a provisional government at almost any moment in January. The police reports of the previous summer had indicated that delay would almost certainly result in some "illegal combination," and six months had passed without meeting any of the agitators' principal demands or taking steps to break up the agitation with police power. But nothing had happened. In late January Riel was still not acting according to prediction even as Stephen's financial crisis reached new, more frightening proportions, and nothing had altered Macdonald's inability to deliver his partner the promised aid.

Here was the context and perhaps also the explanation for the peculiarly provocative content of an important Order in Council that was adopted on January 28. Telegraphed to Dewdney, the news was that Canada would "investigate claims of Half Breeds and with that view [Cabinet] had decided [to make an] enumeration of those who did not participate in Grant under Manitoba Act."[58] The provocation was that only a small minority of the residents of St Laurent could benefit from awards to non-Manitobans. Morever, the government already had the figures: 200 of 1,300 potential claimants.[59] Dewdney was so stunned by the news he refused to pass on the information without alteration. Imagining the purpose of the Order in Council was conciliation rather than provocation, he changed the announcement before transmitting the telegram to St Laurent: "Government has decided to investigate claims of Half Breeds and with that view has already taken preliminary steps." Then Dewdney reminded Macdonald that "the bulk of the French Half Breeds" had "nothing to expect" from the unrevised text. The original news would "start a fresh agitation."[60]

No prime ministerial congratulation came back over the wire thanking Dewdney for his editorial intervention, and Dewdney's text was still far short of the news the Métis wanted. They demanded recognition of their aboriginal title demand, not additional consideration of the matter. Equally important, they wanted news that their claims to river lots were recognized. Here too the telegram from Dewdney was silent. Then on February 6, the Dominion Lands Agent at Prince Albert learned from the Deputy Minister of the Department of the Interior that the river-lot question was about to be

58. PAC, Macdonald Papers, Incoming Correspondence, pp. 42977-42983, quoted by Dewdney to Macdonald in reply, 4 February 1885.

59. Ibid., p. 148567, "Estimated Number of Half Breeds." Although the document is undated, contextual evidence makes clear that the numbers were determined in the summer of 1884. See also the Governor General's recital of the same figures in PAC, RG 7, G 10 (Drafts to Colonial Secretary, Secret and Confidential), vol. 8, Lansdowne to Derby, 21 April 1885.

60. Ibid., pp. 42977-42983, Dewdney to Macdonald, 4 February 1885.

disposed of. He could expect instructions "in the course of a few days."[61]

The claims reported to Winnipeg in June 1884 had passed from Winnipeg to Ottawa in October, and finally back from headquarters to Prince Albert near the end of February 1885. The news the Lands Agent was to report to the claimants was an enormous disappointment to the vast majority of the families hoping for confirmation of titles.[62] They felt they had done their part. All but a small non-co-operating group of forty-five had compromised their original demand for river lots laid out in the old Manitoba pattern. More than 200 settlers had provided evidence of compliance with the boundaries of subdivisions as laid out in the government survey. Eight such claimants received notification that their periods of settlement, extent of cultivation, and value of improvements entitled them to patents. The others were processed as applications for "entry." Consequently, more than sixty per cent of the settlers expecting patent were confronted with an infuriating contradiction: their claims were allowed; patents were denied. They would not become the owners of their land in the eyes of Canada until paying fees, performing more settlement duties, and going through another process of application, inspection, and consideration by the local agent, by the Winnipeg Lands Board, and by the Dominion Lands Branch in Ottawa. Even then they would have to pay for any acreage in excess of the 160-acre maximum allowable "free grant" (some claimants were told that the pre-emption part of their claim would cost $1 per acre, for others the price was $2). Finally, the question of trespass on the lands of the Prince Albert Colonization Company was unresolved; thirty families were excluded from "entry" as well as from patents.[63]

Canada's handling of the river-lot question was far from conciliatory, but the government could defend itself by saying that the claimants received all the consideration they were entitled to expect under the Dominion Lands Act. Indeed, in one respect — waiving the distinction between odd- and even-numbered sections (except in the vicinity of the Prince Albert Colonization Company) — the government could say that the Métis claimants were treated more liberally than the law required.

One last provocation was similarly defensible from the standpoint of rigid adherence to principle. On February 20 the Prime Minister informed Lieutenant Governor Dewdney that the answer to Riel's private claims was a definite no. With uncharacteristic moral outrage Macdonald declared: "We have no money to give Riel. He has a right to remain in Canada and if

---

61. PAC, RG 15, vol. 336, file 84478, A.M. Burgess to Duck, 6 February 1885.

62. See University of Alberta, William Pearce Papers, MG 9/2/4-4, vol. 4, pp. 224-275, 961-962 in relation to Pearce's published report of "All Claims to Land."

63. Their claims were taken up in the autumn of 1885, and accorded the same entry privilege as the others. See University of Alberta Archives, William Pearce Papers, MG 9/2/4-4, vol. 4, pp. 961-962.

he conspires we must punish him. That's all."[64]

The last two provocations together—the personal disappointment of Riel and the general frustration of the land claimants—finally broke Métis patience the day after Lands Agent Duck sent out the last disturbing notification on March 7. On March 8, Riel announced that he thought that the time had come to form a provisional government.

Three days later, Lieutenant Governor Dewdney telegraphed the latest development to the Prime Minister, saying there was a possibility that the declaration was no more than a "bluff" but "if the Half breeds mean business, the sooner they are put down the better." Dewdney advised taking them by surprise. "They are like Indians. When they gather and get excited it is difficult to handle them, but if they are taken unawares there is little difficulty in arresting the leader."[65]

On the same day, March 11, Stephen demanded bold action for the railway, complaining that his finances were "getting beyond all control." Stephen expressed sympathy for Macdonald's political problems, but the CPR president insisted that the time had come for the Prime Minister to do whatever was necessary to alter the current political impasse. "I know and appreciate fully the reason for delaying consideration of our matters till the proper and most favourable time arrives but I am really concerned about ways and means to carry us along in the meantime. . . . I hope you will think of this and bring things to a head as soon as possible."[66]

True to his favourite maxim, "He who waits wins,"[67] Macdonald did nothing, but not with any evident comfort. On March 17, he informed Tupper that "Stephen asks a loan for a year of 5 millions (that Tilley [the Minister of Finance] can't face)" and complained that everyone was reaching the limits of endurance. "How it will end God knows—but I wish I were well out of it."[68] No doubt Stephen and Dewdney were equally perplexed. Unable to get a satisfactory answer to his letters and telegrams, Dewdney pursued his own initiative.

On March 12, the Lieutenant Governor convened a meeting to consider the Riel crisis with four other people in Regina: Hayter Reed (the Indian Commissioner), A.G. Irvine (the Police Commissioner), Hugh Richardson (the Stipendiary Magistrate of the district), and Lawrence Clarke (still Chief Factor at Fort Carlton). The primary concern was Riel's proclamation of intent: whether it was genuine or "a mere matter of

---

64. PAC, Glenbow Dewdney Papers, p. 545, Macdonald to Dewdney, 20 February 1885.

65. PAC, Macdonald Papers, Incoming Correspondence, pp. 43010-43013, Dewdney to Macdonald, 11 March 1885.

66. Ibid., pp. 122735-122742, Stephen to Macdonald, 11 March 1885.

67. See, for example, Macdonald to T. Robertson, in ibid., Letter Book, vol. 23, pp. 85-86.

68. Ibid., Transcripts, vol. 585, Macdonald to Tupper, 17 March 1885.

bluff . . . to frighten the government into making concessions.'' Clarke suggested that since the total force at Riel's command was probably no more than 350 poorly armed men ''with their wives and children, who must be exposed to extreme peril should they be so foolish as to resort to arms,'' and since the government force ''already on the spot'' numbered 120 well-armed police backed by artillery, the Hudson's Bay Company officer thought that the ''only danger to be apprehended . . . would be in the event of Riel attempting to tamper with the loyalty of the Indians.'' In that event, it was agreed that they should arrest the Métis leader ''no matter at what risk.'' And even without Riel's moving towards alliances with the Indians, it was considered that ''Mr. Riel and his band of discontents should not be allowed to keep up senseless agitation, destroying all faith in the country and ruining its peaceable inhabitants.'' Sooner or later they would have to ''settle this matter once for all.'' In Clarke's opinion the question was ''whether this was not the time.'' Under the circumstances of the moment, it was agreed that Clarke should return to Fort Carlton at once, and Irvine would ''start for the 'seat of war' '' several days later, about the time Clarke reached Fort Carlton from Regina.[69]

Arriving at his destination on the evening of March 17,[70] Clarke reported that Riel's movement had ''apparently flattened out'' but there was no doubt as to his ''tampering with Indians.'' Clarke did not think Riel would win many over, but advised the immediate arrest of Riel to prevent any further mischief. ''No better time to deal with leader and followers.''[71] Dewdney responded that he had still ''heard nothing from Ottawa'' and reported that Irvine was departing for Fort Carlton the next day with 100 reinforcements.[72] Then, as rather an afterthought, Dewdney sent Clarke a second telegram on March 17 advising him to make the government's intentions public. ''Put in PA Times that an additional force is being sent. . . . Get paper to enlarge and state scattered that government intend to have peace in the district.''[73]

Clarke passed the instruction on to his new superior officer in Winnipeg, Joseph Wrigley, who responded by telegram that he opposed the newspaper advertisement, at least as a Hudson's Bay Company announcement. Perhaps Wrigley feared that such information would be interpreted as a provocative gesture and lead to criticism of the company later. ''Better for you not to act publicly but leave responsibility on Government.''[74] As a

---

69. Hudson's Bay Company Archives (hereafter cited as HBCA), D.20/33, fo. 67-74, Lawrence Clarke to Joseph Wrigley, 14 March 1885.

70. HBCA, B332/b/1, vol. 1, fo. 96-121, Clarke to Wrigley, 6 July 1885.

71. Ibid., fo. 87, Clarke cypher telegram to Dewdney, 17 March 1885.

72. Ibid., fo. 82, Dewdney cypher telegram to Clarke, 17 March 1885.

73. Ibid., fo. 81, Dewdney cypher telegram to Clarke, 17 March 1885.

74. Ibid., fo. 44, Wrigley cypher telegram to Clarke, 17 March 1885.

result, the action that pushed Riel to take the next step was not a printed word, but verbal communication that Clarke subsequently denied he had ever spoken.

The story Lawrence Clarke later denounced as a "tissue of lies"[75] was that he had encountered a group of Métis near Fort Carlton some time before March 19 and had given them information resembling the news that Dewdney instructed him to spread through the district on March 17. According to popular legend, the Métis asked Clarke if there was any answer yet to their petitions and protest. "His reply was that the only answer they would get would be bullets, and that, indeed, on his way northward, he had passed a camp of 500 policemen who were coming up to capture the Half breed agitators."[76] It is possible that Clarke said only that more police were on the way with the intention of arresting Riel. The rest may have been nothing more than the result of exaggeration in retelling the news at Batoche.

What is certain is that the Métis reacted to Clarke's news as the final provocation. The provisional government emerged on March 19 (with eighty-eight per cent support from the inhabitants of the colony of St Laurent).[77] Despite the risk of police intervention, Riel did not foresee any great danger because the newspapers were full of reports of the possibility of war between England and Russia. With British (and Canadian) forces occupied in a foreign war, surely Canada would dispose of a small domestic crisis peacefully as in 1870. Riel miscalculated. The mobilization for conflict overseas did not occur. Instead, Canada mobilized militia from Halifax to Winnipeg to deal with the Métis, even though Dewdney's dispatches indicated that he thought the police were competent to deal with the situation unfolding in late March.

Macdonald did not anticipate a war against the Métis. At the time of the mobilization (March 23), he cautioned the Minister of Militia, J.P.R.A. Caron, to "remind General Middleton that the [NWMP] Commissioner and Officers are magistrates and well acquainted with the character of the Half-breeds and Indians and must understand the best mode of dealing with them and inducing them to lay down their arms and submit to legal authority."[78] A massive show of force would compel surrender without a fight.

---

75. Ibid., fo. 96-121, Clarke to Wrigley, 6 July 1885.

76. N.F. Black, *History of Saskatchewan and the Old North West* (Regina, 1913), p. 267. The same story appeared in a contemporary account of Clarke's role by James Isbister. See clipping from Winnipeg *Sun*, 19 June 1885, in PAC, Macdonald Papers, Incoming Correspondence, p. 43861.

77. The opponents of Riel are named in Pearce's manuscript copy of "All Claims to Land" (University of Alberta Archives, Pearce Papers, MG 9/2, series 4, vol. 4, pp. 888-901.

78. PAC, Macdonald Papers, Transcripts, vol. 585, Macdonald to Caron, 23 March 1885.

Although Dewdney preferred resolving the problem with local resources ("I would have rather seen the trouble stopped entirely by the police"), the Governor had to concede that the Métis were even less likely to resist if thousands of troops suddenly appeared on the scene, especially if the government met Riel's price and whisked him out of the country before the troops arrived. "How far can I go?" Dewdney asked on March 23.[79]

What Macdonald seems to have envisioned was a sudden dash to the Prairies, a mysterious "escape" of Riel back to the United States, conciliatory gestures to the surrendering Métis, and aid for the railway after it played such a key role in breaking up the "outbreak" so "speedily and gallantly."[80]

On March 26, however, the situation became unexpectedly complicated by bloodshed. Since the Métis believed 500 police were en route to arrest Riel, they prepared to fend off the NWMP in a long siege by sending a force to seize supplies from a store at Duck Lake. Simultaneously, a party of police went to the same place to spoil the attempt. When the two groups came face to face, both sides sent out spokesmen to talk under a flag of truce, but the meeting soon deteriorated into single-champion combat with two men dead, then into general shooting with twelve fallen on the Canadian side and five Métis killed.[81]

The confrontation between police and "half breeds" was followed by sporadic Indian action and raised the spectre of war such as the Americans had fought in the 1860s and 1870s. After March 26, greater prospects of danger and longer delays filled Macdonald with increased dread. "This insurrection is a bad business," Macdonald wrote Dewdney on March 29, "but we must face it as best we may."[82]

Since the Americans were almost as worried as some Canadians that the "outbreak" would become a general Indian war, they offered full cooperation in the movement of troops and supplies and their own cavalry for patrolling the border.[83] Macdonald accepted the transport offer for shipping equipment, but he insisted on the CPR as the vehicle for transporting the unfortunate Canadian volunteers, the first contingent of whom left Toronto on March 30 in two separate trains. When the men reached the north shore

79. Ibid., Incoming Correspondence, pp. 43020-43023, Dewdney to Macdonald, 23 March 1885.

80. "Speedy" and "gallant" were Macdonald's adjectives in Parliament. See House of Commons Debates, 6 July 1885, p. 3117.

81. A detailed, sensational account of the conflict appears in Beal and Macleod, *Prairie Fire*, pp. 151-159.

82. PAC, Macdonald Papers, Letter Books, vol. 23, p. 140, Macdonald to Dewdney, 29 March 1885.

83. See Blake's questions on the matter, House of Commons Debates, 31 March 1885, p. 838; and 1 April 1885, p. 872.

of Lake Superior in the first week of April, they discovered that there were four gaps in the line that had to be crossed by sleigh or on foot. The worst part, however, was one section of isolated railway where the men had to ride on flat cars in the open, bitter cold.[84] Still, in less than two weeks, more than 3,000 troops did reach the Territories ready to be deployed against the "half breeds" and their few Indian allies.

In the fighting that occurred here and there in late April and early May there were several encounters that could be called battles.[85] For more than fifty Canadians and a similar number of "half breeds" and Indians, death was as final as in any global conflict. And yet Macdonald did not exaggerate later when he dismissed most of the military side of the "North West Rebellion" as a "mere riot."

From Macdonald's point of view, the more important aspects of the affair were showing the flag of British authority and proving that the railway had transformed Canada into a country capable of suppressing challenges to its sovereignty in the most remote sections of habitable territory. To be sure, the Opposition made searing accusations of mismanagement, but Macdonald met their charges that the war could have been avoided with counter-charges that his own "half breed" policy had been far more liberal than his opponents.[86] Indeed, on native affairs in general he claimed to be the epitome of enlightened and progressive action, and he moved to substantiate his claim in April with a diversionary franchise bill that included proposals for nearly universal suffrage for white men and extension of the vote to certain single women and the Six Nations of Loyalist Indians in Ontario.[87]

The Liberals were triply embarrassed. Having denounced Macdonald's handling of North West matters, they seemed sympathetic to natives; then, having posed as friends of the Indians and the Métis, they were embarrassed by their own vehement opposition to the inclusion of certain loyal native people in the national franchise because David Mills said they were "savages." Thus, they were set up to be embarrassed the third time when they fought the aid for the railway that had saved the nation from a prolonged war with Canada's native peoples.

The CPR did receive its aid package in July. In the same month, Louis Riel stood trial at Regina where he was held accountable for treason and sentenced to hang. Riel dropped to the end of the hangman's rope in

---

84. Desmond Morton, *The Last War Drum* (Toronto, 1972), pp. 40-44.

85. On the final siege, in particular, see Walter Hildebrandt, *The Battle of Batoche: British Small Warfare and the Entrenched Métis* (Ottawa, 1985).

86. See Blake's seven-hour speech and Macdonald's shorter reply in the House of Commons Debates, 6 July 1885, pp. 3075-3117.

87. See Malcolm Montgomery, "The Six Nations and the Macdonald Franchise," *Ontario History* 57 (1967), pp. 13-25.

Regina on November 16. The railway reached its official completion almost at the same time in a last-spike ceremony on November 7. Still jubilant over the success of his railway, Stephen wrote Macdonald just before Riel's execution to inform the Prime Minister of his pleasure with the rising value of CPR stock over the preceding week and to tell Sir John how "glad" he was that the "mischievous crank Riel is going to have justice meted out to him."[88] No other correspondent with Macdonald was as quick to link the two events so directly, but few people other than Stephen knew how closely the Métis loss had been joined to the railway's gain.

---

88. PAC, Macdonald Papers, Incoming Correspondence, pp. 123001- 123008, Stephen to Macdonald, 14 November 1885.

Louis Riel, ca. 1880
(Public Archives of Canada [PA139073])

"His private land speculation and staunch loyalism both made him an unremarkable candidate for the role of provincial premier."

Conclusion

The loose end of the "North West Rebellion" was Louis Riel. In the summer and autumn of 1885, French Canadians demanded clemency, in part simply because the cry for hanging was so strident in Ontario. With Mackenzie Bowell, Grand Master of the Orange Order of Ontario, on one side in the federal Cabinet and Sir Hector Langevin, a former head of Quebec's St Jean Baptiste Society, at the other extreme, Macdonald was caught in between. He was understandably eager to avoid confrontation with Riel in August 1884 and anxious to get Riel quietly out of the country once the Prime Minister had the exploitable crisis that was the salvation of Stephen's railway. Unfortunately, no one reached the Métis chief in time. When Riel surrendered on May 16, his capture alive meant that there would be a controversial trial and execution.

Macdonald's strategy for bringing the affair to a conclusion that was satisfactory to Ontario without too severely damaging his party in Quebec was to get the matter finished quickly, to permit free ventilation of resentments by members of his own party at the postponed next session of Parliament, and to delay the next general election until the latest possible date in the hope that more manageable distractions would arise in the interim. "He who waits wins."

For the purpose of expediting the execution, Macdonald attempted to downplay the significance of the "outbreak" in August, after having already understated the "gallant and speedy" role of the railway in the recent national mobilization to put down "rebellion." The Governor General had wanted to make a brief statement of commendation in his throne speech proroguing Parliament in July. "Might not a sentence be added testifying to the value of the CPR as a military road?" he asked on July 11.[1] The Prime Minister's reply has not survived in his or Lansdowne's papers, but the text of the speech delivered on July 20 did not mention the railway except as a great national project that was likely to "accelerate the progress

---

1. PAC, Macdonald Papers, Incoming Correspondence, p. 33147, Lansdowne to Macdonald, 11 July 1885.

of settlement and augment the commerce of the Dominion'' now that Parliament had so wisely contributed the last essential subsidy guaranteeing its success.[2] In the new context of the CPR's certain completion (and Riel's inevitable execution), Macdonald wished to downplay the significance of the "outbreak," reducing it from *rebellion* (a political crime likely to receive Crown clemency) to mere *riot* and *murder* (criminal matters on which an appeal to Great Britain would be inappropriate). Here Lansdowne hesitated. At the end of August 1885, the Governor General reminded the Prime Minister that

> we have all of us been doing what we could to elevate it to the rank of a rebellion and with so much success that we cannot now reduce it to the rank of a common riot.
>
> If the movement had been at once stopped with the NWM police the case would have been different, but we were within an ace of Indian war; the progress of the outbreak and its suppression has been described in glowing language of the press all over the world; we brought up troops from all parts of the Dominion; those troops have been thanked by parliament; they are to receive an Imperial medal.[3]

Macdonald had to admit in his reply on September 3 that the proposal suddenly to call the affair by a new name simply for a different political effect was brazen. "I fear you have me with respect to the character given to the outbreak.'' But the Prime Minister reminded the Governor General that important political objectives had been well served by attaching inflated significance to the Métis riot previously. "We have certainly made it assume large proportions in the public eye. This has been done however for our own purposes, and I think wisely done."[4] The implication was that one justifiable manipulation called for another. Consequently, although the execution did not proceed with unseemly haste (there was an inquiry into Riel's sanity), at the last step, royal intervention did not spare Riel as the Crown had pardoned political offenders elsewhere in nineteenth-century British and Canadian history.

Anticipating the next step, Macdonald predicted that Quebec's sympathy for Riel would be an ephemeral phenomenon. He believed that the outrage of the Opposition members was purely artificial, worked up by their contrivance of a thematic similarity between the North West Rebellion and Quebeckers' "own rising in 1837 and their 'Martyrs'.... The attempt now made to revive that feeling in his [Riel's] favour will not extend far and will be evanescent."[5] The Prime Minister was confident that

---

2. *Canada Gazette*, 25 July 1885.

3. PAC, Macdonald Papers, Incoming Correspondence, pp. 42559-42562, Lansdowne to Macdonald, 31 August 1885.

4. Ibid., Letter Books, vol. 23, pp. 271-272, Macdonald to Lansdowne, 3 September 1885.

5. Ibid., pp. 264-267, Macdonald to Lansdowne, 28 August 1885.

the logic of the Toronto *Mail* would appeal, ultimately, even to French Canadians. Macdonald's paper in Toronto had argued that, if there were blame, "if the French-Canadians sought to bring down Sir John A. Macdonald, let them do it on grounds other than the execution of Riel." To destroy the government for hanging a rebel would mean more than the defeat of Macdonald's ministry. According to the *Mail*, "if he should be overthrown simply because he has upheld the majesty of the law . . . then Canadian institutions cannot survive him."[6]

The problem, of course, was that the evidence for exposing the government on the other grounds was not a matter of public record, and did not become open to detailed investigation until 1917 when the surviving bulk of Macdonald's private papers were sold by his widow to the Public Archives of Canada. Even then, many pertinent documents continued to be held in the surrounding warehouses of secrets in Ottawa. Indeed, the secrecy of certain relevant documents was still being maintained by the Canadian Department of Justice one full century later.[7] Enough evidence has emerged, however, to respond to the *Mail's* challenge, to the critical questions raised in the introduction and pursued through the pages of the preceding chapters.

It would appear on the evidence presented that recognition of Métis demands in the Manitoba Act was regarded by the Government of Canada as a kind of contract negotiated under duress. Macdonald admitted to the House of Commons in 1885 that he had never accepted the concept of Métis aboriginal rights in principle, or the notion that Manitoba was to have continued as it began — a predominately Métis province. He declared that the concessions in 1870 were for the sake of taking possession of the territory with as little force as possible:

> to secure peace and order — in fact, to obtain possession of the country — it was necessary to enter into an arrangement. . . . Whether they [the Métis] had any right to those lands or not was not so much the question as it was a question of policy to make an arrangement with the inhabitants of the Province . . . in order to introduce law and order there, and assert the sovereignty of the Dominion.[8]

No matter how inauspicious the beginning, in Macdonald's view, his

---

6. Toronto *Mail*, 20 November 1885. See P.B. Waite's interpretation of the same quotation in the context of his discussion of the execution controversy in *Canada, 1874-1896*, p. 170 and the text of footnote 104, p. 305.

7. On the Justice Department's blanket claim to confidentiality, see James M. Whalen, "The Application of Solicitor-Client Privilege to Government Records," *Archivaria* 18 (1984), pp. 135-141. Whalen's suggestion that access requests are sometimes granted is valid. In the case of the present author, for example, access to thirty-seven files was requested in the spring of 1986. Copies of six were provided. Access to eighty-three pages of thirty-one other files was denied.

8. House of Commons Debates, 6 July 1885, pp. 3112-3113.

government had been consistently more liberal in its handling of Métis matters than the Opposition had been during its term in office from 1874 to 1878. Their entire administration, according to Macdonald, was one vast attempt to "keep down, and crush, and destroy the interests and the rights, or rather the claims of those people."[9] The Liberals' sudden conversion to sympathy for the Métis in 1885 was hypocritical pretence, calculated for partisan gain.

The indictment of the former government by the current administration was valid, as correct as the new Opposition leader's critique of Macdonald. Edward Blake's seven-hour denunciation, delivered on July 6 argued that the Conservatives had provided nothing more than "quasi-recognition." The reality was "neglect, delay and mismanagement."[10]

Each leader knew well the political practice of the other: Blake knew the Conservatives promised accommodation that was vitiated by artful delay; Macdonald correctly criticized the Liberals for brutal denials of existing rights or their stubborn refusals to consider new Métis demands from 1874 to 1878. In the period of the first Macdonald administration, from 1870 through 1873, the land claims of original settlers were neither denied nor honoured. They were held in an administrative limbo while the territory was opened to newcomers whose claims were treated with unusual swiftness and generosity. In the same period of declining Métis power in Manitoba, nothing of any importance in the politics and government of the new province was permitted in strictly Manitoba terms. Even though the people had proven themselves capable of forming institutions of self-government and operating them democratically in 1869-70, they were excluded from the self-governing autonomy enjoyed by the other provinces in Confederation. So long as the Métis were the majority, the Premier was the Royal Governor, an outsider operated from Ottawa. To be sure, the first Lieutenant Governor was sensitive to the wishes of his subjects. But Archibald's was still a colonial administration, and his most important initiative to bolster Métis claims (his handling of the land question in the summer of 1871) was quietly repudiated by his superiors and subsequently subverted by Macdonald's agent, Gilbert McMicken.

In the meantime, Riel and his followers kept waiting, remarkably patiently, hoping for the restoration of the provisional government. Riel considered himself a good Conservative. His private land speculation and staunch loyalism both made him an unremarkable candidate for the role of provincial premier as soon as the amnesty was proclaimed. But the Government of Canada was no more prepared to see restoration of the provisional government than it was ready to accept pre-emptive control of Métis land

---

9. Ibid.
10. Ibid., pp. 3075-3110.

by a Métis controlled legislature.

Macdonald delayed and delayed. The time for implementing the amnesty was never quite right, and there was always one more survey to be conducted before this or that parcel of land could be allotted or patented. In the meantime, the claims of new settlers in Manitoba went ahead smoothly, and newcomers became more and more important in the politics, government, and militia of the new province. As early as 1873, the tide was turning.

The Liberals' preference for straightforward denial over delay or subterfuge was clearly evident in their position on both debates of the Manitoba Act, in 1871 as well as in 1870. Once in power, the Liberals remained true to their original hostility and substituted perpetual loss of political rights and five-years banishment for the vague amnesty promised by Macdonald and Cartier. At the same time, they shifted the burden of proof in the land question from the government to the claimants. Métis "squatters" retained only the right to present the facts of their cases to the Department of the Interior. The claims that were consistent with new settlement-duty criteria received clear titles. Claims that did not meet the criteria of the Department of the Interior were denied and there was no right of appeal. Then the land that was allotted and patented in the name of the children of original settlers went through a process that could not have been better suited to dissolution of their land base unless it were delivered directly to speculators for sale to newcomers. Indeed, most of the patents arriving in Winnipeg were handed directly to such persons, given the requirement that recipients had to work through "attorneys" if patentees were not personally acquainted with the Dominion Lands Agent.

Throughout the period when the Liberals were denying Métis rights, Macdonald's party stood by in acquiescent opposition. Perhaps nothing revealed Macdonald's true position on the Manitoba Act more clearly than his unwillingness to criticize the Liberals' many amendments of the law until they attacked his handling of Métis claims in 1885. Not surprisingly, after the formation of his second ministry late in 1878, Macdonald moved easily in the processes that his immediate predecessors had set in motion. He was happy to call the matter of the Manitoba land question closed in 1882, the year of the largest migration of Manitobans to Saskatchewan. By then, a second opportunity for genuine accommodation was being lost, since Macdonald rejected the scheme of assisting Métis resettlement. The Prime Minister preferred the noble but empty words of an inoperative clause in a statute to actions that would have recognized the Métis as a people with collective rights outside the homestead provisions of the Dominion Lands Act. Finally, Macdonald had sufficient advance warning to prevent the formation of the second provisional government by implementing a programme of conciliation in the autumn of 1884, and he appeared willing to pursue such a policy until the political advantages of doing nothing deflected him from such a course.

The conclusion is that the North West Rebellion in 1885 was not the result of some tragic misunderstanding, but of the government's manipulation of the Manitoba Métis since 1869. Canada appeared to tolerate accommodation when conflict was deemed inexpedient for reasons of state, and aggravation of conflict when confrontation was dictated by the same grounds of expediency. In the theme of Canada and the Métis, there was less noble intention than filled the public ear, and more dishonesty than ever caught the public eye. The presumption of benevolence is not appropriately replaced by one of consistent malevolence, but the exodus of the Métis from their original homeland and their difficulties in resettlement is more explicable by processes of formal and informal discouragement emanating from Canada than by the alleged preference of the Métis for the wandering life of homeless hunters.

Note on Sources and Method

A brief scan of footnotes will show that the work is based primarily on the letters and papers of Sir John A. Macdonald (Public Archives of Canada, MG 26 A). Persons familiar with other studies of Riel or Macdonald will notice that a considerable number of manuscript letters and memoranda appear to be cited here, and not elsewhere. It remains to explain how the main corpus of the collection of Macdonald papers could be available to researchers in the Public Archives of Canada since 1917[1] and remain less than fully exploited — even by such thorough investigators as Donald Creighton, who wrote his two-volume biography of Macdonald in the 1950s.

In Creighton's case, there are several facets to the answer. First and most obviously, he was interested in the whole life of his hero; he did not consider the subject of Canada and the Métis a main theme when so many other matters appeared either more important or more worthy of commemoration in Macdonald's biography.[2]

A second reason that Creighton and the later "Creightonian" historians have not made full use of the Macdonald papers is that preconceptions about Macdonald's "true" significance appear to have narrowed the vision of what is relevant. Some of the material cited here is "newly discovered" only in the sense that another researcher may have seen the same letter or memorandum but, under the presumption of benevolence, such material has been considered either irrelevant or misleading.

A third reason has less to do with the limitations of the historians than the physical inaccessibility of the evidence because the size of the collection is intimidating, to say the least. Focusing on the period of Macdonald's career from 1867 to 1885 there are only thirteen volumes of his Letter Books, but the Incoming Correspondence (called "Political Papers" in the archival finding aid) are organized in 535 roughly chronological volumes

---

1. Creighton, *Young Politician*, p. viii.
2. For Creighton's intentions see his article, "Sir John A. Macdonald and Canadian Historians," *Canadian Historical Review* 24 (1948), pp. 1-13.

running to 276,646 consecutively numbered pages. Clearly, the sheer size of the Incoming Correspondence has precluded researchers from going through the back volumes of the Macdonald papers on a systematic, page-by-page basis—until 1968.

In August 1968 the Public Archives of Canada unveiled a comprehensive author, subject, and chronological index. The first step in the present study was a careful reading of the subject compilation, which involved scanning every line from A to Z. Since particular items can address several or many different subjects at once, it is unlikely that any material relating to the diverse facets of the Macdonald-Métis theme in the Incoming Correspondence was missed. At the completion of the survey, the many references were entered into a machine-readable form and printed by page number to identify duplicate or multiple references to the same item.

Transcription of evidence began with a careful reading of the many items thus identified. In the process, it became evident that the cast of characters in the subject—the personnel who served, appealed to, or succeeded Macdonald in the administration of Métis rights—was a remarkably small circle. At the same time, impressions were formed about each individual's role in the formation and administration of native policy in the period under study. On the chance that other important papers of the same actors existed elsewhere, a systematic search was made of collections outside the Macdonald papers. Footnote references show that some important manuscripts were found in the Governor General's Correspondence with the Colonial Office, Morris papers in the Provincial Archives of Manitoba, the Mills papers at the University of Western Ontario Archives, the Pearce papers in the University of Alberta Archives, and the correspondence of Lawrence Clarke in the Hudson's Bay Company Archives. But the Macdonald papers remained the core material.

Broadening the study from Macdonald's circle of correspondents to the bureaucratic apparatus he headed, the Records of the Department of the Interior, Dominion Lands Branch files (PAC, RG 15) were consulted for every year of the period from 1870 to 1885, and the statistical record of Métis occupancy and persistence was linked to the administrative and legal aspects of Métis dispersal.

During the last stage of the research, transcriptions of the Macdonald Letter Books in the PAC and transcriptions of Macdonald letters in the same archive from collections other than the Macdonald papers were consulted for a comprehensive view of Sir John A. Macdonald's own writing on the subject. A final benefit of the comprehensive index to the Macdonald Papers was its utility in decoding a number of important cypher messages into intelligible English (see the research note on the subject by Timothy Dubé, available from the Prime Minister Section, Manuscript Division, PAC).

The point is that new material is continually coming to hand. As the research and writing of critical studies of Canadian history continues, there can be little doubt that some of the gaps or poorly supported conclusions of the present work will be remedied by succeeding historians' contributions.

Selected Bibliography

Primary Material Cited

1. Private Papers

J.C. Aikins Papers. Archives of Ontario, Toronto. Primarily private correspondence but significant cabinet papers also included.

William Coldwell Papers. Provincial Archives of Manitoba, Winnipeg. MG 2 14. Important eyewitness account of ratification of the "Manitoba Treaty" by provisional government in June 1870.

Joseph Howe Papers. Public Archives of Canada, Ottawa. MG 24 B29. Corresponded officially and as a fellow Nova Scotian with Archibald during his stint as Lieutenant Governor. Valuable material on the emergence of the first Dominion Lands policy.

Sir John A. Macdonald Papers. Public Archives of Canada, Ottawa. MG 26 A. As mentioned in the preceding note on method, the Macdonald Papers were the pivotal collection for the present study, as important for the incoming correspondence as Macdonald's own writing.

Alexander Mackenzie Papers. Public Archives of Canada, Ottawa. MG 19 A 7. Disappointingly little on Canada and the Métis.

Archer Martin Papers. Provincial Archives of British Columbia. Includes notes and correspondence for Martin's study of the Manitoba land question, a book published in 1898 entitled *The Hudson's Bay Company's Land Tenures and the Occupation of Assiniboia by Lord Selkirk's Settlers, with a List of Grantees under the Earl and the Company* (London, 1898).

David Mills Papers. Archives of the University of Western Ontario, London. Important for Mills' correspondence with Archbishop Taché.

Alexander Morris Papers. Provincial Archives of Manitoba, Winnipeg. Best collection of private and official correspondence during his period as Lieutenant Governor.

William Pearce Papers. University of Alberta Archives, Edomonton. MG 9/2. The letterbooks contain copies of many important official reports and other papers that do not appear anywhere in the records of the Department of the Interior in the Public Archives of Canada, Ottawa.

Louis Riel Papers. Provincial Archives of Manitoba, Winnipeg. MG 3. The multi-volume collection of Riel's letters and other works edited by George Stanley, *et al.* (*The Collected Writings of Louis Riel*. 5 vols. Edmonton, 1985) makes Riel material readily accessible but the archival manuscripts are still the only location of letters incoming from Riel's correspondents.

2. Official Papers

Colonial Office Papers. Public Archives of Canada, Ottawa. MG 11 CO42. Microfilm of the British record of correspondence with the Governor General on Canadian matters. Contains copies of materials that have disappeared from the papers of the Canadian writers of such reports.

Records of the North West Rebellion. Hudson's Bay Company Archives, Winnipeg. D.20/33 and B332/b/1. Crucially significant reports, letters and telegrams to government officials not available elsewhere.

Records of the Governor General. Public Archives of Canada, Ottawa. RG 7. The pipeline of official reporting to Britain.

Records of the Department of the Interior. Public Archives of Canada, Ottawa. RG 15. Second only to the Macdonald Papers for finding the story of Canada and the Métis.

Records of the Department of Justice. Public Archives of Canada, Ottawa. RG 13. Letterbooks contain legal opinions on many matters of constitutional significance.

3. Printed Government Records

Canada, *Canada Gazette*

_____, *House of Commons Debates.*

_____, *Senate Debates.*

_____, *Sessional Papers.*

_____, *Journals of the House of Commons.*

_____, *Orders of the Governor General in Council.*

Statutes of Canada.

Statutes of Manitoba.

4. Contemporary Imprints

Codd, Donald. ''Some Reminiscenses of Fort Garry in 1869-70.'' *Great West Magazine* 13 (1899), pp. 294-299.

Denison, G.T. *Reminiscences of the Red River Rebellion of 1869.* Toronto, 1873.

Hind, H.Y. *Narrative of the Canadian Red River Exploring Expedition of 1857 and of the Assiniboine and Saskatchewan Exploring Expeditions of 1858.* 2 vols. London, 1860.

_____. "The Corruption of the Geological Survey." n.p., May, 1883. Copy appears in PAC, RG 15, vol. 295, file 61147.

Macoun, John. *Manitoba and the Great North West.* Guelph, 1882.

Morris, Alexander. *Nova Britannia; or, Our New Canadian Dominion Foreshadowed, Being a series of Lectures, Speeches, and Addresses.* Toronto, 1884.

O'Donnell, J.H. *Manitoba Matters: Being a Short Chapter Devoted and Dedicated to the Davis-Royal Administration, The Autonomy of Provinces no Longer respected, Ottawa Dictates, Manitoba Obeys.* Winnipeg, 1875.

5. Newspapers
Manitoba Free Press.
The Manitoban.
Ottawa Times.
Toronto Mail.
Toronto Globe.

Secondary Works Cited

1. Book and Journal Articles

Creighton, D.G. "Sir John A. Macdonald and Canadian Historians." *Canadian Historical Review* 24 (1948), pp. 1-13.

Dorge, Lionel. "The Métis and *Canadien* Councillors of Assiniboia." *Beaver* 305 (1974), 1:12-19, 2:39-45, 3:51-58.

Ens, Gerhard. "Métis Lands in Manitoba 1870-1887." *Manitoba History* 5 (1983), pp. 2-11.

Flanagan, Thomas. "Louis Riel: Review Essay." *Journal of Canadian Studies* 21 (1986), pp. 157-164.

Gagan, David. "Land, Population, and Social Change: The 'Critical Years' in Rural Canada West." *Canadian Historical Review* 59 (1978), pp. 293-318.

Judd, Carol M. "Native Labour and Social Stratification in the Hudson's Bay Northern Department, 1770-1870." *Canadian Review of Sociology and Anthropology* 17 (1980), pp. 305-314.

Kemp, Douglas. "Land Grants Under the Manitoba Act." Historical and Scientific Society of Manitoba. *Transactions* series 3, No. 9 (1952-53), pp. 33-52.

Lalonde, A.N. "Colonization Companies in the 1880s." *Saskatchewan History* 24 (1971), pp. 101-114.

_____. "Colonization Companies and the North-West Rebellion." In F. Laurie Barron and James B. Waldram, eds., *1885 and After: Native Society in Transition.* Regina, 1986.

Mailhot, P.R. and Sprague, D.N. "Persistent Settlers: The Dispersal and Resettlement of the Red River Métis, 1870-1885." *Canadian Journal of Ethnic Studies* 17 (1985), pp. 1-30.

McLean, D. and Schulman, M. "Lawrence Clarke: Architect of Revolt." *Canadian Journal of Native Studies* 3 (1983), pp. 57-68.

Montgomery, Malcolm. "The Six Nations and the Macdonald Franchise." *Ontario History* 57 (1967), pp. 13-25.

Morton, W.L. "The Red River Parish." In R.C. Lodge, ed. Manitoba Essays. Toronto, 1937.

————. Review of *Le Métis canadien* by Marcel Giraud. *The Beaver* 281 (September 1950), p. 3-7.

Painchaud, Robert. "French-Canadian Historiography and Franco-Canadian Settlement in Western Canada, 1870-1915." *Canadian Historical Review* 59 (1978), pp. 447-466.

Pannekoek, Frits. "The Rev. Griffiths Owen Corbett and the Red River Civil War of 1869-70." *Canadian Historical Review* 57 (1976), pp. 133-149.

Peterson, Jacqueline. "Prelude to Red River: A Social Portrait of the Great Lakes Métis." *Ethnohistory* 25 (1978), pp. 41-67.

Reynolds, G.F. "The Man Who Created the Corner of Portage and Main." Historical and Scientific Society of Manitoba. *Transactions* (1970).

Roberts, A.C. "The Surveys in the Red River Settlement in 1869." *The Canadian Surveyor* (1970), pp. 238-248.

St-Onge, Nicole. "The Dissolution of a Métis Community: Pointe à Grouette, 1860-1885." *Studies in Political Economy* 18 (1985), pp. 149-172.

Sprague, D.N. "The Manitoba Land Question, 1870-1882." *Journal of Canadian Studies* 15 (1980), pp. 74-84.

————. "Government Lawlessness in the Administration of Manitoba Land Claims, 1870-1887." *Manitoba Law Journal* 10 (1980), pp. 415-441.

Spry, Irene, ed. "The Memories of George William Sanderson." *Canadian Ethnic Studies* 17 (1985), pp. 115-134.

Stanley, George. "Last Word on Louis Riel — The Man of Several Faces." In F. Laurie Barron and James B. Waldram, eds. *1885 and After: Native Society in Transition*. Regina, 1986.

Thomas, Lewis H. "A Judicial Murder — The Trial of Louis Riel." In Howard Palmer, ed. *The Settlement of the West*. Calgary, 1977, pp. 37-59.

Woolworth, N.L. "Gingras, St Joseph and the Métis in the Northern Red River Valley, 1843-1873." *North Dakota History* 42:4 (1975), pp. 16-27.

2. Books

Adams, Howard. *Prison of Grass*. Toronto, 1975.

Beal, Bob and Macleod, Rod. *Prairie Fire: The 1885 North-West Rebellion*. Edmonton, 1984.

Benoit, D.P. *Vie de Monseigneur Taché, archevêque de Saint-Boniface*. 2 vols. Montreal, 1904.

Berger, Carl. *The Writing of Canadian History*. Toronto, 1976.

Black, N.F. *History of Saskatchewan and the Old North West*. Regina, 1913.

Brown, Jennifer. *Strangers in Blood: Fur Trade Company Families in Indian Country*. Vancouver, 1980.

Bryce, George. *A Short History of the Canadian People*. London, 1887.

Campbell, M.W. *The North West Company*. Toronto, 1957.

Careless, J.M.S., ed. *Colonists and Canadiens, 1760-1867*. Toronto, 1971.

Creighton, D.G. *Sir John A. Macdonald*. 2 vols. *The Young Politician*. Toronto, 1956. *The Old Chieftain*. Toronto, 1955.

de Trémaudan, A.H. *Histoire de la Nation Métisse dans l'Ouest canadien*. Montreal, 1935.

Flanagan, Thomas. *Louis 'David' Riel: 'Prophet of the New World.'* Toronto, 1979.

_____. *Riel and the Rebellion 1885 Reconsidered*. Saskatoon, 1983.

Friesen, Gerald. *The Canadian Prairies*. Toronto, 1984.

Gagan, David. *Hopeful Travellers: Families, Land, and Social Change in Mid-Victorian Peel County, Canada West*. Toronto, 1981.

Galbraith, J.S. *The Little Emperor: Governor Simpson of the Hudson's Bay Company*. Toronto, 1976.

Gibson, Dale and Lee. *Substantial Justice: Law and Lawyers in Manitoba, 1670-1970*. Winnipeg, 1972.

Giraud, Marcel. *Le Métis canadien: son rôle dans l'histoire des provinces de l'Ouest*. 2 vols. Paris, 1945.

Goldring, Philip. *Papers on the Labour System of the Hudson's Bay Company*. Parks Canada. Manuscript Report No. 362, 1981.

Hedges, James B. *Building the Canadian West: The Land and Colonization Policies of the Canadian Pacific Railway*. New York, 1939.

Hildebrandt, Walter. *The Battle of Batoche: British Small Warfare and the Entrenched Métis*. Ottawa, 1985.

Houston, Cecil J. and Smyth, William J. *The Sash Canada Wore: A Historical Geography of the Orange Order in Canada*. Toronto, 1980.

Howard, Joseph Kinsey. *The Strange Empire of Louis Riel*. New York, 1952.

Lamb, W. Kaye. *History of the Canadian Pacific Railway*. New York,

1977.

MacBeth, R.G. *Making the Canadian West.* Toronto, 1905.

McCallum, John. *Unequal Beginnings: Agriculture and Economic Development in Quebec and Ontario until 1870.* Toronto, 1980.

McKillop, A.B., ed. *Contexts of Canada's Past: Selected Essays of W.L. Morton.* Toronto, 1980.

McLean, Don. *1885: Métis Rebellion or Government Conspiracy?* Winnipeg, 1985.

Mailhot, Philippe R. "Ritchot's Resistance: Abbé Noel Joseph Ritchot and the Creation and Transformation of Manitoba." Unpublished PhD Thesis: University of Manitoba, 1986.

Martin, Chester. *"Dominion Lands" Policy.* Toronto, 1973.

Morice, A.G. *History of the Catholic Church in Western Canada.* 2 vols. Toronto, 1910.

Morton, Desmond. *The Last War Drum.* Toronto, 1972.

Morton, W.L., ed. *Alexander Begg's Red River Journal and Other Papers Relative to the Red River Resistance of 1869-70.* Toronto, 1956.

_____, ed. *Manitoba: The Birth of a Province.* Winnipeg, 1965.

_____. *The Critical Years: The Union of British North America, 1857-1873.* Toronto, 1964.

_____. *The Kingdom of Canada: A General History from Earliest Times.* Toronto, 1963.

_____. *Manitoba: A History.* Toronto, 1957.

Owram, Doug. *Promise of Eden: The Canadian Expansionist Movement and the Idea of the West 1856-1900.* Toronto, 1980.

Patterson, George C. *Land Settlement in Upper Canada.* Toronto, 1920.

Payment, Diane. *Batoche, 1870-1910.* Saint-Boniface, 1983.

Pope, Joseph. *Memoirs of the Right Honourable Sir John A. Macdonald.* 2 vols. Ottawa, 1894.

Pryke, Kenneth G. *Nova Scotia and Confederation.* Toronto, 1979.

Ray, Arthur. *Indians in the Fur Trade: Their Role as Hunters, Trappers, and Middlemen in the Lands Southwest of Hudson Bay, 1660-1870.* Toronto, 1974.

Rea, J.E., ed. *The Letters of Charles John Brydges, 1883-1889.* Publications of the Hudson's Bay Record Society, 33. Winnipeg, 1981.

Silver, A.I. *The French Canadian Idea of Confederation 1864-1900.* Toronto, 1982.

Sprague, D.N. and Frye, R.P., compilers. *The Genealogy of the First Métis Nation.* Winnipeg, 1983.

Spry, Irene, ed. *An Account of John Palliser's British North American Exploring Expedition, 1857-1860.* Toronto, 1960.

Stanley, George. *The Birth of Western Canada*. London, 1936.

———— . *Louis Riel*. Toronto, 1963.

Waite, P.B. *Canada, 1874-1896: Arduous Destiny*. Toronto, 1971.

Warkentin, J. and Ruggles, Richard I. *Manitoba Historical Atlas*. Winnipeg, 1970.

Willson, Beckles. *Lord Strathcona: The Story of His Life*. London, 1902.

Index

Archibald, Adams G.: accepts preferred Métis method of taking 1.4 million acres, 94; complains Manitoba is denied responsible government, 79; critical of OC of 26 May 1871, 94, 96; defends himself over handshaking incident, 78; expected arrival as Lt. Gov. (1870), 67; initial instructions on land question, 90; offers resignation as Lt. Gov., 81; orders first Dominion census of Manitoba, 75; proposes confirmation of titles by deed poll, 93; reacts to scolding by Howe, 97; report on land, 90; reports renewal of trouble between old and new settlers, 102; seeks permission to retire from Manitoba, 101; shakes hand of Louis Riel, 77; urges general amnesty, 76

Bannatyne, A.G.B., 138
Baring Brothers, 168
Batoche. *See* Métis
Begg, James, 138
Blake, Edward, 27, 110; attacks Macdonald's handling of Métis rights (1885), 182; reminds Parliament of BNA Act (1871), 113
Bowell, Mackenzie, 179
Bown, J.Y., 30
British North America Act (1867): section 24, jurisdiction over Indians, 105; section 92(1), provincial constitutions, 59; section 146, admitting new provinces, 28; section 147, representation in the Senate, 62
British North America Act (1871), 62, 111
Brown, George, 19
Bruce, John, 39
Burgess, A.M., 149

Callum, Simon, 134, 138
Cameron, D.R., 40
Campbell, Alexander: devises first Dominion Lands policy (1871), 91; informs Morris province may not legislate for Métis, 105; resentment of Stephen, 153; supports Girard amendment, 126
Canada North West Land Company, 149
Canadian Pacific Railway, 10: in historical interpretation, 10-12. *See also* Stephen, George.
Cartier, George: defends statute confirming Manitoba Act, 63; in first debate of the Manitoba Act, 59; informs Ritchot that petition must precede amnesty, 70; negotiates British Columbia's entry to Confederation, 71; negotiating text of Manitoba Act, 58; negotiating with HBC on terms of transfer, 28; participation in Rebellion of 1837, 79; promises to Ritchot, 61; reaffirms amnesty was promised through British, 84; recommends general amnesty to Lord Lisgar, 71; wins Provencher (1872), 81
Cartwright, Richard, 118
Clarke, Lawrence: advises arrest of Riel